HOW TO
CANCER CELLS

Cookbook

Natalie Mitchell

Nutritionist and Cancer Prevention Coach

Copyrighted material

The information in this book is based on the professional and personal experiences as well as the research of the author. It is not intended as a substitute for consulting with your physician or other health-care provider. Any attempt to diagnose and treat an illness should be under the direction of a health-care professional. The publisher, author and editor are not responsible for any adverse effects or consequences alleged to result or resulting from the use of any of the suggestions, preparations or procedures discussed in this book.

All rights reserved.

ISBN-13: 978-1500476700 (CreateSpace-Assigned)
ISBN-10: 1500476706

Published by Accretive Solutions Ltd

Mail: PO Box HM 2190, Hamilton HMJX, Bermuda

Editor: Colin Barnes

July 2014

Copyrighted material

© Natalie Mitchell

CONTENTS

*"**Food** is Fuel, choose **WISELY!**"*

Unknown

INTRODUCTION

To support and assist readers of my book **"How to Kill Cancer Cells"** as well as anyone generally interested in cancer cure, prevention and keeping healthy, I am pleased to publish this **cookbook** first volume of mouth watering recipes filled with cancer fighting ingredients which are also incredibly healthy for the human body what ever its condition.

The cookbook is also so much more than that, in fact, it is a motivational and educational cookbook which, in addition to 101 recipes, contains much background explanation and knowledge about what foods and ingredients are nutritionally effective in fighting and destroying cancer in the body. You no doubt are wondering why you see a **banana**, **wheatgrass** and **papaya** killing a cancer cell on the cover of my cookbook? All three of them possess strong **antioxidant vitamins** and **alkalizing minerals** that are key nutritionally derived contributors to enabling the body defensive system to effectively destroy cancer cells.

How relevant is this! Japanese Scientific Research, has determined when fully ripe, a banana with the familiar dark spots on its yellow skin produces a substance called TNF (Tumor Necrosis Factor), which has the ability to combat abnormal cells in the body. The more dark the spots it has the higher will be its immunity enhancement quality, hence, the riper the banana the better the **anti-cancer quality**. A yellow skin banana with dark spots on it is 8x more effective in enhancing the defensive powers of white blood cells than a green banana. Bananas are also rich in cancer cell fighting alkaline minerals including potassium, magnesium, calcium, selenium as well as antioxidant vitamins C and E.

Eating 1or more bananas a day has the effect of increasing the strength of your immunity system.

Another of my anti-cancer gunfighters on the book cover, is Wheatgrass which has so much to offer the body that I give you a full spectrum of its benefits in quite some detail later in the cookbook.

You might ask why an **exotic Papaya is participating in taking out the cancer cell?** The enzymes a ripe papaya contains contribute very positively too, so our bodies ability to destroy cancer cells effectively and in Chapter 6 I'll fully explain the details along with recipes for making delicious papaya salads.

It is understandable so many of us fear cancer and worry that we may already have the disease or that we are someday going to suffer from it that many of us wish to have more power and control over our desire to reduce the risk we will suffer from cancer.

My book **"How to Cancer Cells"** and now, this first volume of the **"How to Kill Cancer Cells Cookbook"** are focused on giving readers the knowledge and ability to make changes to our diet that will result in our bodies making cancer cells starve and die.

To do that we have to know specifically which foods possess the incredibly effective power to fight cancer cells and kill them or make them commit suicide. Fortunately, there really **IS MUCH** that each one of us **can do** to control the threat of cancer in our lives and to eliminate it from our body.

After publishing my book **"How To Kill Cancer Cells",** I decided to write this book for you as a result of so many emails I received from thankful patients asking me to write a book with more recipes focused on delicious foods containing powerful cancer cell killing properties.

From travelling around the world, I collected many delicious recipes this last decade and where necessary, I have adapted them to maximize cancer-killing ingredients within the recipes. Your new cookbook means you are equipped to start destroying those nasty cancer cells that we are all born with through every day nutrition and enjoyment of your food.

With the additional knowledge I gained from the study of much well-established and confirmed medical and scientific cancer research and studies over the past century as well as being a constant student myself of cancer cell behavior, I feel very strongly that I should now make vital cancer cell killing food information available to all who want to be proactive in their quest to remain healthy and free from cancer.

I also feel it is important early in the cookbook to share with my readers an understanding of what cancer cells **feed on** and what their **favorite foods are** so you, the reader, armed with this knowledge, can confidently deprive the cancer cells in your body of the fuel they seek in order to multiply on the scale they need to become destructive to body tissue and organs.

The statistic below explains why we are all so much more cognizant today of the cancer threat to our bodies:

This is really quite a stunning statistic: "In 1904 only 1 out of 24 Americans had cancer in their lifetime. Today the cancer rate is 1 out of 2 for men and 2 out of 3 in women."

The clear conclusion is that people in 1904 were much healthier than we are today.

What were they or their bodies doing differently?

Simply put, it is down to this. M**uch of the food** people buy and eat today is quite different from a hundred years ago and is while it may be tasty and appealing, it is not healthy for our bodies and does not meet the needs of our internal cells, organs and tissues for them to function normally year after year. As you will learn in more detail throughout my book, **the root cause of increasing global cancer rates is the increasing level of acidity in the modern diet**. I will be talking about this in some detail here and I do so in depth in my book **"How to Kill Cancer Cells"**.

There are several contributing causes for high acidity in our bodies. Compared with the diet of people a hundred years ago, the modern day diet, in growing numbers of countries, contains a high percentage of processed foods of all kinds. Processed foods are typically high in acidity creating ingredients such as sugar and white enriched flour and are devastingly bad for our bodies over the long term. Other frequently consumed contributors to a state of high acidity in the body are soda drinks, refined carbohydrates, red meat, cheeses, and alcohol. The problem is that Processed foods have low alkalinity levels which is absolutely the opposite to the high alkalinity levels, which the body requires, found in natural foods people predominantly consumed in their diet a century ago such as green vegetables, fresh fruits, spices, etc. Unfortunately today, with our high level of processed food intake, we are literally being pumped full of damaging food additives such as high fructose corn syrup, refined flours, sugar, and artificial sweeteners – all of which are extremely acidic and harmful to the human body.

Sound medical research and study stretching back to cancer disease discoveries beginning as early as the last century support much of the knowledge you will learn in this book. To give you an example, **Dr. Otto Warburg, as early as 1924,** was able to determine that cancer cells are not oxygen breathing and that they have an anaerobic condition. The relevance of this is core to today's cancer avoidance.

While our doctors of medicine and contemporary medical science are doing their best for us when it comes to cancer diagnosis, there continues to be constant research about the different types of cancer, as well as into many other life threatening illnesses, in terms of how best to treat cancer patients and improve cancer survival rates.

It may astound you that even with the medical technology available nowadays doctors can only diagnose active cancer disease in the body when people have already developed **BILLIONS of active cancer cells** in their body.

You will be very interested to learn, therefore, that your every day decisions on what foods to put into your body will no doubt determine during the course of your life, whether or not cancer cells can remain dormant and become destroyed by your body's defenses while your healthy cells remain perfectly healthy and happy.

You are the ONE who decides and acts on what to feed your precious body with. The more you are aware about how much real and effective control you can actually have over your body's health by including the foods recommended in this book in your daily diet, the more power, energy, confidence and improved health you will gain by making the right decisions and choices for achieving a state of sustained health in the years ahead.

Our body is an amazing, complex factory where all organs are interdependent with each other in order to give us the health that often we take for granted. Our immune system acts as our body's defensive mechanism and will function perfectly well if provided with the appropriate body environment to fight in! As much as **70% of your immune system cells** are found in your gut. You can readily make the connection between the quality of your food and your health!

The most important thing is that you are here and reading this book so you are on your way to giving yourself the incredible opportunity to acquire and apply the knowledge you are going to learn in the chapters below, every day from today, the beginning of the rest of YOUR healthy life! Reading my book and cooking healthy delicious cancer preventative foods will give you lifelong tools to tremendously improve the quality of your life and you will start experiencing your health and energy level improving in quite a short period of time if you can follow the advice with a sustained level of diligence and continuity. As you know there is only one thing on this planet, which is impossible to buy or replace, and this is your body's HEALTH! It requires the right knowledge, motivation and most importantly, the concrete actions on your part, which you should have confidence in carrying out, knowing how relevant and effective your choices will be to the degree of health that you enjoy for the rest of your life.

For you to be most successful, it will require your dedication to make changes to your diet no doubt and for you to continually reinforce your positive attitude toward nurturing your precious life. With this book, you have everything you need, at your fingertips, to make a difference. It is all in your hands now as you are the caretaker of your precious Mind, Body and Spirit. Let's start this journey together as I am here to help you understand which food your cells would choose **if they could speak to you and to make sure you have plenty of delicious recipes for doing the right thing!**

Chapter 1

What to avoid - Favorite Foods of Cancer Cells

Before we start with the recipes that **fight** cancer cells I thought it will be very useful for you to know which foods actually **feed** cancer cells.

Way back in 1924 Dr. Otto Warburg discovered the main biochemical cause of cancer, or what **differentiates a cancer cell** from a normal, **healthy cell**. Dr. Otto Warburg was actually awarded the Nobel Prize for this big discovery.

Cancer has only one prime cause. It is the replacement of normal oxygen respiration of the body's cells by an anaerobic (i.e., oxygen-deficient) cell respiration. -Dr. Otto Warburg

What else does Warburg's discovery tell us? It tells us that cancer **metabolizes** much differently than normal cells. Normal cells need oxygen. Cancer cells despise oxygen.

Another thing this tells us is that cancer metabolizes through a process of fermentation.

Warburg was the first to describe in detail the **dependence** of **cancer cells** on **glucose** and **glycolysis** in order to maintain viability following irreversible respiratory damage. He considered **respiration** and **fermentation** as the sole producers of **energy within cells**, and energy alone as the central issue of tumorigenesis.

"We need to know no more of respiration and fermentation here than that they are energy-producing reactions and that they synthesize the energy-rich adenosine triphosphate, through which the energy of respiration and fermentation is then made available for life" Dr. Otto Warburg.

If you've ever made wine, you'll know that fermentation requires **sugar**.

The metabolism of cancer is approximately 8 times greater than the metabolism of normal cells.

The body is constantly overworked **trying to feed cancer**. The cancer is constantly on the verge of starvation and thus constantly asking the body to feed it. When the food supply is cut off, the cancer begins to starve unless it can make the body produce sugar to feed itself.

The wasting syndrome, **cachexia** is the body producing sugar from proteins (you heard it right, not from carbohydrates or fats, but from proteins) in a process called glycogenesis. **This sugar feeds the cancer**. The body finally dies of starvation, **trying to feed the cancer**.

© Natalie Mitchell

The reason Food Therapies for cancer even exist today (beyond the fact that they work) is because the **connection was discovered between sugar and cancer**. There are many food therapies, but not a single one allows many foods high in carbohydrates and not a single one allows sugars, **BECAUSE SUGAR FEEDS CANCER.**

Sugary drinks kill 180,000 people annually through diabetes, cancer and heart disease, a recent Harvard study claims

Sugary drinks aren't just fattening - they're deadly, according to a recent study out of **Harvard confirming this previously known fact**. The study links roughly 180,000 deaths annually in the USA to sugar-sweetened beverages, including **soda**, **sports drinks** and **fruit drinks**.

Specifically, sugary drinks are linked with 133,000 deaths from diabetes, **6,000 deaths from cancer**, and 44,000 deaths from heart disease worldwide.

In the U.S. alone, the research shows that about 25,000 deaths in 2010 were linked to drinking sugar-sweetened beverages, said Gitanjali M. Singh, Ph.D., co-author of the study and a postdoctoral research fellow at the Harvard School of Public Health.

The study was presented on the 19 March 2013 at a meeting of the American Heart Association.

The health effects of drinking sugary beverages have been the topic of heated public debate across the country recently and especially in New York, where Mayor Michael Bloomberg tried unsuccessfully to ban businesses from selling them in sizes larger than 16 ounces.

Bloomberg cited a number of studies linking sugary drink consumption to higher rates of obesity in making his argument for the ban, and he l likely added the new Harvard study to the pile as he fought an appeal. Unfortunately, his appeal was unsuccessful.

The Harvard researchers scrubbed data from a 2010 Global Burden of Diseases study on the consumption levels of sugar-sweetened drinks to measure global intake.
Interestingly, the results revealed that geography may have an impact on how sugary drinks affect certain populations.

Of nine world regions, Latin American and Caribbean countries had the most diabetes-related deaths associated with sugary drinks, while East and Central Europe/Asia claimed the most heart-related deaths.

Overall, among the world's 15 most populous countries, Mexico had the highest rate of deaths associated with sugary drink consumption, with roughly 317 deaths for every million adults.

You might be consuming drinks that have **"0 Sugar"** or **"NO sugar" and note**that there is not much difference in taste and they still taste sweet? The answer is **Artificial Sweeteners** and one of them is a very dangerous one by the name of **Aspartame**.

Study: Aspartame linked to blood cancers

A new human study shows that aspartame use is linked to increased risk of leukemia, non-Hodgkin lymphoma (NHL), and multiple myeloma in men.

A newly published long term study that spans 22 years shows that drinking one or more **aspartame-sweetened** soft drinks per day increases the risk of several blood cancers in men. The study was led by Dr. Eva S. Schernhammer of the Channing Division of Network Medicine, Department of Medicine, Brigham and Women's Hospital and Harvard Medical School in Boston.

Men who consumed one or more aspartame-sweetened sodas per day had an increased risk of NHL and multiple myeloma, compared to men who didn't drink diet soda. This study was published in *The American Journal of Clinical Nutrition.*

The Prime Cause and Prevention of Cancer with two prefaces on prevention

Revised lecture at the meeting of the Nobel Laureates on June 30, 1966 at Lindau, Lake Constance, Germany

By Dr. Otto Warburg Director, Max Planck-Institute for Cell Physiology, Berlin-Dahlem

English Edition by Dean Burk National Cancer Institute, Bethesda, Maryland, USA

"... **for cancer, there is only one prime cause. Summarized in a few words, the prime cause of cancer is the replacement of the respiration of oxygen in normal body cells by FERMENTATION OF SUGAR. All normal body cells meet their energy needs by RESPIRATION OF OXYGEN, whereas cancer cells meet their energy needs in great part by FERMENTATION.**

In every case, during the cancer development, the oxygen respiration always falls, FERMENTATION appears, and the highly differentiated cells are transformed into fermenting anaerobes, which have lost all their body functions and retain only the now useless property of growth and replication. Thus, when respiration disappears, life does not disappear, but the meaning of life disappears, and what remains are growing machines that destroy the body in which they grow…"

The average American consumes an astounding 2-3 pounds of sugar each week, which is not surprising considering that highly refined sugars in the form of **sucrose** (table sugar), **dextrose** (corn sugar), **high-fructose corn syrup** (HFCS), **corn syrup** etc. are typically added into almost all processed foods such as bread, cereals, ketchup, mayonnaise, peanut butter, salad dressings, jams, sauces, premade meals etc.

In the last 20 years **sugar consumption** only in US was increased from **26 pounds** to **135 pounds** per person per Year! The average consumption 1887-1890 was only **5 pounds** per person per year! Now, the average American consumes that in two weeks!

According to the American Cancer Society, **Forty-one thousand (41,000)** Americans (64 people per 100,000) died of cancer in 1900.

Now, each year globally, **12.7 million** people learn they have cancer, and **7.6 million** people die from cancer.

Cancer is the **second** leading cause of **death** in the United States, exceeded only by heart disease.

It kills nearly 547,500 Americans in a single year and that number is rising.

Researchers at Huntsman Cancer Institute in Utah were among the first to discover that **sugar "feeds" tumors**. The research published in the journal *Proceedings of the National Academy of Sciences* said, "It's been known since 1923 that tumor cells use a lot more glucose than normal cells. Our research helps show how this process takes place, and how it might be stopped to control tumor growth," says Don Ayer, Ph.D., a professor in the Department of Oncological Sciences at the University of Utah.

Dr. Thomas Graeber, a professor of molecular and medical pharmacology, has investigated how the metabolism of glucose affects the biochemical signals present in cancer cells. In research published June 26, 2012 in the journal *Molecular Systems Biology*, Graeber and his colleagues demonstrate that **glucose starvation—that is, depriving cancer cells of glucose—activates a metabolic and signaling amplification loop that <u>leads to cancer cell death</u>** as a result of the toxic accumulation of reactive oxygen species (ROS).

Drs. Rainer Klement and Ulrike Kammerer conducted a comprehensive review of the literature involving dietary carbohydrates and their **direct** and **indirect effect** on **cancer cells**, which was published in October 2011 in the journal ***Nutrition and Metabolism***, concluding that cancers are so sensitive to the sugar supply that cutting that supply will suppress cancer. **"Increased glucose flux and metabolism promotes several hallmarks of cancer such as excessive proliferation, anti-apoptotic signaling, cell cycle progression and angiogenesis."**

Eating white sugar, refined flower and processed food causes magnesium mineral deficiencies in the body because the magnesium has been removed in the processing, **making sugar a ripe target as a major cause of cancer because deficiencies in magnesium are not only pro-inflammatory but also pro-cancer**.

Now, I would like you to pay significant attention to why the body stores fat.

The body stores body fat mainly for these 3 reasons:

1. The intake of too many calories from **refined** and **processed carbohydrates** that strip away beneficial fiber or **bad fats.**

2. It is not getting the required **good healthy fats** it needs to run the body smoothly.

3. Interference in the action of the hormone **Leptin, which** plays a key role in our appetite resulting in over-eating.

The **first reason** is quite simple. When we consume more calories than our body requires for energy it stores these excess calories as fat. This is the fat we see on our bellies, hips, and thighs. This fat is the most unhealthy and aesthetically, most of us desperately want to get rid of it.

The **second reason** our body stores fat is because it is not getting the required "good" fats it needs to run smoothly.

The **third reason** is when your brain doesn't get a signal that your stomach is full. I am sure many of you will recognize this feeling, like after eating a big meal, you curiously still feel hungry. The reason is that leptin hormone which is responsible to give a signal to your brain that your tummy is full didn't do its crucial job and didn't deliver the signal to the brain. **Leptin is called the "satisfaction" hormone because it tells your brain that you've had enough to eat**. It can also tell the body to **burn more calories** based on how much you eat.

It is not your fault that you still feel hungry and wish to eat more even after a big meal. The brain is deceived.

© Natalie Mitchell

One of the main reasons for your brain not getting a "satisfaction" message occurs when you consume food which includes **High Fructose Corn Syrup (HFCS).** You will be amazed to find out how much food contains HFCS when you start checking ingredients.

In a review of research, George Bray and colleagues at Louisiana State University found fructose doesn't trip the leptin sensor or promote enhanced production of leptin. In addition, after consuming **high-fructose corn syrup**, participants of some studies had reduced leptin concentrations. Other sweeteners, like glucose, provide satiety signals to the brain that fructose cannot provide, because it is **not transported into the brain**. In an animal study, a diet high in high-fructose corn syrup led to leptin resistance. This causes cells to stop accepting leptin's messages, regardless of how much leptin you have in your body. In both study sets, the results were **significant weight gain** and **habitual consumption of more calories**.

Research published in the December 2008 issue of the "American Journal of Clinical Nutrition" says that prolonged consumption of food and beverages containing fructose-based sweeteners can lead to both overeating and reduce calorie burning by your body. As a result, you can gain weight. Leptin works in the hypothalamus region of the brain, and research has demonstrated that your body's metabolism of high-fructose corn syrup may skip all of the processes that would trigger the work of leptin.

"A diet high in high fructose corn syrup is associated with increased pancreatic cancer risk" Aune D, Chan DSM, Vieira AR, et al. Dietary fructose, carbohydrates, glycemic indices and pancreatic cancer risk: a systemic review and meta-analysis of cohort studies. *Ann Oncol.* 2012;23(10):2536-2546.

Here are the most dangerous ingredients and additives that you should remove permanently from your diet as soon as you can:

- Sugar, flour, enriched white flour, white flour, enriched bleached flour, enriched wheat flour, wheat flour, semolina flour, white rice, maltodextrin, glucose, high fructose corn syrup (HFCS), sucrose (table sugar), dextrose (corn sugar), and levulose
- Artificial Sweeteners - listed as Sucralose, Aspartame, Acesulfame K, and Saccharin

- Trans Fats and Partially Hydrogenated oils
- MSG (also labeled as monosodium glutamate)
- Excess Salt/Sodium in chips, crackers, canned food items, pickles, pretzels, condiments, and salted and sweetened nuts.

Cancer prone tissues are those that have become more **acidic**, whereas **healthy tissues** remain within the normal **alkaline levels that the body works at delivering to cells and tissues**. Optimum alkalinity levels also depend on **correct oxygen levels in the body, which help to neutralize acidity**, while, conversely, abnormal acidity levels prevent oxygen from reaching the tissues that need it. When tissues become devoid of free oxygen, acidity levels rise within the tissue which can then activate otherwise dormant cancer cells.

The way I explain this in more detail, is to talk in terms of the significance of the relationship between the pH level of the body and of the pH level of the different foods that we put into our bodies. Relative to what our bodies required pH levels are, you will understand which foods have higher **alkalinity** values and therefore more **cancer beating power** for our blood cells and tissues than those foods which are more acidic and which, if allowed to continue to be part of our normal diet, will allow cancer cells to continue to be active and potentially multiply.

The pH scale measures how acidic or alkaline a substance is and ranges from 0 to 14, with 7.0 being the neutral state. For this discussion, body pH readings below 7 are **acidic** and above 7 are considered **alkaline**.

You are probably wondering what your body's healthy state pH level should be and what it is currently.

Medical science has determined that blood, lymph and cerebral spinal fluid in the human body are designed to be, and stay healthy in, an alkaline environment at a pH level of 7.4 or higher.

"At a pH level slightly above 7.4 cancer cells within our body become dormant and at the more alkaline level of pH 8.5, cancer cells will actually die while healthy cells will live" (Barefoot, pages 66-67).

To reiterate, as this is key to achieving a cancer resistant body environment and so very important on a daily basis, I recommend that you:

I. **Alkalize your body quickly by consistently eating the right foods and drinks full of Alkaline Minerals and Antioxidant Vitamins that lead to a slightly alkaline body state**

II. **Identify and eliminate all food that contains too much acidity from your diet.**

The chart below shows you **common acidic foods** that many of us consume every day without ever knowing the damage these foods inflict on our blood cells and tissues.

© Natalie Mitchell

Partial List of foods to avoid because they contain TOO much ACIDITY:

Food	Acidity
Tomatoes 	ACIDITY LEVEL: 4.30 - 4.90 Consumable when grown organically and completely ripe
Sweet peppers 	ACIDITY LEVEL: 4.65 - 5.45
Red beetroots 	ACIDITY LEVEL: 5.30 - 6.60
Sorrel 	ACIDITY LEVEL: 4.5

© Natalie Mitchell

Oranges	**ACIDITY LEVEL:** 3.69 - 4.34
Mandarins, tangerines	**ACIDITY LEVEL:** 3.32 - 4.48
Grapefruits	**ACIDITY LEVEL:** 3.00 - 3.75
Strawberries	**ACIDITY LEVEL:** 3.00 - 3.90 Consumable when grown organically and ripe
Raspberries	**ACIDITY LEVEL:** 3.22 - 3.95 Consumable when grown organically and ripe

Blackcurrant	ACIDITY LEVEL: **4.8 – 7.0** Consumable when grown organically and ripe
Redcurrant	ACIDITY LEVEL: **4.8 – 7.0** Consumable when grown organically and ripe
Gooseberries	ACIDITY LEVEL: **2.80 - 3.10**
Pineapples	ACIDITY LEVEL: **3.20 - 4.00**
Kiwis	ACIDITY LEVEL: **3.1 – 3.96**

© Natalie Mitchell

Food	Acidity
Dates	**ACIDITY LEVEL:** **4.14 - 4.88**
Honey	**ACIDITY LEVEL:** **3.70 - 4.20** One teaspoon of honey a week is ok
Cocas, sodas	**ACIDITY LEVEL:** **2.0 – 4.0**
Champagne	**ACIDITY LEVEL:** **2.8 – 3.8**
White wines	**ACIDITY LEVEL:** **3.0 – 3.3**

Pink wines	ACIDITY LEVEL: 3.0 – 3.3
Young red wines	ACIDITY LEVEL: 3.3 – 3.5
Desserts	ACIDITY LEVEL: 1.6 – 3.0
Candies	ACIDITY LEVEL: 1.6 – 3.0
Vinegar	ACIDITY LEVEL: 2.40 - 3.40

© Natalie Mitchell

Pickles	ACIDITY LEVEL:
	5.10 - 5.40

The pH of soda drinks

Here is a chart of the acidity levels of some common Sodas:

SODA NAME	pH
Coke	ACIDITY LEVEL: 2.52
Diet Coke	ACIDITY LEVEL: 3.28

Coca Cola Zero 	ACIDITY LEVEL: 3.28
Pepsi 	ACIDITY LEVEL: 2.53
Diet Pepsi 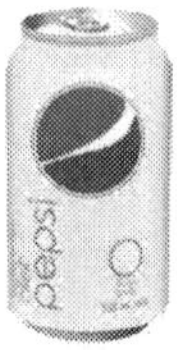	ACIDITY LEVEL: 3.03
Dr. Pepper 	ACIDITY LEVEL: 2.89

© Natalie Mitchell

Diet Dr. Pepper 	ACIDITY LEVEL: 3.16
Cherry Coke 	ACIDITY LEVEL: 2.52
RC Cola 	ACIDITY LEVEL: 2.38
Mr. Pibb 	ACIDITY LEVEL: 2.90

© Natalie Mitchell

Mountain Dew  	ACIDITY LEVEL: 3.22
Diet Mountain Dew 	ACIDITY LEVEL: 3.36
Sprite 	ACIDITY LEVEL: 3.20
7 Up 	ACIDITY LEVEL: 3.20

Diet 7 Up	**ACIDITY LEVEL:** **3.70**
Lemon Brisk	**ACIDITY LEVEL:** **2.86**
Lemon Nestea	**ACIDITY LEVEL:** **2.96**

With knowledge, the right choices are yours to make as you are the ONE who decides what quality of fuel to put in your digestive system!

"Let food be thy medicine and medicine be thy food"

Hippocrates

Chapter 2

Healthy Foods that FIGHT Cancer Cells

Cancer-fighting foods contain natural substances that work by cutting off the blood supply feeding cancer cells. Without a blood supply, cancers cannot grow. With the right foods we can literally starve cancer and avoid unintentionally allowing cancer cells to grow.

Goji Berries as a Super food to destroy Cancer Cells

In one study conducted in 1994 on 79 cancer patients, it was found that they responded better to cancer treatment when **Goji berries** were added to it. Some test tube studies have also found that the antioxidants in Goji berries can prevent and reduce cancer cells

from growing.

Cyperone is a sesquiterpene found in Goji berries. This is said to benefit **blood pressure patients**, those with **heart disease**, ease menstrual discomfort and can even be used to treat patients with **cervical cancer**.

Physalin is a natural compound present in Goji berries. Physalin can act against various types of leukemia. In studies on mice with tumor, it has increased the splenic killer cell activity. This is said to offer broad-spectrum anti-cancer benefits. Antioxidant selenium found in Goji berries can provide cancer protection.

Germanium another nutrient found in Goji berries is said to reduce the growth of tumors and has anti-cancer benefits. Goji berries are also said to reduce the risk or help in the treatment of **testicular cancer**, **lung cancer**, **liver cancer** and **uterine cancer**.

Goji berries are said to have anti-estrogen effects. This means that tumor cells can be more vulnerable to immuno-therapy and radiation. Cancer cells are forced to commit suicide and not proliferate.

Two studies conducted in 2010 have found that polysaccharides which are present in Goji berries can stop the growth of colon, gastric cancer cells and prostate cancer cells and cause their death.

Breast cancer is one common form of cancer. Studies have found that polysaccharides found in Goji berries can prevent breast cancer cells from growing and help them self-destruct.
Goji berries are rich in carotenoids like beta-carotene and zeaxanthin. The latter is known to protect the retina and prevent other **eye disorders**. There are also other antioxidants found in Goji berries which are said to have **anti-aging properties**. Goji berries also contain 18 amino acids of which 8 are essential and which the body cannot produce. It also contains 21 trace minerals which include zinc, copper, iron, magnesium, selenium, mangancsc and phosphorous, vitamin A, C, E, B1, B2 and B6, essential fatty acids like omega-3 and omega6, and many **anti-inflammatory**, **anti-**

fungal, and **anti-bacterial agents**. The ORAC scale which measures **antioxidant levels** in foods gives Goji berries the **number 1 rank**.

Goji berries can be made into tea, added to cereals, salads or soups and used in baking, to make trail mixes, smoothies etc. They have a tangy sweet and sour taste and can be substituted for raisins in many recipes. You can find Goji berry products online, at Chinese herbal stores, through network marketing companies and health food stores like Whole Foods Market, etc.

Ripe Strawberries covered in Dark Chocolate as a double weapon to kill cancer cells

Strawberries destroy cancer cells!

Researchers specializing in the health benefits of plant

compounds have shown that quercetin, a phytonutrient found in abundance in strawberries and other fruits, can induce programmed self-destruction of human cancer cells.

This process, called "apoptosis," is important in cancer prevention because it is one of the primary ways the body eliminates damaged cells. **Quercetin** and whole strawberry extract also inhibited the proliferation of **cancer cells**. The study was published in an edition of the Journal of Agriculture and Food Chemistry.

In this study, researchers sought to identify the mechanisms through which fruit extracts or their components may exert protective effects on human liver cancer cells. Human hepatoma HepG2, a transformed cell line that permits the study of antiproliferative factors for liver cancer research, was used.

Quercetin was the most active polyphenol among the pure compounds tested, showing a dramatic reduction in cell viability (up to 80 percent) after 18 hours of treatment. Significant cell death from treatment with the ripe strawberry extract was also shown to be dose-and time-dependent.

Quercetin and strawberry extract were also shown to **arrest** the cell cycle progression of human hepatoma prior to cell death. This means that cancer cell proliferation was retarded; thus, strawberries and their major phytonutrient, quercetin, may have protective actions at several steps in the process of cancer development.
Quercetin is a member of a large class of plant compounds called **flavonoids**, which have demonstrated anti-cancer, anti-inflammatory and antiviral activity in other studies.

Dark chocolate is packed with flavonoids, a group of phytochemicals that act as **antioxidants** being cancer preventative. Research shows that consuming dark chocolate increases the antioxidants in our blood. In one study comparing the antioxidants among chocolate products, cocoa powder ranked as having the highest of the chocolate products, followed by dark chocolate. Make sure that you buy dark chocolate with no sugar.

I would like you to know, unless you know this already, that **dark chocolate** is known to increase Serotonin and Phenylethyalanine levels in the brain. Phenylethyalanine is a stimulant similar to the body's own dopamine and adrenaline. Phenylethyalanine strikes the brain's mood centers and can induce the emotion of **falling in love**. Serotonin is a "happy" biochemical. It can directly change a person's mood and a person's libido level. Dark chocolate can also gently stimulate the central nervous system and gives an immediate and substantial energy boost thus increasing arousal response and stamina.

Organic ripe strawberries and dark chocolate are also an excellent source of antioxidants which benefit your heart, arteries and your circulation health generally. Many people feel a rush of well being when eating dark chocolate, which boosts production of serotonin and other endorphins and neurotransmitters that result in feelings of deep pleasure, decreased pain, reduced stress, less fatigue, and increased contentment. It's full of libido-boosting methylxanthines. Cancer preventative and sexy ripe organic strawberries clearly should be eaten year round and always dipped in dark chocolate!

Antioxidant Blackberries

"Life offers relatively few unambiguous win-win situations, but here's one: berries, those sweet, natural treats that almost everyone loves may provide potent anticancer compounds."

That's the conclusion of Christine Sardo, who manages clinical trials on berry consumption and cancer prevention for Ohio State University's College of Medicine. "We are promoting the concept of 'fruitraceuticals' as opposed to pharmaceuticals for cancer, and emphasizing prevention vs. treatment," she told about 300 health practitioners at the Nutrition and Health Conference in New York City in 2007. The annual conference, sponsored by Columbia University's College of Physicians and Surgeons and the University of Arizona's School of Medicine, brings together the world's leading nutrition scientists to discuss their latest findings.

The idea of berries as anticarcinogens began in the late 1980s, when Stoner discovered that ellagic acid, found in many fruits and vegetables, inhibited the genesis of tumors. He then found that berries contained high amounts of ellagic acid, and that blackberries in particular had more of this compound than all of the other berries he surveyed.

Berries, said Sardo, may be natural counterparts of synthetic drugs such as Tamoxifen.

"Studies show Tamoxifen can reduce the risk of breast cancer, but the studies have not evolved to look at the chemopreventive action of foods in our diet, of the things we eat every day." That's a mistake, she said, because it may be that a combination of compounds, such as those found in foods, could be more effective than a single agent. Indeed, there are other constituents in berries that can also prevent cancer, said Sardo, including calcium, folic acid, fiber and various phytochemicals.
The blackberry's disease-fighting properties may be energized by a class of compounds called anthocyanins, which have **antioxidant** and **anti-inflammatory** properties. "Anthocyanins are produced only in land-based plants, fruits and vegetables. They don't occur naturally in our bodies. We think that vegetation and fruits produce these compounds to protect themselves from UV sun damage. And while all fruits and vegetables contain anthocyanins, the concentration in berries—especially raspberries and blackberries—is particularly robust" says Russell Mumper, Vice Chair and

Associate Professor of pharmaceutical sciences at UK.
Berries contain a number of healthful compounds including vitamins A, C, E and folic acid; selenium; calcium; polyphenols; and compounds called anthocyanins, which give berries their color. Studies already show people with diets high in fruits and vegetables are healthier, and berries are a particularly tasty fruit.

Antioxidant Blueberries

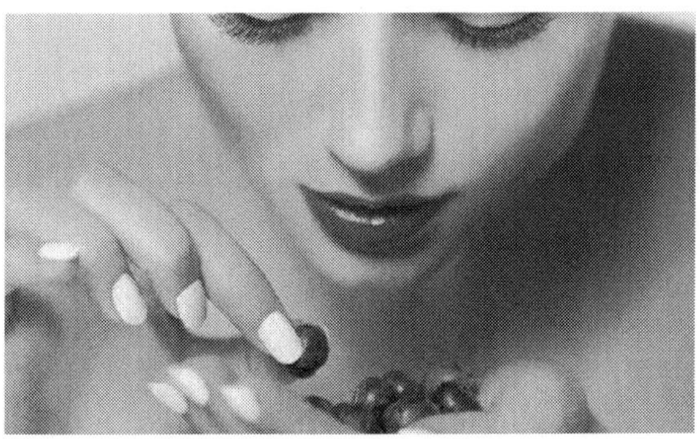

Investigators at the University of Alabama at Birmingham, studying the link between disease and nutrition, believe that eating just one cup of blueberries every day prevents cell damage linked to **cancer**.
Blueberries are full of **antioxidants** and **flavonoids** that help prevent **cell damage**. Antioxidants work by neutralizing free radicals, atoms that contain an odd number of electrons and are highly unstable. Free radicals can cause the type of cellular damage that is a big factor in cancer development.

Blueberries are rich in one particular type of flavonoid called **anthocyanins.** These compounds are water-soluble pigments that are red, violet or blue depending on their pH level. Blueberries and apples both get their beautiful colors from anthocyanins.

In plants, anthocyanins act as antioxidants and protect the plant from oxidative damage. In cells, they perform a **similar function**. They are also rich in **vitamin C**, which supports the immune system and can help the body to absorb iron. And fresh, ripe blueberries provide the most health benefits.

Elderberries fight cancer cells too

Ripe elderberries have been used for their medicinal benefits for thousands of years throughout North America, Europe, Western Asia and North Africa. In the Middle Ages, it was considered a Holy Tree due to its ability to improve health and longevity.

In Israel, Hasassah's Oncology Lab has determined that elderberry stimulates the body's immune system and they are **treating cancer** and AIDS patients with it. The wide range of medical benefits (from flu and colds to debilitating asthma, diabetes, and weight loss) is probably due to the enhancement of each individual's immune system.
Elderberries contain organic pigments, tannin, amino acids, carotenoids, flavonoids, rutin, viburnic acid, vitaman A and B and a large amount of vitamin C. They are also mildly laxative, a diuretic, and diaphoretic. Flavonoids, including quercetin, are believed to account for the therapeutic actions of the elderberry flowers and berries. According to test tube studies2 these flavonoids include anthocyanins that are powerful antioxidants and protect cells against damage.

Magic Apricot Kernels

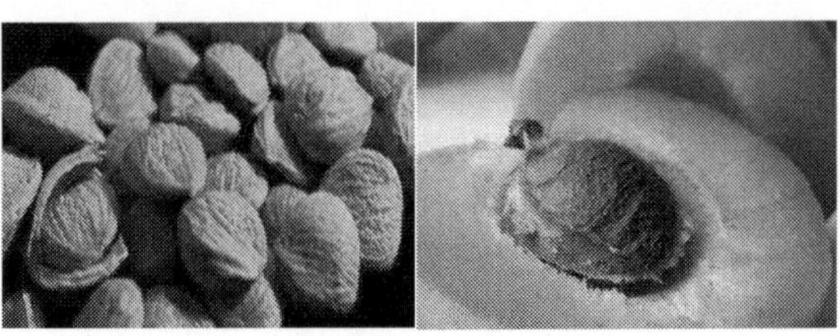

The apricot seed contains **Vitamin B17**. Vitamin B17 is the **anticancer vitamin**. Some researchers have found that cancer and sickle cell anemia are caused by a **deficiency of vitamin B17**. Just as scurvy is caused by a deficiency of vitamin C, pernicious anemia is due to a deficiency of vitamin B12 and folic acid, and pellagra is caused by a deficiency of vitamin B3.

Vitamin B17 kills cancer cells without harming normal cells, **making it nature's version of chemotherapy**.

Various documents from the oldest civilisations such as Egypt at the time of the Pharaohs and from China 2,500 years before Christ mention the therapeutic use of derivatives of **bitter almonds.** Egyptian papyri from 5,000 years ago mention the use of "aqua amigdalorum" for the treatment of some **tumours** of the skin. But the systematised study of Vitamin B-17 really did not begin until the first half of the past century, when the chemist Bohn discovered in 1802 that during the distillation of the water from bitter almonds hydrocyanic acid was released. Soon many researchers became interested in analysing this extract, which they called AMYGDALIN (from amygdala = almond).

I would suggest to you eating at least some of the B-17-containing food and seeds, but not eating more of the seeds by themselves than you would be eating if you ate them in the whole fruit. Example: if you eat **three apricots** a day, **the seeds in the three apricots are sufficient B-17**. You would never eat a pound of apricot seeds. Other foods containing **magic vitamin B 17** are wild blackberry, choke cherry, wild crab-apple, Swedish cranberry, apple seeds, cherry seeds, peach seeds, plum seeds, pear seeds, nectarine seeds, fava beans, etc.

Almonds are cancer cell killers and boost energy too

Almonds contain zinc, selenium, and vitamin E, selenium and vitamin E contain cancer cells killing properties, you can read more in depth about alkalizing minerals and antioxidant vitamins in my book **"How To Kill Cancer Cells"**.

Selenium can help with infertility issues and, with vitamin E, help heart health. Zinc is a mineral that helps produce men's sex hormones and can boost libido.

Interestingly, Almonds have long been purported to increase passion, act as a sexual stimulant, and aid with fertility.

Healthy Avocado super fruits

These super fruits are rich in vitamin E, which has antioxidant properties (cancer cells killers), potassium (an alkalizing-cancer cell destroying mineral), and vitamin B6, which may prevent or delay heart disease and promote better blood flow. Avocados are also a really good source of heart-healthy monounsaturated fats. Anything that helps your heart and circulation contributes toward a healthy sex life. Men with heart disease are twice as likely to have erectile dysfunction because both conditions can result from artery damage.

As an additional health benefit, eating a diet high in the omega-9 fats, of which avocado is one of the best sources, has been shown to have the potential to reduce blood levels of 'bad' low-density lipoprotein cholesterol, at the same time as raising 'good' high-density lipoprotein cholesterol.

Omega-9 fat also aids in the absorption of fat-soluble vitamins and antioxidants from the food they are eaten with.
Many people would be surprised that a food high in fat and calories would be considered good for weight loss. However research has shown that monounsaturated fatty acids are more likely to be used as slow burning energy than stored as body fat.

This slow burning energy and the feeling of fullness that you get from eating an avocado is one of the reasons they are known for reducing hunger and appetite.

1. Smoldering Guacamole

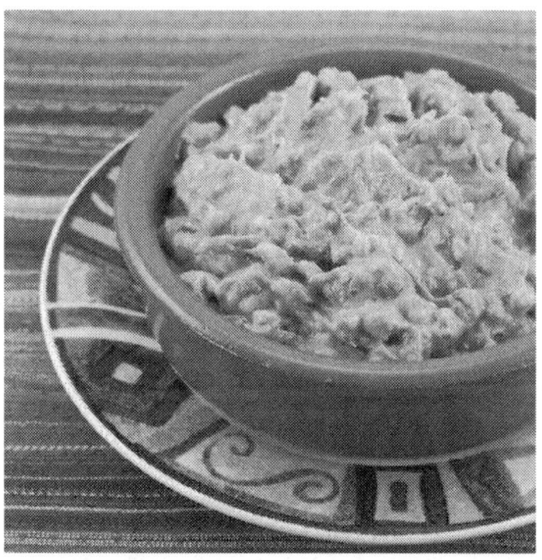

Ingredients

Serves 2

- 1 1/4 lbs **avocado** (ripe, about 3, halved and pitted)
- 1 **scallion** (medium, minced, white and light green parts only)
- For "spicy" include 1/2 **jalapeno chilies** (medium, seeded and minced)
- 1 tbsp **chopped fresh cilantro** (finely)
- 1 tbsp **lime juice** (freshly squeezed, plus more as needed)
- 1 tsp **sea salt** (plus more as needed)

Preparation

1. Scoop the flesh from the avocados into a medium bowl with a tablespoon. Mash the avocado flesh with the back of a large fork or a potato masher to make a chunky paste.

2. Add the remaining ingredients and stir well to combine.

3. Taste and season with additional lime juice and sea salt as needed.

4. Serve immediately or place a sheet of plastic wrap directly on the surface of the guacamole and refrigerate for up to 2 hours. (The plastic wrap will keep the surface of the guacamole from turning brown.) ENJOY!

2. Avocado, Arugula, radish and cucumber salad

Ingredients

Serves 2

- 6 cups arugula leaves
- 1 cucumber medium size
- 2 avocado, peeled and sliced
- 5 radishes

For the dressing

- 2 tbs lime juice, about 1/2 lime or lemon
- 4 tbs olive oil
- 1/2 tsp mild curry spice
- 1/2 tbp turmeric
- Sea salt

Preparation

1. Combine all the ingredients for the salad dressing in a jar, close it tight and shake until the ingredients are well mixed.
2. Toss the arugula leaves with the half of the dressing
3. Add the avocado slices, cucumber slices and radishes slices to the arugula mix, drizzle the remaining dressing on top. Serve immediately. ENJOY!

Organic Arugula as a champion in fighting cancer cells

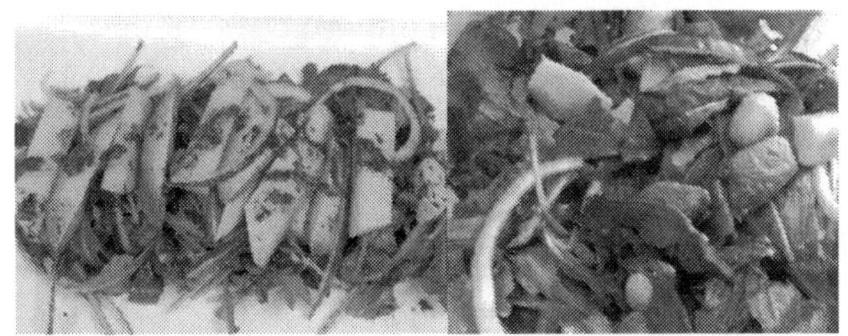

Organic arugula is an anti-cancer cruciferous green and contains two cancer fighters called **kaempferol** and **quercetin.** Researchers have shown that diets containing arugula can reduce the risk of lung cancer. Arugula is best used raw as a salad.

Arugula, which is a highly recommended ingredient to any and every salad, has been heralded as an arousal aid since the 1st century AD. Greek philosophers such as Pliny, Dioscorides, and others identified it as a food with the ability to **increase libido**. The Romans even consecrated arugula to the God Priapus, a God of fertility.

Arugula is one of the historically renowned "**love drugs**" that has been **verified by medical research**. Today, research reveals that the trace minerals and antioxidants packed into dark, leafy greens are essential for our sexual health because they *inhibit the* *introduction of potentially libido-reducing contaminants* into your system — making them essential for the health and responsiveness of your genital organs. Italian cuisine is quite rich in arugula so maybe we now know one of the reasons why Italians are quite famous for being sexy!

3. Arugula, Mango and Avocado Salad

I love the colors in this salad; the mix of arugula, mango, avocado, red onions, cilantro, and red chili peppers make it look fun. I've always enjoyed salads and am fortunate that my loved one enjoy salads too even on those days that he decides to be a picky eater. He will still eat his salad and ask for more, he really likes the onions and can't get enough of them.

Ingredients

Serves 3-4

- 6 cups arugula leaves
- 1 mango, peeled and cut into long slices
- 1 avocado, peeled and sliced
- ½ red onion, sliced
- 1 tbs lime juice

For the spicy vinaigrette

- 1 tbs champagne vinegar
- 2 tbs lime juice, about ½ lime
- 4 tbs olive oil
- ½ tsp cumin
- 2 tbs finely chopped cilantro
- 1 red chili or hot pepper, sliced
- Sea salt and pepper

Preparation

1. Combine all the ingredients for the salad dressing in a jar, close it tight and shake until the ingredients are well mixed.
2. Soak the onion slices in warm water with a dash of salt and 1 tbs lime juice for about 10 minutes.
3. Rinse and drain the onions slices.
4. Toss the arugula leaves with half of the vinaigrette.
5. Add the avocado slices, mango slices and onion slices to the arugula mix, drizzle the remaining vinaigrette on top. Serve immediately. ENJOY!

4. Warm Arugula, Shrimp and Cucumber Salad

Ingredients

Serves 2

- 6 cups arugula leaves
- 1 cucumber medium size
- 2 avocado, peeled and sliced
- 20 tiger shrimps
- 2 cloves of garlic

For the dressing

- 2 tbs lime juice, about 1/2 lime or lemon
- 4 tbs olive oil
- 1/2 tsp turmeric
- Sea salt

Preparation

1. Combine all the ingredients for the salad dressing in a jar, close it tight and shake until the ingredients are well mixed.
2. Heat the olive oil and cook tiger shrimps with pressed garlic for about 2 min
3. Toss the arugula leaves with shrimps and garlic as well as hot olive oil and add the cucumber slices and to the arugula mix. Serve immediately. ENJOY!

Organic Asparagus

Asparagus is a healthy food to include in your diet and does have many benefits, including phytonutrients that can protect against cancer.

Also asparagus has been a known aphrodisiac from ancient days. It is rich in folate, also called vitamin B9 that helps increase your production of histamine which plays an essential role in sexual libido in men and women. This phallic shaped vegetable aphrodisiac contains the phytochemical "glutathione", which has excellent **antioxidant properties**. Asparagus also has a good supply of Vitamin E, considered to stimulate production of sex hormones and be essential for a healthy sex life. Besides being an aphrodisiac, asparagus is a rich treasure of many health benefits. It is also used successfully as a detoxifying and anti-aging vegetable.

5. Poached Egg, Hollandaise and Grilled Asparagus

A British spring-time classic; sweet asparagus, rich hollandaise, brought together with a perfectly poached egg. Heaven!

Ingredients
Serves 2

For the asparagus:

- 16 asparagus spears, woody ends trimmed
- 2 tbsp olive oil
- sea salt and freshly ground black pepper
- 25g/1oz butter

For the hollandaise:

- 2 tsp freshly squeezed lemon juice
- 2 tsp white wine vinegar
- 2 large free-range eggs, yolks only
- pinch sea salt
- 125g/4½oz butter, melted

For the poached eggs:

- 1 tbsp white wine vinegar
- 4 free-range eggs

Preparation

1. For the asparagus, bring a pan of salted water to the boil, add the asparagus spears and cook for 1-2 minutes.
2. Drain, return the asparagus spears to the pan, off the heat, and drizzle with olive oil. Shake the pan to coat the asparagus spears, then season, to taste, with salt and freshly ground black pepper.
3. Heat a griddle pan over a medium to high heat. When the pan is smoking, add the seasoned, blanched asparagus and griddle for 3-4 minutes, or until tender.
4. Add the butter to the pan and, when foaming, shake the pan to coat the asparagus spears in the butter.
5. For the hollandaise, in a separate, non-reactive pan, heat the lemon juice and white wine vinegar until just boiling.
6. Place the egg yolks and a pinch of salt into a food processor. Set the motor to run slowly, then gradually add the hot lemon and vinegar mixture to the egg yolks in a thin stream, until all of the mixture has been incorporated into the egg yolks.
7. With the processor still running, gradually add the melted butter to the mixture in a thin stream, until completely incorporated.
8. Season, to taste, with salt and freshly ground black pepper. Set aside and keep warm (cover the mixture to prevent a skin from forming on the surface).
9. For the poached eggs, bring a small pan of water to a gentle simmer then add the vinegar.
10. Stir the simmering water vigorously to create a vortex,

then carefully crack two of the eggs into the water. Poach for 2-3 minutes, or until the eggs are cooked to your liking, then carefully remove from the pan using a slotted spoon and set aside to drain on kitchen paper.

11. Repeat the process with the remaining two eggs.

12. Alternatively, if using later, drop the poached eggs straight into iced water and chill in the fridge until ready to use. Bring a pan of water to the boil, then add the poached eggs and cook for 1 minute just to heat through. Drain onto kitchen paper.

13. To serve, divide the asparagus spears equally among four serving plates. Place one poached egg on top of each serving of asparagus. Drizzle over the hollandaise sauce and serve immediately. ENJOY!

More on Cancer Cell fighting Bananas

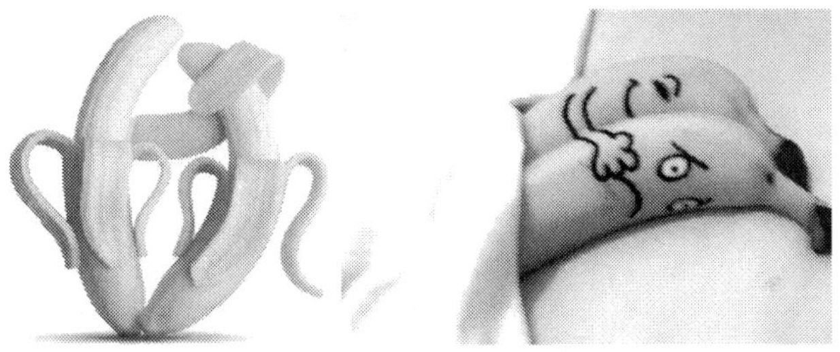

Being literally a power-packed food, ripe bananas are good sources of dietary fiber, **cancer cells fighting** antioxidants and alkalizing minerals like Vitamin C and E, potassium, calcium, magnesium, selenium, etc.

Bananas are equally a very good source of Vitamin B-Complex like riboflavin which are important for the conversion of carbohydrates into energy and which is also said to help in the manufacture of sex hormones such as **testosterone**. Bananas are also rich in bromelain, an enzyme purported to increase libido and reverse impotence in men.

Seafoods eliminate cancer cells

A 22-year study of the relation between fish intake and colon cancer in over 20,000 men published in the American Journal of Clinical Nutrition. This study found that eating fish was not related to the number of colon cancer cases. But among men diagnosed with colon cancer, those consuming fish five or more times a week had a 48 percent lower risk of prostate cancer death than did men consuming fish less than once weekly.

As experts explore the role between the healthy fats in fish and cancer prevention, eat up because "perhaps the best reason to eat...fish on a regular basis is that they are good sources of protein without the heavy dose of saturated fat and calories that usually come with it," according to the American Institute for Cancer Research.

Recent scientific evidence suggests that mussels, clams, and oysters deliver two types of amino acids that spark the release of sex hormones in both men and women. Oysters are also a good source of protein, Vitamin C, phosphorus, riboflavin, niacin, Vitamin B12, iron, copper, manganese and selenium.

Wild salmon, mackerel, herring, sardines and bluefish are rich in omega-3 fatty acids, which are essential for a healthy heart. Being high in iodine, shrimp and other types of seafood are vital to the thyroid gland, which is vital for energy. Studies have shown that populations which eat fish regularly live longer and have less chronic disease than populations that do not.

We have to make sure to preserve all the good nutrition of fish by cooking it correctly which means where oil is used in the recipe, only cooking the fish with olive oil or coconut oil, as fish that is battered and fried in any other oils or slathered with butter, or blanketed in creamy sauces becomes just another vehicle for putting unwanted fat and excess calories into the body.

6. Spicy Coconut Shrimp Bisque

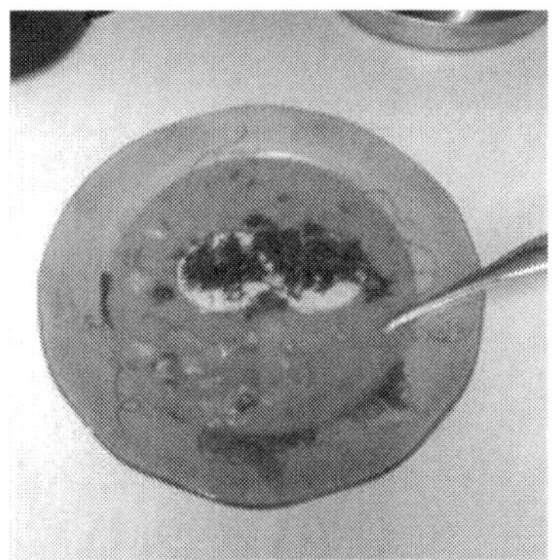

Ingredients

Original recipe makes 6 servings

- 2 tablespoons butter
- 1 pound large shrimp, shelled and deveined, shells reserved
- 2 1/2 cups filtered water
- 2 tablespoons butter
- 1/3 cup green onions, chopped
- 1/3 cup chopped celery
- 1/4 cup diced fresh jalapeno pepper
- 1/4 cup whole grain flour
- 1/2 cup coconut milk
- 1/4 teaspoon red curry paste, or to taste
- 1 dash fish sauce, or to taste
- 2 ounces rice crackers
- 1 tablespoon thinly sliced fresh basil

Preparation

1. Melt 2 tablespoons butter in a saucepan over medium heat. Stir in shrimp shells; cook, stirring, until shells turn pink, 2 minutes. Pour in filtered water and bring to a simmer; cook 20 minutes. Remove from heat and set aside.

2. Melt 2 tablespoons butter in a large saucepan over medium heat. Stir in green onions, celery, and jalapeno; cook, stirring, until mixture is slightly softened, about 5 minutes. Reduce heat to medium low, stir in whole grain flour and cook 3 minutes.

3. Pour shrimp shell mixture through a mesh strainer. Increase heat to medium-high and bring to a simmer.

4. Stir coconut milk, red curry paste, and fish sauce, bring to a simmer and cook for 15 minutes. Stir in shrimp, decrease to heat to low and simmer until shrimp are cooked through, 3 to 4 minutes. Ladle bisque into bowls, place a rice cracker in the middle, and top the cracker with sliced basil. ENJOY!

7. Crab Salad Stuffed Avocados

Ingredients
Serves 8-10 people as an appetizer or 4-5 people as an entree salad

For the crab salad

- 1 pound of cooked crab meat
- ½ red onion, finely chopped
- ½ cucumber, finely diced
- 4 radishes, finely diced
- Juice of 2 limes
- 2 tablespoons of olive oil
- 2 tablespoons of finely chopped cilantro
- Sea salt and pepper to taste

For the stuffed avocados:

- 4-5 ripe but firm avocados
- ½ green lime

To garnish:

- lettuce or salad greens,
- cilantro leaves,
- chopped green onions or chives,
- radishes

Preparation

To prepare the crab salad:

1. Mix the cooked crab meat with diced onions, diced cucumbers, diced radish, lime juice, olive oil, chopped cilantro, and sea salt/pepper.
2. The salad can be prepared in advance and kept refrigerated until just ready to assemble the avocados.

To prepare the crab stuffed avocados:

1. Cut the avocados in half, remove the seeds and peel the avocados. Sprinkle each avocado half with a little lime (or lemon) juice to prevent the avocados from browning too quickly.

2. Fill the center of the avocados halves with the crab salad. Serve the crab stuffed avocados over lettuce leaves and garnished with chopped chives (or green onions) and radishes.

ENJOY!

Fancy Ginger has a weapon too

Thanks to research from the University of Michigan and nearly three centuries of medicinal use, we can now utilize ginger root to not only kill ovarian cancer cells, but also prostate cancer cells with zero toxicity.

Truly among the great natural medicines of the world, ginger has long been used to treat inflammation and nausea, but the results presented in a session at the American Association for Cancer Research show that in every single instance where ginger powder was used to treat cancer cells, they all died as a result of being exposed to the compound. In medical lingo this is called apoptosis (cancer cell suicide.) When ginger is present, the cells even attack one another.

While ginger has been deemed a great natural remedy for those who are undergoing chemotherapy, it can also be used in larger quantities to treat cancer of its own accord.

Another study showing ginger's ability to fight ovarian cancer concludes with:

"Ginger inhibits growth and modulates secretion of angiogenic

factors in ovarian cancer cells. The use of dietary agents such as ginger may have potential in the treatment and prevention of ovarian cancer."

Ginger has also been proven to treat prostate cancer. The British Journal of Nutrition published the results of an American study recently in which ginger extract (zingiber officinale) killed human prostate cancer cells while healthy prostate cells were left alone. Whole ginger extract was revealed to **shrink prostate tumor size by a whopping 56%.**

Further adding to the **benefits of ginger**, the spice has no toxicity when consumed even in high doses, and does not cause people to endure the very uncomfortable side effects of chemo and radiation treatments.

The powerful and high prized medicinal ginger roots, raw, cooked or crystallised, stimulates the circulatory system and relaxing blood vessels. The pungent principles (including the volatile oil gingerol) are the most medicinally potent because they inhibit prostaglandin and leukotriene (products in the body that influence blood flow and inflammation). They also give ginger its pungent aroma.

8. Chicken with Ginger

Ingredients

- 1 three-inch piece fresh ginger, peeled and cut into 1/8-inch-thick matchsticks (1/2 cup)
- 2 tablespoons olive oil
- 1 1/2 pounds boneless, skinless organic chicken breasts, cut into 1 1/2-inch chunks
- 1 large onion, thinly sliced
- 2 cloves garlic, minced
- 1/4 cup fish sauce
- 1/2 cup sliced scallions

Preparation

1. Soak ginger in cold water 10 minutes; drain.
2. Heat olive oil in a skillet over high heat; brown chicken in two batches, 6 to 8 minutes. Set aside.
3. In same skillet over medium heat, cook ginger, onion, and garlic, stirring until browned, 8 to 10 minutes. Add fish sauce cook over high heat until thick, 3 to 4 minutes.
4. Add chicken; stir to warm. Remove from heat; stir in scallions. ENJOY!

Fabulous Figs

It's rare for a natural molecule to garner the attention of medical researches for two completely different cancer-fighting properties, but the compound **psoralen** has done just that. Found in figs, celery

and other fruits and vegetables, psoralen is already used to treat lymphoma-as well as skin conditions as psoriasis-based on its ability to stop DNA from copying itself and triggering cell death when combined with UV light.
Now researches at Duke University have found that UV light activation of psoralen also has the ability to kill breast cancer cells that overproduce the protein HER2. About one-third of breast tumors are HER2-positive, along with stomach, ovarian, and other types of cancer. The most promising drugs for HER2-positive cancer, such as lapatinib and trastuzumab, can block the function of HER2 on the surface of cells, but they can't recognize HER2 deep within the cells. Over time the tumors can become resistant to these drugs. In contrast, psoralen activated with UV light can block all the HER2 in cells, eventually leading to their death.

These delicious and rather sexy fruits have a long history of being a fertility booster. Not only are they extraordinarily good for you as an aphrodisiac, they are also packed with both soluble and insoluble fiber, which is important for maintaining heart health. High-fiber foods like figs help fill you up, not out, so it's easier to achieve that sexy belly profile.

Figs are also a superb source of magnesium, iron, and calcium.

Foods Rich in Psoralen

- Anise seeds
- Carrots
- Celeriac
- Celery
- Chervil
- Cilantro
- Coriander seeds
- Cumin seeds
- Dill
- Fennel seeds
- Figs

- Lemons
- Limes
- Mustard seeds
- Parsley
- Parsnips
- Parsley root

9. Figs and Arugula Salad

Ingredients

Original recipe makes 4 servings

- **4 cups arugula**

- 8 fresh figs, quartered
- 2 tablespoons toasted pine nuts
- 2 tablespoons honey
- 2 tablespoons balsamic vinegar

Preparation

1. Toss the arugula, figs, and pine nuts together in a large bowl.

2. Drizzle honey and balsamic vinegar over salad before serving. ENJOY!

Heavenly Sweet potatoes

Sweet potatoes are rich in potassium which helps fight high blood pressure, which is associated with a higher risk of erectile dysfunction. Sweet potatoes are also rich in beta-carotene, providing the body with useful doses of vitamin A, which is suspected to be helpful for those with infertility. As I mentioned above potassium being an alkaline mineral helps the body stay free of cancer as it assists in alkalizing the body.

Mouthwatering Watermelon

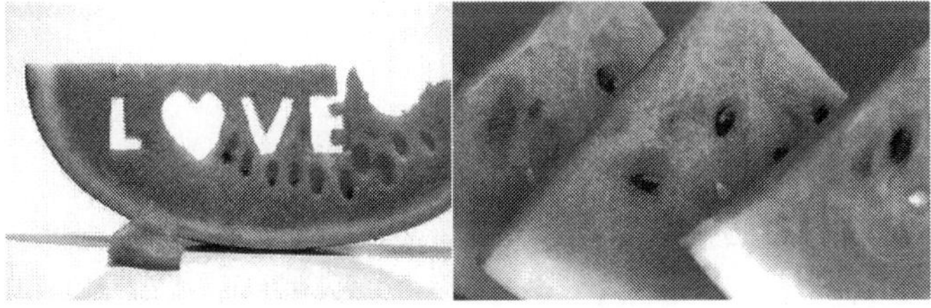

Watermelon has a good dose of antioxidants, about 80 percent of your daily vitamin C, and 30 percent of your vitamin A, or beta carotene. Watermelon also contains lycopene, the famous cancer-

fighting substance.
Consumption of the watermelon, papaya and cantaloupe (taken together) was found to be associated with a lower risk of breast cancer in one 2009 study of Chinese women.

This popular summer fruit is low in calories but high in potentially libido-boosting phytonutrients. In 2008, Texas A&M research suggested that the lycopene, citrulline, and beta-carotene found in watermelons may help relax blood vessels, and provide a natural enhancement for reviving up your sex drive.

Saw Palmetto - Prostate Gland support

*The use of **Saw Palmetto** by the American Indians, especially in the Southern States where the saw palmetto plant grows, has been around for thousands of years, and has been used for prostate health for thousands of years.*

Enlarged prostate and prostate cancer is caused, not by testosterone, but by excessive *dihydrotestosterone* (DHT). This is where saw palmetto works and can make a big difference.

According to Dr. Moerck, the medical literature contains as many as 100 clinical studies on saw palmetto. One of the first prostate drugs on the US market was actually saw palmetto, released by Eli Lilly Company back in the early 1870's.

"The mechanism of action of saw palmetto is not fully clear," Dr.

Moerck says. *"We are certainly not making any drug claims, but the evidence suggests that there is a reduction in the conversion of testosterone into the dihydrotestosterone (DHT), and therefore, men that take saw palmetto will have slightly higher levels of testosterone in their body... That's a good thing..."*

It turns out that if you don't have enough testosterone in your body it can cause all kinds of problems like gaining weight, breast enlargement in men, and problem with urinating.

According to the Creighton University School of Medicine, the first documented use of Saw Palmetto to benefit men's sexual health traces its use back to the Mayan and Seminole Indians of North America. These North American natives used Saw Palmetto in the form of a tonic to increase men's sex drive, enhance fertility, cure impotence, and reduce urinary track issues. The Saw Palmetto tonics also contained extracts from **nettles** and **pumpkin seeds**, which many believed enhanced the effects of the primary ingredient. Pumpkin seeds have long been valued as an important natural food for men's health. This is in part because of their high **zinc** content, which is important for prostate health (where it is found in the highest concentrations in the body), and also because pumpkin seed extracts and oils may play a role in treating benign prostatic hyperplasia (BPH, or enlarged prostate). Research suggests that both pumpkin seed oil and pumpkin seeds may be particularly beneficial in supporting **prostate health**.
"Alone or in combination with other herbs such as ***pygeum*** *(Prunus africana),* ***stinging nettle*** *(Urtica dioica), pumpkin seeds (Cucurbita pepo) and* ***devil's claw*** *(Harpagophytum procumbens), for example,* ***saw palmetto*** *is commonly used in Western Europe for the treatment of BPH* "(Buck, 2004; Schulz et al., 2004; Katz, 2002).

Another nutrient that has been found to offer significant protection against **prostate cancer** is **vitamin K2.** You can supply your body with vitamin K2 by including in your diet chicken, eggs and fresh butter (in small portions).

Testosterone is a sex hormone found in not only men, but also in women and this hormone plays a vital role in supporting your libido, or sex drive, as well as monitoring the growth and health of your muscular system. Testosterone is manufactured by your pituitary gland as well as your hypothalamus.

Saw Palmetto is beneficial for men and women.
For women, the most common benefit attributed to Saw Palmetto is the inhibition of an enzyme called 5-alpha-reductase. Many women, particularly during and after menopause, suffer a lack of Testosterone. Symptoms are many, including low libido, poor sexual response, muscle weakness, lack of endurance and - importantly - loss of zest for life! A host of compounds are found in the fruit of this plant which boost female hormonal health.

Saw palmetto's primary active compounds are fatty acids with other active constituents found in it like carotenes, tannins, polyphenolic compounds and phytosterols. Some of the proposed uses of saw palmetto include reducing inflammation, protecting the prostate from cancer cell development as well as enhancing urine production. Saw palmetto is used popularly in Europe for symptoms associated with benign prostatic hypertrophy (enlargement of the prostate).

New research from Switzerland now reveals that the herb does something the pharmaceuticals don't: **it improves older men's sexual function.** In the study, published in Phytotherapy Research, 82 men charted their BPH symptoms and sexual functioning and then took Saw Palmetto (320 mg/day). After eight weeks, they reported significantly decreased BPH symptoms and improved sexual function.

© Natalie Mitchell

Chapter 3

Your Cancer fighting kitchen - what to keep it stocked with always - and what to banish from it

Before we reach the recipe chapters, I think it is good and appropriate that I share some words of advice and recommendations about what you will want to make sure you always keep a stock of in your kitchen cabinets. This will allow you to readily cook more delicious and healthy meals every day and to make the most of the recipes contained in this first Cookbook.

To be able to cook many of the dishes created from my recipes, my assumption is that for many readers of the Cookbook, a few changes will be required to be made regarding the future choice of the basic cooking ingredients that you purchase at the grocery store and keep at home.

I say this because the right choices, always, for your basic ingredients will be critical to being able to follow my recipes accurately so please do make sure that your kitchen is always stocked with the necessary every day ingredients that will be always be needed in your new kitchen to make your healthy cooking both fun and easy and which will allow you to see in a few months your beautiful body being transformed too as a result of your sustained and more knowledgeable recipe selections!

I am going to start by explaining why most of the oils commonly used in the home kitchen as well as in store bought and store cooked foods are actually really, really bad and unhealthy for you and why you need to avoid ever using them in your kitchen whenever possible.

Before I do, please note I stress that good quality, first pressed Olive oil and Coconut oil are the only two oils that you should ever cook with and use to prepare dressings and marinades with, the reason being that these oils are the only oils suitable from a health perspective for your body. The good news is that Olive oil and Coconut oil will keep you healthier as well as enhance the taste of the delicious and healthier food that you cook from this day forward.

For olive oil, I recommend good quality "first pressed, extra virgin olive oils" and the greener the colour of the oil the better it is. I suggest you avoid buying any olive oils that appear yellowish in colour and these tend to be quite definitely inferior in quality and taste as a result of being blended with other oils. You will want to have a selection of both un-flavoured olive oil and olive oil with a bit of spice or pepper added to it.

My knowledge based opinion is that the practise of only ever cooking with natural olive oil and coconut oil is a key nutritional component to prolonging our longevity as I will explain further below.

Astonishingly, much of the prepared and processed food we buy contains or is cooked with other cheaper oils that are incredibly damaging for our body cells.

Globally, most foods eaten by people are cooked with and contain a variety of different vegetable oils (and margarine, made from these oils). These health damaging vegetable oils are extracted from cheap to commercially produce seeds like rapeseed (canola oil) soybean (soybean oil), corn, sunflower, safflower, etc. Vegetable oils were practically non-existent in the human diet until the early

1900s when new chemical and mechanical processes allowed them to be extracted in large volumes.

Here's why they need to be eliminated from your kitchen: **Vegetable cooking oils** such as corn oil, soy oil, soybean oil, canola oil, sunflower oil etc., chemically **break down under cooking heat temperatures** (approximately above 60 C, which is 140 F) and produce dangerous "free radicals"

Even though the heated, oxidised oils look the same as non-oxidized vegetable oils, the chemical structure of the oxidised oils breaks down **to produce masses of "free radicals" which then coat the food the oxidised oil was cooked in. To remain healthy, we must make sure we avoid ingesting "free radicals" in our food intake.**

The fat content of the human body is about 97% saturated and monounsaturated fat, with only 3 % polyunsaturated fats. Half of that three percent is Omega-3 fats, and that balance needs to be there in our food intake. Unfortunately, the common vegetable cooking oils sold in your grocery store contain very high levels of polyunsaturated fats which are a big contributor to bad cholesterol levels in the body, and these oils have almost completely replaced many of the saturated fats in our diets since the 1950s.

The health problem for the human body through the ingestion of these highly undesirable oils comes about from the fact that polyunsaturated fats are highly unstable and **oxidize** easily in the body if they haven't already oxidized during processing. This is quite damaging to our health as **these oxidized fats cause inflammation and mutation in body cells.**

In one study performed at the University of Western Ontario, researchers observed the effects of ten different dietary fats ranging from most saturated to least saturated. What they found is that saturated fats produced the least number of cancers, while omega-6 polyunsaturated fats produced the most. Numerous other studies have also shown that polyunsaturated fats stimulate cancer while saturated fat does not and that saturated fats do not break down to form free radicals.

Blaming saturated fat for heart disease "is the greatest biomedical error of the twentieth century."

Dr George Mann in the forward of Fat: "It's Not What You Think"

It gets worse. Refined vegetable oils, mostly polyunsaturated, bought in the store contain few, if any, nutrients for the body in addition to the hazards of oxidizing and introducing free radicals to the body when ingested with food cooked in them.

In contrast, olive oil and coconut oil, which are the only healthy cooking oils,) are totally natural whole oil foods complete with a nutritional profile (i.e. containing bio-available nutrients) and are a product of nature, not commercialization. The huge benefit of healthy cooking oils is that they remain stable when heated and cooked and do not degrade into a modified chemical structure producing masses of free radicals. It is also important to note that plant sources of saturated fat also do not convert into bad cholesterol.

My dear reader, these are the reasons why I have to recommend most strongly to you that going forward, you only use **extra virgin olive oil when you marinate, fry, cook and roast. Olive oil is also the healthiest salad dressing**. Coconut oil will be as suitable to cook with as olive oil (although not always as readily available at the grocery store). I recommend that **every other vegetable oil should be banished forever from your kitchen and never again used for cooking food or dressing purposes**.

© Natalie Mitchell

I will also share with you that studies have shown that pure, authentic extra virgin olive oil also helps ease body inflammation, protect against heart disease, stroke, and cancer, as well as soothe achy joints, lower blood pressure and bad (LDL) cholesterol.

Now that we've established which oils it is vitally important to keep in our kitchen to cook with and why, let's move on to other nutritionally sound, basic ingredients that will be handy for you to always have in your kitchen. Nutritionally optimal choices are listed below:

1. Flour.
    - Granola flour and / or Buckwheat
    - Whole wheat flour

    Banish: any white or white enriched and bleached flour and bread as well as any enriched wheat flour

2. Salt.
    - Use only Sea salt in or on your food

    Banish: Regular table salt (sodium chloride)

3. Eggs.
    - Use only Organic, free range eggs. You can always tell the higher quality eggs because they tend to have the darker, healthier egg yolks.

4. Milk.
    - Use only non-dairy milks such as Almond milk or other non-dairy milk made from natural cereals and nuts such as hazel nut, coconuts

      Banish: Cow, Goat and Soy milk as well as yoghurt, dairy creams and cheese of any kind)

5. Butter.

   Being casein protein free, dairy butter in small quantities is actually good for you and the only dairy product which is.

   Banish: Any margarines and any butter spreads containing vegetable oil.

6. Salmon.
    - Use only Wild salmon, fresh or smoked.
    - Avoid farm-raised salmon, which are fed on low cost, unnatural feed like soy and corn.

8. Olive oil.
    - First pressed, Extra virgin please

      Avoid olive oil blended with other vegetable oils

9. Coconut oil.

10. Coconut cream.

11. Coconut milk.

12. Ripe Avocado.

13. Lemon.

© Natalie Mitchell

14. Lime.

15. Stevia, an alternative to refined sugar.

Banish forever white sugar and avoid any food or drink with added sugar as well as any foods containing added fructose of any kind.

Spices:

1. Curry powder (choose the strength according to you taste)
2. Coriander
3. Cumin
4. Green, yellow and red curry paste
5. Garlic
6. Turmeric
7. Cayenne pepper
8. Chili
9. Ginger
10. Lemon grass
12. Cumin
13. Fish sauce
14. Lime juice

Essential equipment for healthy kitchens & sexy Cooks will include a good:

1. Blender
2. Food Processor
3. Juice maker
4. Garlic press
5. Vegetable Steamer
6. Corkscrew for the Cook's wine!

This may be useful too;

Quantities measurement converter:

Butter

A cup of butter weighs 8 ounces and, 1 ounce = 28.34 grams, so one cup of butter weighs 227 grams.

1/4 cup of butter = 57 g

1/3 cup of butter = 76 g

1/2 cup of butter = 113 g

Dry Goods

Whole grain Flour

Cups	Grams	Ounces
1/8 cup (2 tbsp)	16g	0.563 oz
1/4 cup	32g	1.13 oz
1/3 cup	43g	1.5 oz
1/2 cup	64g	2.25oz
2/3 cup	85g	3oz
3/4 cup	96g	3.38 oz
1 cup	128g	4.5 oz

Liquids
1 tsp = 6ml
1 tbsp = 15ml
1/8 cup = 30ml
1/4 cup = 60ml
1/2 cup = 120ml
1 cup = 240ml

Dried ingredients
1 tsp = 5g
1 tbsp = 15g
1oz = 28g

© Natalie Mitchell

1 cup flour = 150g
1 cup caster sugar = 225g
1 cup icing sugar = 115g
1 cup brown sugar = 175g
1 cup sultanas = 200g

Butter
1/8 cup = 30g
1/4 cup = 55g
1/3 cup = 75g
1/2 cup = 115g
2/3 cup = 150g
3/4 cup = 170g
1 cup = 225g

Oven temperatures
275°F = 140°C
300°F = 150°C
325°F = 165°C
350°F = 180°C
375°F = 190°F
400°F = 200°C
425°F = 220°C
450°F = 230°C

© Natalie Mitchell

"HEALTHY Looks Good on YOU!"

Whole Foods Market

Chapter 4

Recipes that help your body Kill Cancer Cells

Straight to the point...You wake up in the morning and crave a power breakfast that will fill you with energy and fight any cancer cells by bringing them their most hateful food full of **alkalizing minerals** and **antioxidant vitamins**. Here are some delicious and quick to make breakfast recipes you will enjoy!

Awesome, power -packed Breakfast recipes

10. Wild smoked Salmon, fried or scrambled Eggs on whole grain toast with ripe avocado slices

Ingredients

1 serving:

- 2-3 organic eggs
- 2-3 slices of smoked wild salmon
- Sea salt added to taste
- 1 tablespoon olive oil
- 1 half ripe avocado sliced

Preparation

1. Heat the olive oil in a skillet and fry the eggs to your own preferences.
2. As soon as the fried eggs are cooked place them on sliced whole grain bread or toast. Add slices of ripe avocado and wild salmon and serve immediately. ENJOY!
3. Please make sure that the ingredients of the whole grain bread you buy do not include soy, high fructose corn syrup, corn syrup, any white flour or white sugar. I'll explain later in the book more in details why you should avoid those ingredients in any food product.

11. Wild Salmon, eggs and hummus on whole grain bread

Ingredients

1 serving

- 2-3 organic eggs
- 2-3 slices of wild, smoked salmon
- Sea salt to taste
- 1 tablespoon olive oil
- 1 avocado

Preparation

1. Heat the olive oil and cook the eggs to your preference. As soon as the eggs are cooked place them on freshly sliced whole grain bread.
2. Add the hummus and wild salmon. For variety I add sometimes big green olives and marinated garlic (great thing for our hearts!) Don't worry about the smell of garlic, as it doesn't have any smell when marinated! Serve immediately.
3. If you really a big man or just feeling very hungry in the morning as some of us do, you can add a slice of bread with crab meat or mushroom pate. ENJOY!

Why whole eggs are good for us. Free-range eggs contain plentiful amounts of amino acids and are an excellent source of protein for relatively few calories. Eggs are good sources of the essential amino acids methionine, isoleucine and lysine. They are a good source of tryptophan, an essential amino acid involved in the production of the mood-enhancing neurotransmitter serotonin.

Whole eggs provide your body with a source of fat-soluble vitamins, including A, D and E, significant quantities of certain B complex vitamins, including B-6, B-12, folate and riboflavin and alkaline and cancer preventative minerals such as **calcium, magnesium**, iron, zinc and **selenium**.

12. Omelet with Spinach, Mushrooms and

Red Onion

Ingredients

Original recipe makes 2 servings

- 1 (8 ounce) carton liquid egg substitute
- 1/4 teaspoon sea salt
- 1/8 teaspoon ground black pepper
- 1/8 teaspoon garlic powder
- 1 teaspoon olive oil
- 1/2 cup chopped fresh mushrooms
- 1 tablespoon chopped red onion
- 1/2 cup chopped fresh spinach, or more to taste

Preparation

1. Whisk egg substitute, sea salt, black pepper and garlic powder together in a bowl.

2. Heat olive oil in a nonstick skillet over medium heat; cook and stir mushrooms and red onion until tender, 4 to 5 minutes.
3. Add spinach; cook until spinach wilts, 3 to 4 minutes. Pour in egg mixture; swirl pan around to evenly distribute egg mixture.
4. Cook until egg is fully cooked and set in the middle, 5 to 10

© Natalie Mitchell

minutes.

5. Cut into wedges. ENJOY!

13. Omelet with Wild Salmon and Arugula

Serves 2-3

Ingredients

- 1 teaspoon olive oil
- 4 eggs
- 2 cups of arugula
- 1 4-oz fillet of wild, smoked salmon
- 1/2 teaspoon sea salt
- 1/2 teaspoon ground black pepper
- 1 tablespoon of capers, rinsed and dried

Preparation

1. Preheat a nonstick pan with the olive oil over medium heat
2. In a medium mixing bowl, beat the eggs; add the salt and pepper
3. Add the arugula and wild smoked salmon. Mix well
4. Pour the omelet mixture into the pan and cook for ~3-4

minutes. When the edges are crisp and coming off of the pan, gently take a wooden spatula and slide it underneath and all around the omelet so that you know parts of the omelet are not stuck to the pan (makes for easy flipping).

5. If you feel comfortable enough to flip, go for it! I try to keep it safe and take a large plate (wider than the pan), place the plate over the pan, and then using an oven mitt, flip the omelet onto the plate. Then slide the omelet back into the pan (uncooked side facing down), and cook for another 1-2 minutes.
6. Sprinkle on top with capers. ENJOY!

14. Porridge with almond milk and nuts

If you don't feel like eating eggs in the morning then real porridge oats cooked with hazelnut, almond, oat, millet, or any other cereal milk might be another breakfast option for you. As I pointed out earlier, please avoid cow milk, soy or goat milk of any kind as well as any dairy or soy yoghurt. You might exclaim "I like my milk and yogurt in the morning!" Well, I promised to keep you healthy so please be patient as I will explain in detail with supported research a bit later in the book why I ask you to avoid these ingredients.

Ingredients

Serves 4

- 60g (1/3 cup) almond kernels

- 40g (1/4 cup) pistachio nut kernels
- 4 (about 80g) fresh dates, pitted, roughly chopped
- 750ml (3 cups) almond milk
- 140g (1 1/2 cups) whole grain rolled oats
- Pinch of sea salt
- 125ml (1/2 cup) pure organic maple syrup
- Extra almond milk, to serve

Preparation

1. Preheat oven to 180°C. Spread the almonds and pistachio nuts in a single layer over a baking tray.
2. Cook in preheated oven, tossing once, for 8 minutes or until lightly toasted and aromatic. (See microwave tip).
3. Transfer to a chopping board and set aside for 10 minutes to cool slightly.
4. Roughly chop and place in a small bowl. Add the dates and stir to combine.
5. Place the almond milk, oats and sea salt in a medium heavy-based saucepan.
6. Stir over high heat until the mixture comes to the boil.
7. Reduce heat to low and simmer, uncovered, stirring occasionally, for 10-12 minutes or until the mixture thickens.
8. Spoon the porridge into serving bowls and sprinkle with the nut and date mixture.
9. Drizzle with maple syrup and serve with extra almond milk.

To make you more energetic you can add almonds, cashew, walnuts or any nuts according to your own taste.

Nuts and **legumes** are abundant sources of amino acids. Walnuts, almonds, Brazil nuts, cashews and peanuts are all rich sources of the essential amino acid L-argininc. Arginine is known to **boost immune function**, assist in **muscle metabolism** and muscle mass and enhance collagen production and bone growth. Almonds and cashews are also top sources of isoleucine, another essential amino acid that stabilizes blood sugar and increases energy. Almonds and peanuts also boast high levels of the amino acid phenylalanine, which is thought to enhance mood.

Nuts contain “good” fat and this is one of the best ways to burn unwanted fat in the Again I will go more into details later in the book.

Of course the simplest breakfast and again a very filling one would be a whole grains cereals with one of your favorite cereal milks. Please make sure to buy packaged cereals with as little sugar as possible. I don't want to scare you but you should know that sugar is one of the favorite foods for cancer cells. Being a cancer preventative coach, I feel I should share this information with you even early in the book. Please keep in mind that 4 grams of sugar is the equivalent of 1 teaspoon of sugar. So when people drink a bottle or can of Coke, it contains 39 gr of sugar which is approximately 10 teaspoons of white sugar! Don't worry about the past - we learn all our life and I didn't know this information 12 years ago either and was consuming a lot sugar myself and had much less energy.

To make them more enjoyable and interesting, you can add to your cereals, sliced bananas, blueberries, papaya, mango, ripe strawberries as well as different nuts.

15. Another satisfying breakfast idea - South Beach Buckwheat or Granola Pancakes!

There's something about buckwheat pancakes that takes us back to an earlier time—pioneer days, log cabins, pot belly stoves, and all that. Perhaps it's because buckwheat used to be a lot more popular a hundred years ago, in fact 20 times the acreage was cultivated in 1918 compared with today. In spite of the name, there is no "wheat" in buckwheat. It's not even a grain or grass. Yet in many ways it behaves like wheat, and its flour produces wonderfully, unexpectedly fluffy pancakes, with a rich, warm, earthy taste. We experimented quite a bit with this recipe, including an egg, excluding an egg, all buckwheat flour, or half buckwheat, half all-purpose flour, and you know what? It's all good. My favorite combination includes an egg and uses half white flour and half buckwheat flour. The combos without the egg or with all buckwheat flour were also fluffy, flavorful, and eat-way-too-many-able. Buckwheat has zero gluten in it, so if you are at all gluten-sensitive, you shouldn't have a problem with buckwheat (just use all buckwheat flour instead of the mix in the following recipe.) Griddle's on!

Ingredients

- olive oil for coating the pan
- 3/4 cup (100g or 3.5 oz) buckwheat or granola flour

- 3/4 cup (100g or 3.5 oz) whole grain flour (can sub with buckwheat or granola flour for a 100% buckwheat or granola pancake if you wish)
- 1 1/2 tsp or 1 1/4 packets Stevia
- 1/2 teaspoon sea salt
- 1 banana
- 1 teaspoon baking soda
- 3 Tbsp unsalted butter, melted
- 1 egg (optional)
- 2 cups (475 ml) almond milk

Preparation

1. Heat a well-seasoned griddle, cast iron skillet, or stick-free pan on medium heat. The pan or griddle should be ready for the batter as soon as it is mixed.
2. Whisk together the dry ingredients—the flours, Stevia, sea salt, baking soda—in a large bowl.
3. Pour the melted butter over the dry ingredients and start stirring.
4. Beat the egg with a fork and stir it into half of the almond milk.
5. Add the almond milk / egg mixture to the dry ingredients, then slowly add in the rest of the almond milk as needed to get to the right consistency for your batter (you may not need all of the almond milk). Stir only until everything is combined. Do not over mix. A few lumps are fine.
6. Put a small amount (a half teaspoon) of olive oil on the pan or griddle and spread it around with a paper towel to coat.
7. Ladle the batter onto the hot surface to the desired size, about 4-5 inches wide. (A 1/4 cup measure will ladle about a 4-inch pancake.) Reduce the heat to medium-low. Allow the pancake to cook for 2-3 minutes on this first side. Watch for bubbles on the surface of the pancake. When air bubbles start to rise to the surface at the center of the pancake, flip the pancake. Cook for another 1-2 minutes, or until nicely browned.
8. Keep your pancakes warm on a rack in the oven set on "warm," or stack them on a plate and cover with a towel as you make more. Spread more oil on the pan as needed between batches of pancakes.

9. Serve with banana and organic maple syrup. ENJOY!

16. Swiss Mountain Buckwheat Pancakes with mushrooms and spinach

This recipe is good either for lunch or dinner!

Serves: 4

Ingredients

Pancakes :

- 275ml Almond Milk
- 1 egg
- 55g whole wheat flour
- 55g buckwheat flour
- 1tbsp olive oil

Filling :

- 50g whole wheat flour
- 50g butter
- 275ml Almond milk
- ¼ tsp nutmeg
- A pinch of sea salt
- 100g sliced chestnut mushrooms
- 3 large handfuls of baby spinach leaves

- Olive oil

Preparation

To make the filling:
1. Preheat the olive oil in a small saucepan. Add whole wheat flour to the pan and stir to create a paste-like consistency. Continue cooking for a further 30 seconds.
2. Gradually add in the almond milk, stirring vigorously until you have a smooth sauce.
NB. Make sure to stir continuously to prevent lumps forming.
3. Drizzle the olive oil in a small frying pan on a high heat. Fry the mushrooms until brown. Throw in the spinach leaves and allow wilting.
4. Stir the mushrooms and spinach into the white sauce and stir.
5. Add in the nutmeg and season to taste.

To make the pancakes:
1. To make the pancakes, place the two types of flour into a large bowl and make a small well in the middle of the bowl.
2. Lightly whisk the egg into almond milk. Pour some of the egg mixture into the middle of the well and begin to whisk. Continue adding the liquid and whisking until you have a smooth batter.
3. Melt the butter in a non-stick frying pan and add in a ladle of the pancake batter. Swirl the pan to evenly coat the base. Flip the pancake to cook both sides until golden. Repeat until all the batter is used.
4. Spoon some of the mushroom and spinach filling into the middle of the pancakes and fold the sides in to create a parcel. ENJOY!

Lunch ideas

Delicious Soups for lunch

The greatest form of comfort food, soups arc a celebration of the freshest produce available in season. They can be therapeutic, warming, wild and experimental, sweet or tangy, luscious, indulgent, immunity boosting, spoiling and why not. Best thing about them? They come in all colors & textures possible and can be incredibly healthy. From smooth and creamy, to thick and hearty, perfect for every mood and occasion.

17. Pumpkin Soup

"This delicious, cream-like soup is great for Thanksgiving dinner and any time of year!"

Ingredients

Original recipe makes 8 to 10 servings

- 6 cups organic vegetable stock
- 1 1/2 teaspoons sea salt
- 4 cups pumpkin puree
- 1 teaspoon chopped fresh parsley
- 1 cup chopped onion
- 1/2 teaspoon chopped fresh thyme
- 1 clove garlic, minced
- 5 whole black peppers

Preparations

1. Heat organic vegetable stock, sea salt, pumpkin, onion,

thyme, garlic, and pepper. Bring to a boil, reduce heat to low, and simmer for 30 minutes uncovered.

2. Puree the soup in small batches (1 cup at a time) using a food processor or blender.

3. Return to pan, and bring to a boil again. Reduce heat to low, and simmer for another 30 minutes, uncovered. Pour into soup bowls and garnish with fresh parsley.

18. Pea & Mint Soup

Ingredients

- 1 bunch spring onions, trimmed and roughly chopped
- 1 medium potato, peeled and diced
- 1 garlic clove, crushed
- 850ml organic vegetable stock
- 900g young peas in the pod (to give about 250g/9oz shelled peas)
- 4 tbsp chopped fresh mint
- 1 tbsp fresh lemon or lime juicc

Preparation

1. Put the spring onions into a large pan with the potato, garlic and organic vegetable stock. Bring to the boil, turn down the heat and simmer for 15 minutes or until the potato is very soft. For the garnish, blanch 3 tbsp of the shelled peas in boiling water for 2-3 minutes, drain, put in a bowl of cold water and set aside.

2. Add the remaining peas to the soup base and simmer for 5 minutes – no longer, or you will lose the lovely fresh flavor of the peas.

3. Stir in the mint and lemon or lime juice, cool slightly then pour into a food processor or liquidizer and whizz until as smooth as you like and season with sea salt and pepper.

4. To serve the soup cold, cool quickly, then chill – you may need to add more stock to the soup before serving as it will thicken as it cools. To serve hot, return the soup to the rinsed-out pan and reheat without boiling).

19. Parsnip and Apple Soup

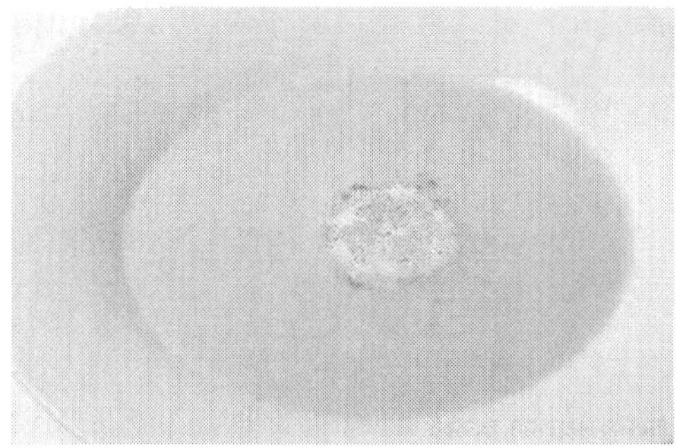

Ingredients

Serves 5

- 25g butter
- 1 medium onion, chopped
- 1 large garlic clove, crushed
- 450g parsnip, chopped
- 250g dessert apples peeled, cored and chopped
- 1/2 tsp ground coriander
- 1.2l organic vegetable stock
- 70ml coconut cream

Preparation

1. Melt the butter in a large pan then add the onion and garlic for 3-4 minutes until softened.
2. Add apples and parsnips for a further 3-4 minutes. Add coriander and stir for 30 seconds. Pour in stock, season well and bring to the boil. Reduce heat, cover and simmer for 25 minutes.
3. Remove from the heat, wait for it to cool then blend it in the food processor until almost smooth (so as to keep a little texture)
4. Return soup to the pan, stir in the coconut cream and reheat gently, but don't boil.
5. Serve straight away. ENJOY!

20. Ukha (Russian Fish Soup)

© Natalie Mitchell

A wonderful fish soup. Very popular in Russia and easy to make. Try it with pike, perch or salmon.

Ingredients

Serves 4

Original recipe makes 4 servings

- 4 cups organic vegetable stock
- 2 potatoes, cubed
- 1 onion, chopped
- 1 bunch fresh parsley, chopped
- 4 ounces salmon, perch, pike or cod fillets, cubed
- 1 lemon, juiced
- Sea salt and pepper to taste

Preparation

1. Put 4 cups of organic vegetable stock in a large saucepan and bring to a boil over high heat.
2. Add the potatoes, onion and parsley. Heat for 10 to 15 minutes and add the fish.
3. Heat for 10 more minutes, then squeeze in lemon juice and season with sea salt and pepper to taste.

© Natalie Mitchell

21. Carrot and Sweet Potato Soup with Ginger and Coriander

Ingredients

Serves 4

- 1-2 tbsp olive oil
- 1 medium onion, chopped
- 2 tbsp finely minced fresh ginger root
- 3 big carrots, peeled and cubed
- 1 big sweet potato, peeled and cubed
- 3 cups of organic vegetable stock (plus more water if needed)
- 1 tbsp ground coriander
- sea salt, to taste
- freshly ground black pepper, to taste
- chili flakes, to taste
- 2 garlic cloves, finely grated
- serve with cold pressed extra virgin olive oil, freshly ground black pepper and some fresh coriander

Preparation

1. In a big stockpot, add olive oil and onions and cook on medium to high heat until translucent.

2. Add ginger and cook for 30 seconds.
3. Add carrots and sweet potato and cook for 1-2 minutes, stirring.
4. Add organic vegetable stock (and more water if needed to cover the veggies) and bring to a boil. Once it's boiling, lower heat, add coriander, season with sea salt, pepper and chili flakes (if using) and simmer until carrots and potato are tender.
5. Turn off heat and allow soup to partially cool, then add it to the blender and puree it.
6. Return to the pot, add grated garlic and stir.
7. Warm it up again before serving. ENJOY!

22. Asparagus soup

Ingredients

Serves 4

- 3 pounds fresh asparagus, rinsed
- 8 cups organic vegetable stock
- 4 tablespoons unsalted butter
- 1 cup minced shallots
- 1 cup minced leeks, whites only, well rinsed

- 1 tablespoon minced garlic
- 1/2 teaspoon sea salt
- 1/4 teaspoon ground white pepper

Preparation

1. Trim the attractive top tips from the asparagus, about 1 to 1 1/2 inches in length. Cut the woody stem ends from each spear and reserve. Cut the remaining tender stalks into 1/2-inch pieces.

2. In a medium pot, bring the stock to a boil. Add the tough woody stems, lower the heat and simmer to infuse with asparagus flavor, 20 to 30 minutes. Remove with a slotted spoon and discard, reserving the stock.
3. In a medium stockpot, melt the butter over medium-high heat. When foamy, add the shallots and leeks and cook until tender, about 3 minutes.
4. Add the garlic and cook until fragrant, about 1 minute. Add the chopped asparagus stalks, sea salt and pepper, and cook, stirring, for 2 minutes.
5. Add the organic vegetable stock and simmer until the asparagus are very tender, 15 to 20 minutes. Remove from the heat.
6. With a hand-immersion blender or in batches in a food processor, puree the soup until smooth. Adjust the seasoning, to taste.
7. If serving right away, return to medium heat. Cook, stirring, until the soup is warmed through, about 3 minutes.
8. Alternatively, if serving the soup later, let cool at room temperature. Cover and refrigerate. ENJOY!

23. French Onion Soup

The trick to a great French onion soup is starting with good stock. French onion soup is usually made with chicken stock or beef stock. Another important element is the proper caramelization of the onions. Caramelizing onions requires at least thirty minutes of slow cooking the onions over medium high heat. The browning, or caramelizing, of the onions brings out the sweetness in them.

Serves 4-6.

Ingredients

- 6 large red or yellow onions, peeled and thinly sliced root to stem
- Olive oil
- 1/8 teaspoon of Stevia
- 2 cloves garlic, minced
- 8 cups of organic chicken stock
- 1/2 cup of dry vermouth or dry white wine
- 1 bay leaf
- 1/4 teaspoon of dry thyme
- Sea salt and pepper

Preparation

1. In a large saucepan, sauté the onions in the olive oil on medium high heat until well browned, but not burned, about 30-40 minutes (or longer).
2. Add the brown sugar about 10 minutes into the process to help with the carmelization.

3. Add garlic and sauté for 1 minute. Add the stock, vermouth or wine, bay leaf, and thyme. Cover partially and simmer until the flavors are well blended, about 30 minutes.

4. Season to taste with salt and pepper. Discard the bay leaf.

5. To serve you can either use individual oven-proof soup bowls or one large casserole dish. Ladle the soup into the bowls or casserole dish. ENJOY!

24. Leek and Potato Soup

Ingredients

- 1 tablespoon extra-virgin olive oil
- 2 cups diced onion
- 4 large leeks, cleaned and sliced, plus 1 cup julienned, for garnish
- Sea salt and freshly ground black pepper
- 3 tablespoons butter
- 3 tablespoons whole grain flour
- 1 quart organic chicken stock

- 3 tablespoons white wine
- 4 cups peeled, quartered or diced new potatoes, plus 2 cups julienned shoestring-style, for garnish
- 2 tablespoons minced chives, for garnish

Preparation

1. Heat olive oil in a skillet over medium heat. Add the onion and leeks, sauté for 2 minutes.
2. Season with sea salt and pepper. Add butter. When melted, stir in whole grain flour to make a roux. Whisk in organic chicken stock.
3. Add wine and new potatoes. Bring to a simmer and cook until potatoes are tender.
4. Meanwhile, add 3 inches of olive oil to a Dutch oven, or a saucepan. Heat the oil to 350 degrees F.
5. Add julienned potatoes and fry until golden brown. Remove and place on plate lined with paper towels.
6. Season with sea salt. Repeat the process for the julienned leeks.
7. If desired, puree the soup with a hand blender for a smoother consistency. Season with sea salt and pepper. Garnish with shoestring potatoes, leeks and chives. ENJOY!

25. Chicken and Lentil Soup

Ingredients

Makes 4 servings

- 1 cup Green Lentils, rinsed, drained
- 2 cups organic vegetable stock
- 4 cups Water
- 2 organic Chicken Breast Fillets
- 1 Onion, finely chopped
- 2 Celery Sticks, leaves intact, chopped
- 2 Carrots, finely chopped
- 1 Bay Leaf
- 1/4 cup Chopped Flat-leaf Parsley and Kale

Preparation

1. Place the lentils in a large saucepan and cover with water. Bring to the boil over high heat. Drain and rinse under cold water.

2. Bring the organic vegetable stock and water to the boil in the saucepan over high heat. Remove from heat and add chicken. Place over low heat and simmer, covered, for 15 minutes or until cooked. Use a slotted spoon to transfer the

chicken to a plate.

3. Increase heat to high. Add the lentils, onion, celery, carrot and bay leaf. Bring to the boil. Reduce heat to low. Simmer, covered, for 45-50 minutes or until lentils are tender. Season to taste.
4. Shred the chicken and return to the soup. Ladle among bowls. Top with parsley and Kale. ENJOY!

Salads for Lunch

26. Paradise Salad

Ingredients

Makes 4 servings

- 2 teaspoons curry powder (preferably Madras-style)
- 1/4 cup light mayonnaise
- 1/4 cup coconut cream
- 2 teaspoons mango chutney
- 1 teaspoon minced peeled fresh ginger
- 1/2 teaspoon grated orange peel
- 3 cups 1/2-inch pieces cooked skinless boneless chicken breast
- 1 cup halved seedless red grapes
- 1 cup ripe strawberries
- 1 mango chopped
- 1 avocado chopped

© Natalie Mitchell

- Some curly lettuce leaves or arugula
- 4 small clusters seedless red grapes

Preparation

1. Stir curry powder in small skillet over medium heat until fragrant, about 30 seconds. Transfer to medium bowl.
2. Add light mayonnaise, coconut cream, mango chutney, minced ginger, and grated orange peel. Whisk to blend.
3. Stir in chicken, grapes, chopped strawberries mango and avocado. Season salad to taste with salt and pepper.
4. Place lettuce leafs or arugula on each of 4 plates. Divide salad among leaves.
5. Garnish each plate with grape cluster. ENJOY!

27. Shrimp and Mango Salad

This salad is delicious served immediately at room temperature. It's even better after being chilled for an hour to combine the flavors.

Ingredients:

Serves 4

- 1 pound **grilled shrimp**, chopped
- 3 large mangoes, peeled and cut into chunks
- 1/2 small red onion, thinly sliced
- 3 tablespoons chopped cilantro
- 1/2 jalapeño pepper, seeded and chopped (optional)
- Juice of 2 large limes

- Sea salt to taste

Preparation:

1. Place all the ingredients but the salt in a large bowl. Stir to combine.
2. Season with the sea salt and serve. ENJOY!

28. Smoked Salmon and Fennel Salad Lake Garda style

A simple, elegant and delicious starter. Sliced baby fennel is marinated in seasoned lemon juice, then served with smoked salmon. This dish is perfect for dinner parties.

Ingredients

Serves: 3

- 100-120g sliced wild smoked salmon
- 250g baby fennel, green tops removed and reserved, thinly sliced
- 1/4 teaspoon chopped fennel leaves

- 1/2 lemon, juiced
- 1 pinch sea salt
- 1 pinch ground black pepper
- chopped dill for garnish
- extra virgin olive oil for drizzling

Preparation

Prep: 15 minutes › Extra time:5 minutes marinating › Ready in:20 minutes

1. Combine sliced fennel, fennel leaves, lemon juice, sea salt and pepper in a bowl. Mix well using your hands. Let sit for 5 minutes or until fennel is slightly softened.
2. Divide the wild smoked salmon onto three plates. Arrange the lemon-seasoned fennel on the top or the side. Sprinkle with chopped dill and drizzle with olive oil. ENJOY!

29. Arugula, Radish and Fennel Salad

Ingredients

Serves 2

- 6 cups fresh arugula leaves
- 1 fennel medium size
- 5 radishes

For the dressing

- 2 tbs lime juice, about 1/2 lime or lemon
- 4 tbs olive oil
- 1/2 tsp medium curry spice
- 1/2 tbp turmeric
- Sea salt

Preparation

1. Combine all the ingredients for the salad dressing in a jar, close it tight and shake until the ingredients are well mixed.
2. Toss the arugula leaves with the half of the dressing
3. Add the fennel slices and radishes slices to the arugula mix, drizzle the remaining dressing on top.
4. Serve immediately. ENJOY!

30. Tuna Carpaccio with Capers, Olives, Lemon Zest, Arugula and Olive Oil

© Natalie Mitchell

Ingredients

Serves 2

- 1/2 pound of the freshest sashimi grade yellowfin tuna
- Arugula
- 1 lemon, zested, optional
- 1/2 lemon juice
- Extra virgin olive oil (light)
- 1/2 cup Kalamata olives, pitted and diced
- 2 tablespoons capers, salt-packed and rinsed
- Chopped parsley leaves
- A pinch of sea salt
- Pepper to taste

Preparation

1. Thinly slice the tuna and place in a bowl. Season with a pinch of sea salt mixed with light extra virgin olive oil and lemon juice.

2. Tip: Place the tuna in the freezer for half an hour to firm it up before you slice – it's slices thinner and easier

3. Toss the arugula with the zest, olive oil and season with sea salt and pepper. Place the tuna on top of the greens and sprinkle the olives around the tuna. Garnish with capers and chopped parsley.

4. Serve immediately. ENJOY!

31. Napoleon of Tuna Tartar

© Natalie Mitchell

Ingredients

Serves 4

Tartare:

- 8 ounces freshest yellow fin tuna
- 4 baby gherkins
- 1 teaspoon capers
- 1 shallot
- 1 tablespoon extra-virgin olive oil
- 1/2 teaspoon lemon juice
- Sea salt and freshly ground black pepper
- 2 pappadams

Pickle:

- 1 tablespoon rice vinegar
- 1 cup water
- 1 sprig fresh thyme
- 1 sprig fresh rosemary
- 1 bay leaf
- 3 black peppercorns
- Pinch sea salt
- 1 teaspoon mustard

© Natalie Mitchell

Garnish:

- 1/4 teaspoon truffle oil
- 4 sprigs fresh dill
- 4 caper berries

Preparation

For the tartare:

1. Dice the tuna into small pieces.
2. Finely chop the gherkins, capers and shallot and add to the tuna.
3. Mix in the olive oil, lemon juice, sea salt and pepper.
4. Form into quenelles and store in the refrigerator.
5. Cut the pappadams into 4 and deep-fry until golden.

For the pickle:

1. Add to a saucepan the pickle ingredients except for the mustard.
2. Cook on low heat for 2 min.
3. Mix in the mustard.

Presentation on the plate:

1. Stack the tuna quenelles in layers on top of the pappadams and arrange the gherkins around the side.
2. Finish with a drizzle of truffle oil, a sprig of dill and a caper berry on top of the tuna. ENJOY!

30. Thai Green Curry Mussels

Clean the mussels with a stiff brush under cold running water. Remove the beard, the little tuft of fibers the mussel uses to connect to rocks or pilings, by cutting and scraping it with a knife or scissors. You may also pull it sharply down toward the hinged point of the shells with your fingers.

Ingredients:
Serves 4

- 1 can (14 fl. oz.) coconut milk
- 1 Tbs. Thai green curry paste
- 1 stalk lemongrass
- 1 lime leaf (optional)
- 1 Tbs. Asian fish sauce
- 1 1/2 lb. mussels, scrubbed and debearded if necessary
- 3 Tbs. slivered fresh basil or mint leaves

Preparation

1. In a wok or large saucepan over medium-low heat, combine 1/4 cup of the coconut milk and the curry paste.
2. Cut the bottom one-third of the lemongrass stalk into 1-inch pieces. Crush the pieces with the flat side of a chef's knife. Add to

the wok along with the lime leaf. Increase the heat to medium and bring the curry mixture to a simmer.

3. Cook, stirring occasionally, until fragrant, about 5 minutes.

4. Add the remaining coconut milk, 1/2 cup water and the fish sauce to the curry base and stir.

5. Discard any open mussels that do not close to the touch, then increase the heat to high and add the mussels. When a few start to open, cover the wok and cook for 2 minutes. Uncover and, using a slotted spoon, transfer the opened mussels to individual bowls. Cover the wok again and continue to cook until the remaining mussels open, about 2 minutes more.

6. Transfer the mussels to the bowls, discarding any that have failed to open. Ladle the broth over the mussels, garnish with the basil and serve immediately. ENJOY!

31. Arugula, Papaya and Avocado Salad with Pomegranate-Lime Vinaigrette

Ingredients

Serves 4

- See recipe for Pomegranate-lime vinaigrette dressing below
- 5 cups baby arugula, washed and dried
- 1 Haas avocado, peeled and diced
- 1/2 small, ripe papaya, peeled and diced
- 1 small red onion, halved and sliced

Pomegranate-Lime Vinaigrette

Ingredients

- 1 tablespoon rice wine vinegar
- 1/4 cup fresh pomegranate juice, seeds reserved for salad
- 2 teaspoons lime juice, freshly squeezed
- 1 tablespoon honey
- 1 teaspoon Dijon mustard
- 1 teaspoon garlic, minced
- Cayenne pepper to taste
- 1/2 cup olive oil
- Sea salt and black pepper to taste

Preparation

1. Make the dressing - Whisk first 7 ingredients (vinegar through cayenne) in a bowl. Let sit for 5-10 minutes to meld flavors.
2. Whisk in the olive oil and season to taste with salt and pepper. Set aside.
3. Make the salad - Combine ingredients for salad in a large bowl.
4. Add half of the dressing and toss thoroughly.
5. Add additional dressing as needed or serve a little extra on the side. Enjoy!

32. Chicken, Avocado and Mango Salad (one of my favorites!)

Ingredients:

For 2 servings:

- 1 cup shredded, cooked organic chicken
- 1 tablespoon water
- 1 tablespoon and 1 teaspoon lime juice
- 2 tablespoons chili garlic sauce
- 1 ripe medium mango - peeled, seeded and diced
- 1/2 ripe avocado - peeled, pitted and diced
- 1/4 (10 ounce) package spring lettuce mix
- 1 teaspoon honey

Preparation

1. In a saucepan over medium-high heat, stir together the honey and water. Bring to a boil, then pour into a medium bowl.

2. Stir in the garlic chili sauce and lime juice. Set the dressing aside.

3. In a large bowl, toss together the organic chicken, diced mango and avocado.
4. Arrange the spring salad mix on serving plates, then top with a few spoonfuls of the chicken mixture. Pour dressing over the top. ENJOY!

33. Lobster Avocado Salad

Ingredients

Serves 4

- Two 1 1/2-pound lobsters
- 3 tablespoons rice vinegar
- 1/2 teaspoon American Yellow Mustard
- 1/4 teaspoon finely grated fresh ginger
- 3 tablespoons olive oil
- Sea salt and freshly ground pepper to taste
- 1 bunch watercress (6 ounces), large stems discarded
- 1 Hass avocado, peeled and cut into chunks
- Spring onion

Preparation

1. In a large pot of boiling water, cook the lobsters until they turn bright red, about 12 minutes. Drain and let cool. Twist off the tails and claws. Crack the claws and remove the meat; cut into large pieces. Using kitchen scissors, slit the tail shells lengthwise up the center and remove the tail meat. Remove the black intestinal tract and discard. Cut the tail meat into 1-inch medallions. Cover and refrigerate the lobster meat.

2. In a large bowl, combine the vinegar with the mustard and ginger. Whisk in the oil until emulsified, then season with sea salt

and pepper. Add the watercress and lobster and toss gently, then add the avocado and toss just until dressed. Serve chilled. ENJOY!

34. Warm Sweet Potato, Mushroom and Spinach Salad

This warming, slightly spicy, sweet potato mushroom and spinach salad is just perfect for winter days. I love hot, filling dishes when it is cold outside! Mushrooms are an amazing addition to any dish as they add a fantastically filling, almost meaty, texture to everything. I also love how juicy and tender they become after they're stir fried with salt and olive oil. Yum! They're great at absorbing extra flavors too, which means here they pick up the subtly, spicy tastes given off by the slices of jalapeño pepper which they're cooked with. Their spicy, meatiness combines perfectly with the sweet, tender nature of the sweet potato cubes, the soft lime infused spinach and the ever-so-slightly crunchy quarters of juicy cherry tomatoes to create an amazingly simple but insanely delicious plate of goodness.

Everything on this plate will make your body love you, from the iron rich spinach to the B vitamin filled mushrooms and the antibacterial jalapeño peppers. All the ingredients are just amazing. Although it's the sweet potatoes that get me most excited. I love that they're so amazingly filling like normal white potatoes but then they have these extra specially awesome health benefits as well as aphrodisiac properties ☺. They're bursting with all kinds of goodness. Not only are they one of nature's richest sources of beta-carroteine (super important for your body to…., but they're also fantastic providers of Vitamins A and C, antioxidants, fiber, potassium, manganese and B6. As a result they have awesome anti-inflammatory properties and help to control your blood sugar. So there really are too many reasons to tuck into a huge plate of these deliciously sweet beauties!

Ingredients

Serves 2

- 1 large organic sweet potato (orange variety)
- a dozen chestnut mushrooms
- 2 bowls of (cooked) spinach
- 2 jalepeno peppers
- 1 red onion
- apple cider vinegar
- cinnamon
- paprika
- sea salt
- extra virgin olive oil

Preparation

1. Slice the sweet potatoes into bite-sized cubes and place them on a baking tray. Drizzle with olive oil, sea salt, paprika and cinnamon.
2. Bake for 15-20 minutes at 190C, until they're deliciously soft.
3. While these cook, slice the mushrooms into pieces and gently stir fry them with olive oil, salt, two teaspoons of apple cider vinegar, the chopped jalapeño pepper (remember to discard the seeds before chopping) and red onion. This should take about 7 minutes. Just before the end add the spinach and allow it to wilt.

This is a very quick process; it will only take one or two minutes to become perfectly soft.

4. Once everything is cooked mix it all together and serve.

ENJOY!

35. Warm Spinach Salad

Ingredients

- Serves 3-4
- 3 tablespoons extra-virgin olive oil
- 1 lb mushrooms (cleaned and trimmed)
- 5 asparagus (leaned and cut)
- 3 shallots, thinly sliced
- 2 cloves garlic, chopped
- 3 tablespoons sherry vinegar
- 2 pounds triple washed spinach, stems removed
- Sea salt and freshly ground black pepper
- Freshly grated nutmeg to taste
- 4 hard-boiled eggs, quartered lengthwise

Preparation

1. Heat the olive oil in a large skillet over medium-high heat. Once hot, add the mushrooms, asparagus, shallots and garlic to the pan.
2. Cook for 3 to 4 minutes then deglaze the pan with vinegar, turn the spinach into pan and wilt down a bit but do not fully cook the spinach, just give it a few turns with tongs. Season the greens with sea salt, pepper and nutmeg.
3. Place spinach on a serving dish and top with quartered eggs. Serve immediately. ENJOY!

36. Zucchini, Spinach and Mushroom Salad

Ingredients

Serves 4

- 6 cups spinach or arugula leaves
- 4 golden zucchini (large, sliced into long, thin strips)
- 1 lb mushrooms (cleaned and trimmed)
- 2 tbs olive oil
- 8 sprigs fresh chervil (chopped)
- 3 tbsps lemon juice
- Sea salt
- Black pepper

For the dressing

- 2 tbs lime juice, about 1/2 lime or lemon
- 4 tbs olive oil
- 1/2 tsp medium curry spice
- 1/2 tbp turmeric
- Sea salt

Preparation

1. Combine all the ingredients for the salad dressing in a jar, close it tight and shake until the ingredients are well mixed.
2. Toss the spinach leaves with the half of the dressing
3. Heat the olive oil and cook mushrooms and zucchini for 3-4 min. Add the fresh chervil, cooked mushrooms and zucchini to the spinach mix, drizzle the remaining dressing on top.
4. Serve immediately. ENJOY!

37. Bermuda Fish Cake

Ingredients

Serves 4

- 3 ounces chopped onion
- 1/2 ounce chopped garlic
- 1 tablespoon olive oil

- 1 ounce curry powder
- 1 ounce fresh chopped thyme
- 1 ounce fresh chopped parsley
- 1 pound cooked, roughly smashed potatoes (no cream or milk, only with butter)
- 8 ounces salted cod fish (soaked and rinsed 3 times over the previous 24 hours in the refrigerator, poached in water for 8 minutes)
- Coconut cream
- Sea salt and pepper, to taste
- 2 ounces whole grain flour
- Olive oil, for frying

Preparation

1. In a heavy bottom pan, sauté the onion and garlic on low to medium heat until cooked.
2. Add the curry powder and herbs and cook for 1 minute.
3. Add the potato and flaked cod fish to the pan and mix together. Season with sea salt and pepper.
4. Add enough coconut cream to make the mixture workable. On a floured surface, shape the fish cakes and fry in shallow oil on each side for 5 to 6 minutes over a medium heat. ENJOY!

38. Antiguan Crab Cake

© Natalie Mitchell

Ingredients:

Serves 4 to 6

- 1 pound crabmeat, picked free of shells
- 1/3 cup crushed whole grain crackers
- 3 green onions (green and white parts), finely chopped
- 1/4 cup light mayonnaise
- 1 egg
- 1 teaspoon Worcestershire sauce
- 1 teaspoon dry mustard
- 1/2 lemon, juiced
- 1/4 teaspoon garlic powder
- 1 teaspoon sea salt
- Dash cayenne pepper
- Whole grain flour, for dusting
- 1/2 cup extra virgin olive oil
- Your favorite dipping sauce, for serving

Preparation

1. In a large bowl, mix together all ingredients, except for the whole grain flour and olive oil. Shape into patties and dust with whole grain flour.
2. Heat oil in a large skillet over medium heat. When oil is hot, carefully place crab cakes, in batches, in pan and fry until browned, about 4 to 5 minutes. Carefully flip crab cakes and

fry on other side until golden brown, about 4 minutes.
3. Serve warm with preferred sauce and arugula or spinach. ENJOY!

39. Thai Shrimp Cake

Dried coconut, fresh ginger, fish sauce, and a couple of dashes of Sriracha lend Asian flavor to Thai Shrimp Cakes.

Ingredients
Serves 4

- 2/3 cup whole wheat bread crumbs, divided
- 1/4 cup minced unsweetened dried coconut, divided
- 2 tablespoons minced green onions
- 2 tablespoons finely chopped fresh cilantro
- 2 teaspoons fish sauce
- 2 teaspoons Sriracha (hot chile sauce)
- 1 1/2 teaspoons grated peeled fresh ginger
- 1 teaspoon lime juice
- 1 large egg, lightly beaten
- 1 garlic clove, minced
- 8 ounces peeled and deveined shrimp, chopped

- 1 tablespoon olive oil
- 1 lime, quartered

Preparation

1. Combine 1/3 cup whole wheat bread crumbs, 2 tablespoons coconut, and next 8 ingredients in a large bowl. Add shrimp; stir just until combined. Using wet hands, shape mixture into 4 equal balls. Combine remaining panko and coconut in a shallow dish. Coat balls in panko mixture; press to form 4 (4-inch) patties.

2. Heat a large nonstick skillet over medium-high heat. Add oil; swirl to coat. Add patties; cook 4 minutes on each side or until desired degree of doneness. Serve with lime.

Quinoa is one of the best proteins for lean muscles and reduced fat mass!

Quinoa is nutritionally rich: One cup of cooked quinoa contains 222 calories and provides the following nutrients:

- 8.2grams protein
- 40 grams carbohydrate
- 31 mg calcium
- 2 mg Zinc
- 2.75mg Iron
- 120 mg magnesium
- 5.2 grams dietary fiber

Given its strong protein and iron content it's especially good for vegetarians and vegans.

If you are on a gluten free diet it's worth trying Quinoa. It's also easy to digest.

Unwashed Quinoa can taste bitter. Quinoa is coated in a natural compound called saponins (a soap like substance). This compound help protect it while it is growing and ensures the seed is not eaten by birds, as saponin produces a bitter taste. As a result Quinoa needs to be washed before being eaten. While most commercially sold Quinoa is pre-washed, its worthwhile rinsing Quinoa before cooking just to make sure it contains no saponins.

Quinoa can be germinated to boost its nutritional value
Germinating Quinoa activates natural enzymes and multiplies the vitamin content. Better yet, the germination period is short, requiring only 2 to 4 hours soaking in water to make it sprout. Germination makes Quinoa soft, making it great for use in salads.

The great thing about this recipe for Quinoa with Zucchini and Onions is that this dish can be served hot or cold. The other night I made this as a side dish, and the next day I enjoyed the leftovers for lunch (and probably will today too). In addition to its versatility, this recipe is easy to prepare, involving cooking the Quinoa and frying the Zucchini and Onions and then combining it all together with some parsley, lemon juice and pine nuts. I didn't have pine nuts to hand, so I substituted toasted slivered almonds, which worked just as well.

40. Quinoa with Zucchini and Onions

Serves 4 as a meal and between 6 and 8 as a side.

Ingredients

- 800g of zucchini (courgettes), cut into 5mm thick slices
- a knob of butter
- 2 tablespoons of olive oil
- 3 red onions, peeled, cut in half and then sliced thinly
- a few sprigs of thyme, leaves only
- 3 garlic cloves, finely chopped
- 200g of white quinoa
- a good handful of flat leaf parsley, roughly chopped
- a squeeze of lemon juice
- 50g of pine nuts, lightly toasted
- sea salt and freshly ground pepper

Preparation

1. Place a large frying pan over a medium heat, add the oil and butter and once the butter has melted add the zucchini, onions, thyme and salt and pepper. Cook for 20 to 25 minutes, stirring from time to time, until the zucchini and tender and starting to turn golden. Add the garlic and fry for another couple of minutes.

2. While the zucchini and onions are cooking, rinse the quinoa in several changes of cold water and then place in a saucepan along with plenty of cold water and a pinch of salt. Bring to the boil and then reduce the heat and simmer for 12 minutes or until the quinoa is tender and the long white kernels are coming away from the seeds. Tip into a sieve and leave to drain and steam.

3. Combine the quinoa and zucchini and onions and toss to mix well. Add the parsley, lemon juice, salt and pepper and stir well. Check the seasoning and adjust as necessary. Serve topped with toasted pine nuts.

   Notes
   You will need to ensure you have a very large frying pan to

cook the zucchini and onions so that they cook properly rather than steam. If you don't have pine nuts to hand then substituted slivered almonds will work well too. ENJOY!

41. Quinoa Salad with Asparagus and Baby Artichoke

Ingredients:
Serves 4

- 8 baby artichokes
- 1 tablespoon olive oil
- 1 cup white quinoa
- 2 cups organic vegetable broth (or water)
- 1/2 cup asparagus pesto
- 1/2 pound asparagus (trimmed, cut into 1 inch pieces and blanched)
- 1 cup chickpeas (drained and rinsed)
- 1 splash lemon juice

Preparation

1. Peel the leaves from the artichokes until you get to the paler, tender, inner leaves. Cut the top third off and discard and cut the artichoke in half.
2. Heat the oil in a pan.
3. Add the artichoke hearts and sauté until tender, about 6-8 minutes.

4. After rinsing the quinoa in several changes of cold water, add the quinoa and broth, bring to a boil, reduce the heat and simmer, covered, until the quinoa is tender, about 15-20 minutes.
5. Mix everything and serve. ENJOY!

42. Quinoa Salad with shrimp and cucumber

This salad, with its gingery lime dressing, scallions, cilantro and a little bit of heat, has Asian overtones. Serve it as a side dish or a light lunch or supper. Vegetarians will enjoy this without the shrimp, which otherwise garnish the top of the salad.

For the dressing:
Serves 4

- 2 tablespoons freshly squeezed lime juice
- 1 tablespoon seasoned rice wine vinegar
- 1 teaspoon minced fresh ginger (more to taste)
- 1 small garlic clove, minced
- Sea Salt to taste
- Pinch of cayenne
- 2 teaspoons olive oil
- For the salad:
- 3 cups cooked quinoa (3/4 cup uncooked)
- 4 scallions, white and light green parts, sliced thin
- 1 small cucumber, halved, seeded and thinly sliced on the diagonal
- 1/4 cup chopped cilantro

- 12 to 16 cooked medium shrimp, peeled

Preparation

1. In a small bowl or measuring cup, whisk together the lime juice, rice wine vinegar, ginger, garlic, salt, cayenne and olive oil.
2. In a salad bowl, combine the quinoa, scallions, cucumber, and cilantro. Toss with the dressing and divide among salad plates. Top each portion with 3 or 4 shrimp, and serve. ENJOY!

Advance preparation: The cooked quinoa will keep for 3 or 4 days in the refrigerator. You can make the dressing and prep the ingredients for the salad a few hours ahead.

Cultivated for over 5,000 years quinoa is steadily increasing in popularity due to its nutty texture, rich flavor and health benefits.

Quinoa is a high protein grain that's also calorie dense, which means it's ideal for those looking to build **lean muscle** as well as **reducing fat mass**. The protein it contains is made up of all 9 essential amino acids, which means it's a complete protein that will help build lean muscles and repair them when necessary.

A study conducted in the 2011 issue of Food Chemistry magazine found that quinoa is rich in ecdysteroids and a 2010 study published in the Journal of Steroid Biochemistry found that ecdysteroids encouraged increased **muscle mass** and actively **reduced fat mass**.

Researchers have recently taken a close look at certain antioxidant phytonutrients in quinoa, and two flavonoid—quercetin and kaempferol—are now known to be provided by quinoa in especially concentrated amounts. In fact, the concentration of these two flavonoids in quinoa can sometimes be greater than their concentration in high-flavonoid berry like cranberry.

One of the best reasons to enjoy quinoa is because it has a high-protein content, which makes it a great **cholesterol-free and low-fat** source of protein for vegetarians and vegans. According to the USDA nutrient database, **1 cup of cooked quinoa (185 g) contains 8.14 grams of protein**. Quinoa has significantly greater amounts of both lysine and isoleucine (especially lysine), and these greater amounts of lysine and isoleucine allow the protein in quinoa to serve as a complete protein source.

Fat in Quinoa:

Quinoa is typically considered to be a valuable source of certain health-supportive fats. About 25% of quinoa's fatty acids come in the form of oleic acid, a heart-healthy monounsaturated fat, and about 8% come in the form of alpha-linolenic acid or ALA—the omega-3 fatty acid most commonly found in plants and associated with decreased risk of inflammation-related disease.

One cup of cooked quinoa provides 3.4 grams of fat. By comparison, 185 grams cooked lean ground beef provides 33 grams of fat.

Quinoa definitely deserves to be shown more appreciation and its benefits are numerous:

- **It is one of the most protein-rich foods we can eat.** It is a complete protein containing all nine essential amino acids.

- **Contains almost twice as much fiber as most other grains.** Fiber helps to prevent heart disease by reducing high blood pressure and diabetes.

- **Contains Iron.** Iron helps keep our red blood cells healthy and is the basis of hemoglobin formation. Iron carries oxygen from one cell to another and supplies oxygen to our muscles to aid in their contraction.

- **Contains lysine.** Lysine is mainly essential for tissue growth and repair.

- **Is rich in magnesium.**
- **Is high in Riboflavin (B2).** B2 improves energy metabolism within brain and muscle cells and is known to help create proper energy production in cells.
- **Has a high content of manganese.** Manganese is an antioxidant, which helps to prevent damage of mitochondria during energy production as well as to protect red blood cells and other cells from injury by free radicals.

Quinoa exists in white, red and black colors. My favorite is the red which is not as crunchy as the black one but a little more interesting to chew than the softer, white quinoa. I would recommend you rinse the quinoa before cooking to remove the quinoa's natural coating which can taste a little bit bitter.

43. Balsamic Roasted Vegetable Couscous Salad

Ingredients

Serves 3-4

© Natalie Mitchell

- 2 carrots (halved lengthways and thickly sliced)
- 2 courgettes (halved lengthways and thickly sliced)
- 10 chestnut mushrooms (halved)
- 1 onion (small, halved and thickly sliced)
- 3 cloves garlic (unpeeled)
- 1 handful green beans (fine, halved)
- 3 sprigs thyme
- 3 sprigs rosemary
- 1 handful coriander (torn)
- 1 pinch smoked paprika
- 1/2 tsp fennel seeds
- pepper
- extra virgin olive oil
- 4 tbsps balsamic vinegar
- 1 handful rocket leaves
- 1 handful watercress
- 250 grams couscous
- 400 ml organic vegetable stock (boiling)
- sesame oil

Preparation

1. Place all the vegetable and herbs into a large oven-proof casserole dish, drizzle with olive oil and the balsamic vinegar and sprinkle with the paprika and fennel then toss around, place the lid on and roast for 30 minutes on 190C
2. Remove the lid, stir and roast for a further 15 minutes until beginning to brown.
3. Prep the couscous by placing it in a large bowl and covering with the stock and olive oil ...I use a little lemon infused olive oil... cover and set aside for 5 minutes take the veggies out of the oven and set aside. I like to use the casserole dish as the main vessel for the final dish, so pour the couscous and salad leaves into the veggies, sprinkle over a little sesame oil and toss it all together coating the couscous in all the gorgeous oils and juices eat and of course, ENJOY!

44. Couscous Salad with Chicken and Chopped Vegetables

Ingredients

Serves 4

- 1 1/2 cups water
- 1 tbsp olive oil (divided)
- 3/4 tsp sea salt
- 1 cup couscous (uncooked)
- 1/2 cup zucchini (finely chopped)
- 1/2 cup mushrooms (chopped)
- 1 1/2 cups rotisserie chicken (chopped skinless, boneless)
- 1/2 cup carrots (1/8-inch-thick diagonally cut)
- 1/4 cup green onions sliced (thinly)
- 3 tbsps dried currants
- 3 tbsps chopped fresh mint (finely)
- 1/8 tsp black ground pepper (freshly)
- 3 tbsps fresh lemon juice
- 1 tbsp honey
- 1 cup coconut cream
- 1 tbsp white wine vinegar

Preparation

1. To prepare salad, bring water, 1 teaspoon oil, and salt to a boil in a medium saucepan; gradually stir in couscous. Remove from heat; cover and let stand 5 minutes. Fluff with a fork. Place in a large bowl; cool to room temperature.
2. Heat a large nonstick skillet over medium-high heat. Add remaining oil to pan. Add zucchini, and mushrooms; sauté 4 minutes. Add chicken, carrot, onions, currants, mint, and black pepper to couscous; toss gently to combine.
3. To prepare dressing, combine coconut cream and remaining ingredients, stirring with a whisk. Drizzle over couscous mixture, tossing gently to combine. ENJOY!

45. Warm kale and quinoa salad

Ingredients

Serves 3-4

- 1 cup Quinoa
- 1 Leek, sliced
- 3-4 Garlic cloves, minced.
- 1 Carrot, diced.
- 2 Zucchini, diced
- 1 cup Button Mushrooms, diced

- 1 bunch Dinosaur Kale (or other leafy green) coarsely chopped.
- 1 cup Garbanzo beans
- pinches dried Oregano
- Sea Salt and Pepper to taste
- Extra Virgin Olive Oil
- Juice of half a lemon
- 1 handful pine nuts
- 1 cut ripe avocado

Preparation

1. In a saucepan, boil 2 1/2 cups of water. Reduce heat to medium, add pre washed quinoa, a dash of sea salt, and let simmer with the lid half-on. The quinoa will take about 15 - 20 minutes, when the grain is translucent with a spiral-like germ.

2. In the meantime, heat some olive oil in a frying pan. Sauté the leeks and most of the garlic until softened. Add carrots. After a few minutes, add the mushrooms and zucchini. Season with the oregano and salt and pepper to taste. When softened, transfer to a large bowl.

3. In the same pan, without wiping any of the juices, sauté the remaining garlic and add the kale, turning it often. Season with a dash of sea salt and pepper, and some of the lemon juice. Transfer to the bowl with the rest of the cooked veggies.

4. Add the garbanzo beans and toss. Add the quinoa about a cup at a time. Toss in the pine nuts. Check salt and pepper taste. Drizzle with some remaining olive oil and some lemon juice, if desired. Add cut avocado on the top and ENJOY!

46. Warm Scallop Salad with Mushrooms and Zucchini

Ingredients

Serves 4

- 2 anchovies (minced)
- 1 tsp grated lemon zest (finely)
- 1 1/2 tbsps fresh lemon juice
- 5 tbsps extra-virgin olive oil
- sea salt
- freshly ground pepper
- 1 zucchini (medium, halved lengthwise and sliced crosswise 1/4 inch thick)
- 1/2 lb oyster mushrooms
- 16 sea scallops (large)
- 1 shallots (large, thinly sliced)
- 1/4 cup dry white wine
- 1 tbsp unsalted butter
- 1 head Boston lettuce (torn into pieces)
- 2 tbsps chives (minced)
- 2 tsps tarragon (chopped)
- bottarga (Finely grated, optional)

Preparation

1. In a small bowl, combine the anchovies with the lemon zest,

lemon juice and 2 tablespoons of the olive oil. Season with salt and pepper.

2. In a large skillet, heat 1 tablespoon of the olive oil. Add the zucchini, season with salt and cook over high heat until browned in spots; transfer to a large plate. Add 1 tablespoon of the olive oil and the mushrooms to the skillet; season with salt and pepper, cover and cook over moderate heat until starting to brown. Uncover and cook until tender and browned; transfer to the plate. ENJOY!

3. Season the scallops with salt and pepper. Heat the remaining 1 tablespoon of olive oil in the skillet until shimmering. Add the scallops and cook over moderately high heat until browned on the bottom. Turn the scallops and cook for 1 minute longer; transfer to a small plate. Add the shallot to the pan and cook until softened. Add the wine and simmer, then stir in the zucchini and mushrooms and reheat. Swirl in the anchovy dressing, any scallop juices and the butter.

4. Arrange the lettuce on plates and top with the scallops and vegetables. Garnish with the chives, tarragon and *bottarga* and serve. ENJOY!

47. Mung Bean Sprouts Salad with Parsley Root and Carrot

Mung bean sprouts contain various vitamins, in addition to an assortment of minerals including **calcium, iron, and potassium.** They are free of cholesterol, and are ideal for anyone counting calories. You may have noticed bean sprouts are gaining popularity as a health food, appearing in a wide variety of dishes from salads to soups, wraps or just as a healthy snack. Making sprouts at home is easier than you think and they are generally fresher and better than any store bought one.

Ingredients

- 100 g Mung bean sprouts
- 100 g Parsley root, finely grated
- 50 g Carrot, finely grated
- 8 Belgian endive leaves
- 1 tbsp Pomegranate seeds
- Lemon Juice
- Olive oil
- Sea Salt and pepper

Preparation

1. Peel and finely grate parsley root and carrot with a mandolin. Arrange Belgian endive leaves in a salad bowl. Place the grated vegetables in the center. Scatter the mung bean sprouts and pomegranate seeds over.
2. Add the olive oil, lemon juice and sea salt and pepper to taste and toss gently the grated vegetables, mung bean sprouts and pomegranate seeds together. ENJOY!

48. Whole wheat Penne with Arugula and Avocado

Ingredients:
Serves 2

- 200 g Whole wheat penne
- 3 cup Baby arugula leaves
- 3-5 Garlic cloves, sliced
- 40 g Walnuts, toasted
- One Avocado
- 70 ml Olive oil
- Sea salt and freshly ground pepper

Preparation:

1. Bring a large pot of water to a rapid boil. Add 1 teaspoon of sea salt and the pasta to the boiling water and stir. Boil gently uncovered, stirring occasionally. Follow package directions and cook until "al dente" stage, chewy but not hard.
2. Meanwhile, combine arugula, garlic slices, walnuts in a food processor. With the machine running, slowly drizzle in olive oil and process until evenly blended. Season pesto well with sea salt and freshly ground black pepper. Mix until evenly combined.
3. Drain pasta and return to the pot. Add arugula pesto and sliced avocado and toss well. Serve immediately. The pesto will keep about 1 week in a tightly sealed container in the refrigerator. ENJOY!

49. Venice Whole-Wheat Spaghetti in Anchovy Sauce (Bigoli in Salsa)

© Natalie Mitchell

Ingredients

Serves 4

- 8 oz. salt-packed anchovies (about 32 fish)
- 1½ cups tocai friulano or other dry Friuli white wine
- ½ cup extra-virgin olive oil
- 1 large yellow onion, peeled, halved, and thinly sliced
- 12 oz. whole wheat spaghetti
- Sea salt

Preparation

1. Soak anchovies in ½ cup of the white wine and 2 cups water in a large bowl for 30 minutes. Gently pull anchovies apart into lengthwise halves from the head end and remove and discard spines and all tiny bones. Wash anchovies in the soaking liquid, discard the soaking liquid, set aside 6 halves for garnish, then cut remaining halves into small pieces and set aside.

2. Heat oil in a large skillet over medium heat. Stir in onions and anchovies, breaking up anchovies with the back of a wooden spoon, until onions are very soft and anchovies have "melted," about 10 minutes. Add remaining 1 cup wine and stir, scraping up any brown

bits stuck to bottom of skillet. Reduce heat to low, cover, and cook for about 30 minutes, stirring occasionally.

3. Meanwhile, cook spaghetti in a large pot of lightly salted (the anchovies are very salty) boiling water over high heat until pasta is just tender, about 8 minutes. Drain, add pasta to sauce, mix well, and serve garnished with reserved anchovies and parsley, if you like. ENJOY!

50. Whole-Wheat Spaghetti with Lemon, Basil, and Wild Salmon

Ingredients
Serves 4

- 1/2 pound whole-wheat spaghetti pasta
- 1 clove garlic, minced
- 2 tablespoons extra-virgin olive oil
- 1/2 teaspoon sea salt, plus more for seasoning
- 1/2 teaspoon freshly ground black pepper, plus more for seasoning
- 1 tablespoon olive oil
- 4 x (4-ounce) pieces wild salmon
- 1/4 cup chopped fresh basil leaves
- 3 tablespoons capers

- 1 lemon, zested
- 2 tablespoons lemon juice
- 2 cups fresh baby spinach leaves

Preparation

1. Bring a large pot of salted water to a boil over high heat. Add the pasta and cook until tender but still firm to the bite, stirring occasionally, about 8 to 10 minutes. Drain pasta and transfer to a large bowl. Add the garlic, extra-virgin olive oil, salt, and pepper. Toss to combine.

2. Meanwhile, warm the olive oil in a medium skillet over medium-high heat. Season the salmon with salt and pepper. Add the fish to the pan and cook until medium-rare, about 2 minutes per side, depending on the thickness of the fish. Remove the salmon from the pan.

3. Add the basil, capers, lemon zest, and lemon juice to the spaghetti mixture and toss to combine. Set out 4 serving plates or shallow bowls. Place 1/2 cup spinach in each bowl. Top with 1/4 of the pasta. Top each mound of pasta with a piece of salmon. Serve immediately. ENJOY!

51. Grilled Brussels Sprouts

Ingredients

Serves 4

- 1 pound Brussels sprouts, as uniform in size as possible

- 1 tablespoons olive oil
- 1 tablespoon minced garlic
- 1 teaspoon dry mustard
- 1 teaspoon smoked paprika
- 1 teaspoon sea salt
- 1/4 teaspoon freshly ground black pepper

Preparation

In order to facilitate even cooking, it is important that the Brussels sprouts be as uniform in size and shape as possible.

1. Heat grill to medium temperature.
2. Cut off the stem end of the Brussels sprouts and remove any yellowing outer leaves. Place the Brussels sprouts into a large, microwave safe mixing bowl and heat in the microwave on high for 3 minutes. Add the olive oil, garlic, mustard, paprika and sea salt and toss to combine. Allow the sprouts to cool until you can handle them.
3. Skewer 4 to 5 Brussels sprouts onto each metal skewer with the stem ends facing in the same direction, leaving at least 1/2-inch in between each sprout. Place the skewers onto the grill with stem end closest to the flame. Cover and cook for 5 minutes. Turn the skewers over and continue to cook for another 5 minutes.
4. Serve as is or for additional flavor, remove the sprouts from the skewers, return them to the original mixing bowl and toss with any of the remaining oil and garlic mixture before serving. ENJOY!

52. Sautéed Brussels Sprouts and Shallots

Ingredients

- 2 tablespoons olive oil
- 1 cup thinly sliced shallots
- 2 garlic cloves, minced
- 3/4 pound Brussels sprouts, trimmed and thinly sliced lengthwise
- 1/4 teaspoon sea salt
- 1/8 teaspoon freshly ground black pepper

Preparation

1. Heat a large stainless steel skillet over medium-high heat. Add oil to pan; swirl to coat. Add shallots sauté 3 minutes or until almost tender, stirring occasionally.
2. Add garlic; sauté 30 seconds, stirring constantly.
3. Add Brussels sprouts; sauté 5 minutes or until brown, stirring occasionally. Sprinkle with salt and pepper, toss. ENJOY!

53. Brussels Sprouts with Currants and Pine Nuts

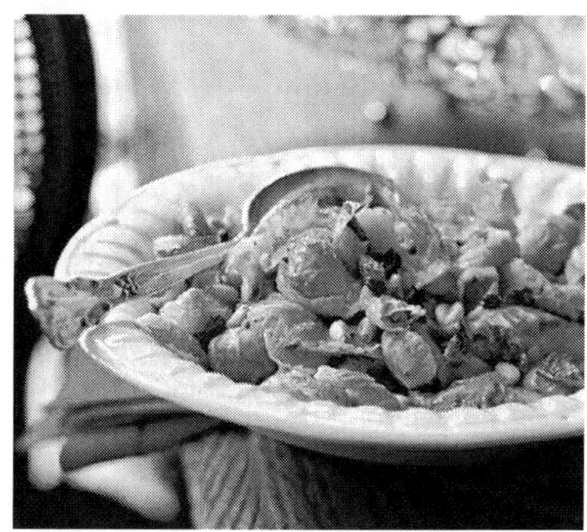

Ingredients

- 1 1/2 pounds Brussels sprouts, trimmed
- 1 tablespoon pine nuts
- 1 tablespoon butter
- 1/4 cup finely chopped shallots
- 2 tablespoons dried currants
- 1 teaspoon chopped fresh thyme
- 1/4 teaspoon sea salt
- 1/4 teaspoon freshly ground black pepper
- 1/2 cup fat-free, less-sodium chicken broth

Preparation

1. Separate sprouts into leaves, leaving just the center intact. Set aside.

2. Heat a large nonstick skillet over medium-high heat. Add nuts to pan; cook 2 minutes or until toasted, stirring constantly. Coarsely chop nuts.

© Natalie Mitchell

3. Melt butter in pan over medium-high heat. Add shallots to pan, sauté 1 minute or until golden, stirring frequently. Stir in Brussels sprouts centers and leaves, currants, thyme, salt, and pepper; toss to combine. Add broth. Cover, reduce heat, and cook 7 minutes.
4. Increase heat to medium-high. Uncover; cook 4 minutes or until liquid evaporates and sprout centers are tender, stirring frequently.

5. Remove from heat; sprinkle with nuts.

54. Brussels Sprouts Curry with Pumpkin and Pomegranate (Delicious!)

My promise you is that healthy, sustaining food can always be delicious and here below is a one example of a quick and very easy vegetable curry made with Brussels sprouts and pumpkin. It is most flavorful and delicious served with warm homemade wholegrain bread or brown, black rice:

Ingredients

- 30 g Ginger
- 1 Onion
- 1 clove Garlic
- 350 g Brussels sprout
- 350 g Pumpkin
- 1 tbsp Olive oil
- 2 tsp Curry powder
- 200 ml Coconut milk
- 200 ml Vegetable stock
- Sea salt according to your taste
- 1-2 tsp Lime juice
- 2 tbsp Cilantro or parsley, chopped
- Some pomegranate seeds

Preparation

1. Finely dice the ginger, onion, and garlic. Rinse the Brussels sprouts and remove any wilted outer leaves. Trim the woody bottoms and cut in half. Cut the pumpkin into inch pieces.
2. Heat olive oil in a pan together with diced ginger, onion and garlic. Cook until aromatic, about 2 minutes.
3. Add in Brussels sprouts and pumpkin. Cook for 5 minutes. Sprinkle the curry powder over and stir until well blended.

4. Pour in coconut milk and vegetable stock. Bring to a boil and cook, covered, over medium-heat for 15 minutes.

5. Season with sea salt and lime juice. Garnish with cilantro leaves and pomegranate seeds.

Let's take a closer look at Brussels sprouts as you might wonder why I am emphasizing and providing you with many Brussels sprouts recipes. Quite often this vegetable is overlooked and the studies and findings in relation to its sexual health improvement, body detox and cancer preventative qualities telling us that this is a delicious and rather special, cruciferous vegetable

© Natalie Mitchell

Here is the background on this wonderful vegetable: **Brussels sprouts** contain indole-3-carbinol, which works to transform estrogen in the body into a substance that helps create testosterone..

I3C is a short form of indole-3-carbinol, a phytochemical that stops the production of 'bad estrogen' and promotes conversion of 'good estrogen' into testosterone. An enzyme known as aromatase is the main culprit behind the transformation of testosterone to estrogen. I3C disables aromatase, resulting in the restricting of the conversion of testosterone.

Brussels sprouts are now known to top the list of commonly eaten cruciferous vegetables in terms of health benefit. Their total glucosinolate content has been shown to be greater than the amount found in mustard greens, turnip greens, cabbage, kale, cauliflower, or broccoli. **Glucosinolates** are important **phytonutrients** for our health because they are the chemicals starting points for a variety of **cancer-protective substances**. All cruciferous vegetables contain glucosinolates and have great health benefits for this reason. But it's recent research that's made us realize how especially **valuable** Brussels sprouts are in this regard.

You'll find nearly 100 studies in PubMed (the health research database at the National Library of Medicine in Washington, D.C.) that are focused on **Brussels sprouts**, and over half of those studies involve the significant health benefits of this cruciferous vegetable in **relation to cancer prevention**. This connection between **Brussels sprouts** and **cancer prevention** exists since Brussels sprouts provide special nutrient support for three body systems that are closely connected with **cancer development** as well as **cancer prevention**.

These three systems are:

1. The body's detox system
2. Its inflammatory/anti-inflammatory system.

3. Its antioxidant system

Research has shown that the cancer protection we get from Brussels sprouts is largely related to four specific cancer-preventive components in a special combination found in this cruciferous vegetable.

A recent study has shown improved stability of DNA inside our **white blood cells** after daily consumption of **Brussels sprouts in the amount of 1.25 cups**. Interestingly, it's the ability of certain compounds in Brussels sprouts to block the activity of sulphotransferase enzymes that researchers believe to be responsible for these DNA-protective benefits.

If you have not previously been very fond of this vegetable because of its taste or smell, I am happy to show you that you can cook them in several very delicious ways:

Brussels Sprouts and Detox Support

The detox support provided by Brussels sprouts is quite extensive. *First*, there is evidence from human studies that **enzyme systems in our cells** required for **detoxification** of **cancer-causing substances** can be activated by compounds made from **glucosinolates** found in Brussels sprouts.

Second, the body's detox system **requires** ample supplies of **sulphur** to work effectively, and Brussels sprouts are **rich** in sulphur-containing nutrients. Sulphur is connected with both the **smell** and **taste** of Brussels sprouts, and too much sulphur aroma is often associated with overcooking of this vegetable. Sulphur-containing nutrients help support what is commonly referred to as Phase 2 of detoxification. *Third*, our body's **detox system** needs strong **antioxidant support** - especially during what is called Phase 1 of detoxification. Brussels sprouts are able to provide that kind of support because they are an excellent source of **vitamin C**, a very good source of **beta-carotene** and **manganese**, and a good source of **vitamin E**. Brussels sprouts also contain a wide variety of antioxidant phytonutrients, including many antioxidant flavonoids. Finally, there is evidence that the DNA in our cells is protected by naturally occurring substances in Brussels sprouts, and since many environmental toxins can trigger unwanted change in our DNA, Brussels sprouts can help prevent these toxin-triggered DNA changes.

Brussels Sprouts and Inflammatory/Anti-inflammatory Support

Chronic unwanted inflammation is also a risk factor for **many types of cancer**. Exposure to **environmental toxins**, chronic overuse of prescription or **over-the-counter medications**, chronic excessive stress, chronic lack of exercise, chronic lack of sleep, and a **low quality diet** can all contribute to our risk of **unwanted inflammation**.

Brussels sprouts and lots of other green vegetables and fruits can help us avoid chronic, excessive inflammation through a variety of nutrient benefits.

Glucosinolates found in Brussels sprouts help to regulate the body's **inflammatory/anti-inflammatory system** and prevent unwanted inflammation.

A second important anti-inflammatory nutrient found in Brussels sprouts is **vitamin K**. Vitamin K is a direct regulator of inflammatory responses, and we need optimal intake of this vitamin in order to avoid chronic, excessive inflammation.
As a comparison: the amount of **Vitamin K** in organic **Brussels sprouts** is **218.9** mcg and in organic **carrots** is **10.7** mcg.

A third important anti-inflammatory component in Brussels sprouts is not one that you might expect. It's their **omega-3** fatty acids. We don't tend to think about vegetables in general as **important sources** of omega-3s, and certainly no vegetables that are as low in total fat as Brussels sprouts. But 100 calories' worth of Brussels sprouts (about 1.5 cups) provide about **430 milligrams** of the most basic omega-3 fatty acid (called alpha-linolenic acid, or ALA). That amount is more than one-third of the daily ALA amount recommended by the **National Academy of Sciences** in the Dietary Reference Intake recommendations, and it's about half of the ALA contained in one teaspoon of whole flaxseeds. Omega-3 fatty acids are the building blocks for the one of the body's most effective families of anti-inflammatory messaging molecules.

Brussels Sprouts and Antioxidant Support

As mentioned earlier, Brussels sprouts are an important dietary source of many **vitamin antioxidants**, including vitamins C, E, and A (in the form of beta-carotene) as well as the **alkaline minerals** such as **potassium, calcium magnesium, selenium** etc. Flavonoid antioxidants like isorhamnetin, quercitin, and kaempferol are also found in Brussels sprouts, as are the antioxidants **caffeic acid** and **ferulic acid**. In fact, one study examining total intake of antioxidant polyphenols in France found Brussels sprouts to be a more important dietary contributor to these antioxidants than any other cruciferous vegetable, including broccoli. Some of the antioxidant compounds found in Brussels sprouts may be somewhat rare in.

Dinner choices

If you feel like you need to provide your body with more sustainable food at lunch or dinner then soups or salads than let's look to food that will provide a good source of protein for your lean beautiful body and lean muscles. We shouldn't forget about the importance of amino acids in this discussion.

Amino acids are described as the "building blocks of protein," and they are important to the synthesis of proteins and the **overall functioning of the body**. In particular, there are 10 amino acids classified as **"essential,"** which means they are not naturally made by the human body. These amino acids must be acquired through the foods you eat, reports the University of Arizona Department of Biochemistry, or your body will begin to break down existing protein, such as **muscle tissue**. Unlike fat, amino acids can't be stored in the body for later use. Therefore, it is doubly important that you include these amino acids in your diet on a consistent basis.

Wild Fish

Wild fish of any kind is one of the top sources of many of the good amino acids. Fatty fish such as salmon, tuna, herring and sardines are also rich in omega-3 fatty acids, which may have benefits in protecting against heart disease. Fish are abundant in the essential amino acids isoleucine, lysine and methionine.

55. Lemon Rosemary Wild Salmon

Ingredients

Original recipe makes 2 servings

- 1 lemon, thinly sliced
- 4 sprigs fresh rosemary
- 2 wild salmon fillets, bones and skin removed
- sea salt to taste
- 1 tablespoon olive oil, or as needed
- 20 asparagus

Preparation

1. Preheat oven to 400 degrees F (200 degrees C).

2. Arrange half the lemon slices in a single layer in a baking dish. Layer with 2 sprigs rosemary, and top with salmon fillets. Sprinkle salmon with sea salt, layer with remaining rosemary sprigs, and top with remaining lemon slices. Drizzle with olive oil.

3. Bake 20 minutes in the preheated oven, or until fish is easily flaked with a fork.
4. Steam asparagus for 10 min and then serve it with salmon. ENJOY!

56. Balsamic-Glazed Wild Salmon Fillets

"A glaze featuring balsamic vinegar, garlic, honey, white wine and Dijon mustard makes baked salmon fillets extraordinary."

Ingredients

Original recipe makes 6 servings

- 6 (6 ounce) salmon fillets
- 4 cloves garlic, minced
- 1 tablespoon white wine
- 1 tablespoon honey
- 1/3 cup balsamic vinegar
- 4 teaspoons Dijon mustard
- sea salt and pepper to taste
- 1 tablespoon chopped fresh oregano

Preparation

1. Preheat oven to 400 degrees F (200 degrees C). Line a baking sheet with aluminum foil, and spray with non-stick cooking spray.

2. Coat a small saucepan with non-stick cooking spray. Over medium heat, cook and stir garlic until soft, about 3 minutes. Mix in white wine, honey, balsamic vinegar, mustard, and salt and pepper. Simmer, uncovered, for about 3 minutes, or until slightly thickened.

3. Arrange salmon fillets on foil-lined baking sheet. Brush fillets with balsamic glaze, and sprinkle with oregano.

4. Bake in preheated oven for 10 to 14 minutes, or until flesh flakes easily with a fork. Brush fillets with remaining glaze, and season with salt and pepper. Use a spatula to transfer fillets to serving platter, leaving the skin behind on the foil.
5. You can steam broccoli for 10 min and roast sweet potato for 40 min in the oven. ENJOY!

57. Wild Garlic Salmon

"A large wild salmon filet, steamed in foil and cooked either in the oven or barbecue. It's seasoned with minced garlic, fresh baby dill, lemon slices, fresh ground pepper and green onions."

Ingredients

Original recipe makes 4 to 6 servings

- 1 1/2 pounds wild salmon fillet
- salt and pepper to taste
- 3 cloves garlic, minced
- 1 sprig fresh dill, chopped
- 5 slices lemon
- 5 sprigs fresh dill weed
- 2 green onions, chopped

Preparation

1. Preheat oven to 450 degrees F (230 degrees C).
2. Place salmon fillet on top of one piece of foil. Sprinkle salmon with salt, pepper, garlic and chopped dill. Arrange lemon slices on top of fillet and place a sprig of dill on top of each lemon slice. Sprinkle fillet with chopped scallions.
3. Cover salmon with second piece of foil and pinch together foil to tightly seal. Place on a baking sheet or in a large baking dish.
4. Bake in preheated oven for 10 to 15 minutes, until salmon flakes easily. ENJOY!

58. Grilled Sea Bass

Ingredients

Serves 4

- 4 sea bass fillets, scaled and pin-boned and cut into half
- 3 tbsp of olive oil
- Sea salt
- freshly ground black pepper

- Crispy okra
- 1/4 tsp of turmeric
- 1/2 tsp of chili powder
- 1/4 tsp of chat masala
- 1/2 tsp of carom seeds
- 3/4 tbsp of coriander stalks, chopped
- 10 okra, trimmed and thinly sliced
- 1/2 lemon, juiced
- 4 tbsp of whole grain flour
- olive oil
- sea salt

Coconut rice

- 250g of basmati rice
- 2 tbsp of olive oil
- 2 tbsp of unsalted butter
- 1 tsp of black mustard seeds
- 1 tsp of ginger, finely chopped
- 1 tsp of green chili
- 10 curry leaves, finely shredded
- 1 banana shallot, finely sliced
- 4 tbsp of coconut, grated
- 1/2 lemon, juiced
- 1 tbsp of fresh coriander, chopped
- Sea salt

Dhal sauce

- 70g of red lentils
- 70g of yellow lentils
- 2 tbsp of olive oil
- 1/2 tbsp of cumin seeds
- 1/2 tbsp of garlic, finely chopped
- 1 tsp of ginger, finely chopped
- 1 tsp of green chili, finely chopped
- 1/2 tsp of turmeric

- 1/2 tsp of red chili powder
- 2 tbsp of onion, chopped
- 1 tbsp of unsalted butter
- Sea salt

Preparation

1. First make the dhal sauce. Wash the lentils under cold running water, then place in a deep pan and cover with 4 times their volume of water. Leave to soak for an hour
2. Put the lentils on the heat and bring to the boil. Reduce the heat, cover and simmer until the lentils are soft and broken down, skimming off any scum from the surface. Add more water, if necessary, to prevent the lentils sticking to the base of the pan
3. Heat the olive oil in a separate pan and add the cumin seeds. When they begin to splutter, add the garlic, ginger and green chili and sauté until the garlic begins to color lightly
4. Add the turmeric, red chili powder and the chopped onions, and sweat. Season with sea salt and stir together well
5. Blitz the lentils until smooth, put back on the heat and add the butter, adjust the seasoning and keep warm
6. For the coconut rice, cook the basmati rice slightly less than the packet instructions tell you so it retains a little bite. Drain thoroughly
7. Heat the oil in a heavy-based pan, add the butter and sprinkle in the mustard seeds. When they begin to pop, add the ginger, green chili and curry leaves. Sauté for 30 seconds, then add the shallot and grated coconut. Reduce the heat and sauté until the shallot is softened but not colored
8. Now add the cooked rice, lemon juice and salt. Toss the rice until heated through, then remove from the heat, and stir in the chopped coriander
9. For the okra, mix together the spices and coriander stalks and toss with the okra. Add the lemon juice and some salt and set aside for 2 minutes. Add the whole grain flour a little at a time until it lightly coats the okra
10. Deep-fry in olive oil heated to 175°C until golden and crisp, then drain on kitchen paper (if you don't have a thermometer, check

it is hot enough by adding a cube of bread to the oil. It should start to bubble and fry, but not burn, the moment it has been added)

11. Season the sea bass fillets with sea salt and pepper. Heat the oil on a large, flat griddle (or in a heavy-based frying pan) over a medium heat and add the fish, skin-side down

12. Fry for about a minute, until seared underneath, then turn and cook the other side. Remove from the pan and leave to rest for 2 minutes

13. Place a ring mold on each serving plate and fill with the rice. Top with the fish, and arrange the okra over it. Spoon the dhal sauce around the fish, making a moat. ENJOY!

59. Sea Bass with Jerusalem artichoke purée, roasted garlic and red wine

Ingredients
Serves 4

Sea bass

- 4 sea bass fillets
- sea salt
- pepper
- olive oil

Jerusalem artichoke purée

- 200g of Jerusalem artichoke, peeled
- 150ml of coconut cream
- sea salt
- pepper

Red wine jus

- 200ml of red wine
- 1 sprig of fresh thyme
- 50g of shallots, sliced
- 200ml of organic chicken stock

Roasted garlic

- 1 head of garlic, roughly chopped
- olive oil
- Sea salt

Beans

1. 100g of butter beans
2. 100g of flageolet bean
3. 20ml of coconut cream

Preparation

1. For the Jerusalem artichoke purée, place the Jerusalem artichokes in a pan and add enough water to cover. Place over a medium heat and bring to a simmer. Add a pinch of salt and leave to cook slowly until the artichokes are tender - this should take at least an hour
2. For the red wine jus, place a large pan over a low heat. Add the red wine, thyme and shallots and cook until almost completely reduced. Once nearly dry, add organic chicken stock and reduce again until a syrup consistency is achieved - this process should take approximately 1 hour, so start right away after step 1
3. Wrap a broken head of garlic in foil with a little olive oil and place on a bed of sea salt on a baking tray. Place in an oven set to 180°C/gas mark 4 for 20 minutes
4. Once the artichokes are soft, drain well, and then place back in the pan with the coconut cream. Bring to the boil and reduce slightly. Season to taste and blend until smooth - pass through a sieve if still lumpy. Keep warm until ready to serve

5. For the sea bass, place a large pan over a medium-high heat. Once the pan is scorching hot, add the sea bass fillets, skin-side down, and cook until the skin is crispy, this should take around 3 minutes

6.Turn the fillets over, season, and then cook on the other side until the fish is delicately cooked through - this should take no longer than a minute. Turn off the heat and allow the fish to rest in the pan - any residual heat from the pan should finish the cooking process effectively

7. Meanwhile, heat the flageolet and butter beans in a pan with the coconut cream until boiling. Remove from the heat

8. Pass the red wine jus through a sieve and set aside

9. To serve, arrange the beans in the center of each plate and lay the fillets of sea bass on top. Drizzle the fish in the red wine jus and spoon the purée around the outside of each plate. Garnish with the roasted garlic and deep-fried rocket. ENJOY!

60. Monkfish with garlic and chili

Ingredients

Serves 4

- 4 monkfish fillets, scaled and pin-boned and cut into half
- 4 cloves garlic finely chopped

- lemon peel finely chopped
- 1cup parsley finely chopped
- red chili
- olive oil
- sea salt

Preparation

1. Marinate monkfish fillets with finely chopped garlic, parsley, lemon peel, chili and sea salt. Put it into refrigerator for 3-4 hours.

2. Then, shallow-fry the monkfish cheeks in hot olive oil until slightly brown. Drain and set aside.

3. Garnish with some parsley and serve warm. ENJOY!

61. Pepper-Crusted Tuna Steak and Wasabi Potatoes

Ingredients

For the wasabi smashed potatoes:

- 4 russet potatoes, cubed
- 1 tablespoon wasabi (use less if sensitive)
- 1/4 cup coconut milk
- Pinch sea salt and freshly cracked black pepper

For the sauce:

- 1/2 cup Marsala wine
- 2 tablespoons honey2 teaspoons olive oil
- 4 cloves garlic, crushed
- 4 knobs ginger, peeled

For the pepper-crusted tuna steak:

- 4 yellowfin sushi-grade tuna steaks, 1-inch thick
- 1/4 cup freshly cracked black pepper
- 4 tablespoons olive oil

Preparation

To make the wasabi smashed potatoes:

Boil potatoes in sea salt water until fork tender, about 10 to 15 minutes. Strain and place in a big bowl. Add wasabi, coconut milk, sea salt, and pepper and smash together. Don't over-mash.

To make the sauce:

Heat a saucepan on medium, add marsala wine, honey, olive oil, garlic, and ginger, bring to a boil. Reduce the heat to low and simmer for 5 minutes. Strain the sauce to remove garlic and ginger.

To make the Pepper-Crusted Tuna Steak:

Coat the tuna steaks evenly on all sides with freshly-cracked black pepper. In a frying pan, heat the olive oil on high heat until smoking. Place steaks in frying pan and baste with the sauce you made. For medium rare steak: cook for 1 minute, flip and cook for another minute, or cook longer according to your preference.

Slice tuna against the grain to sever muscle, making tuna even more tender. Serve with a generous scoop of wasabi smashed potatoes. Drizzle the sauce over both. ENJOY!

62. Grilled Yellowfin Tuna with Romaine Avocado and Mango

Here's a healthy summer dish with everything you need - grilled yellowfin tuna, romaine lettuce and tropical fruit. The fish will cook on a hot grill pan quickly so you can have this impressive meal on the table in a snap.

Ingredients

Serves 4

- 4 cups packaged chopped romaine lettuce
- cup refrigerated sliced mango, chopped
- sliced avocado, chopped
- 1/3 cup chopped red onion
- 2 tablespoons chopped fresh cilantro
- 2 tablespoons fresh lime juice
- 3 tablespoon olive oil
- 1/2 teaspoon sea salt, divided
- 3/8 teaspoon freshly ground black pepper, divided
- 8 (4-ounce) Yellowfin tuna steaks
- 4 lime wedges (optional)

Preparation

1. Combine first 6 ingredients in a large bowl; add 1 teaspoon olive oil, 1/4 teaspoon sea salt, and 1/8 teaspoon pepper, tossing to combine.

2. Heat a large heavy grill pan over medium-high heat with olive oil. Rub 2 teaspoons olive oil over tuna; sprinkle tuna evenly with remaining 1/4 teaspoon sea salt and 1/4 teaspoon pepper. Add tuna to pan; cook 3 minutes on each side or until desired degree of doneness. Arrange 1 1/2 cups salad on each of 4 plates; top each serving with 2 tuna steaks. Serve with lime wedges, if desired. ENJOY!

63. Grilled Yellowfin Tuna with Lemon and Garlic

Ingredients

Serves 4

- 1 oz fresh tuna steaks
- 1 lemon
- 2 tbsps fresh lemon juice
- 2 cloves garlic (minced)
- sea salt
- pepper

- olive oil

Preparation

1. Arrange fish in a shallow, non-reactive dish.
2. Whisk together marinade ingredients in a small bowl, reserving the zest; pour over steaks.
3. Cover and refrigerate for 1 to 1 1/2 hours, turning frequently.
4. Place fish on a well-greased grill or grilling basket and grill over medium coals for about 3 to 4 minutes, basting frequently with marinade.
5. Turn and cook for 3 to 4 minutes longer, or until fish is nicely grilled on the outside but still pink or somewhat translucent in the center.
6. Place on serving dish and top with zest. ENJOY!

64. Bermuda style Grouper With Banana and Almonds

Ingredients

Serves 6

- cup olive oil
- 1/2 whole grain flour
- 6 8-oz fresh grouper filets, boned and skinned
- cup sliced almonds
- 4 bananas, 1/4-in.sliced

© Natalie Mitchell

- Sea salt and freshly ground black pepper
- 1/2 chopped fresh parsley for garnish
- 1/2 cup butter
- 1/2 cup dark Rum
- cup coconut cream

Preparation

1. In a large skillet, heat the olive oil over medium to high heat.
2. Place the whole grain flour in a shallow plate, add the sea salt and pepper and mix until combined.
3. Dredge the fish fillets in the flour mixture and sauté in the hot skillet until they are golden brown.
4. Drain the oil from the skillet and add the dark rum. Flambé immediately and cook for 20 seconds to burn off some of the alcohol.
5. Add the coconut cream and half the butter seasoning lightly with salt and pepper. Cook everything for approximately 5 min. Remove the skillet from the heat and allow to rest.
6. In a separate pan melt the remaining butter and then add the almonds. Let the almonds sauté for then add the sliced bananas. Let everything cook for 2 minutes.
7. Place the cook fish fillets on a platter and top with the almonds and bananas.
8. Drizzle the sauce around and over the fish. Add a little rum on top and garnish parsley. Serve hot. ENJOY!

65. Venison Stroganoff with Coconut Cream

"This is an easy and very good venison recipe that my family loves"

Ingredients

Original recipe makes 4 servings

- 1 pound venison, cut into cubes
- sea salt and pepper to taste
- garlic powder to taste
- 1 red onion, chopped
- 1/2 pound mushrooms
- 1 (16 ounce) package uncooked egg noodles
- 1 (8 ounce) container coconut cream
- 2 cups basmati rice
- 1tsp olive oil

Preparation

1. Season venison with sea salt, pepper and garlic powder to taste. Sauté red onion and mushrooms in a large skillet; when soft, add venison and brown. Drain when venison is no longer pink. Reduce heat to low and simmer.

2. Meanwhile, bring a large pot of lightly salted filtered water to a boil. Add basmati rice and 1 tsp olive oil and cook for 20 minutes on the low heat.

3. When rice is almost done cooking, stir coconut cream into meat mixture, cook another 2-3. Pour meat mixture over hot cooked noodles and serve. ENJOY!

66. Veal Escalopes in Marsala Sauce with rosemary potatoes and sauté spinach Saltimbocca Alla Romana

Literally translated, saltimbocca *means* ***"Jump in the mouth,"*** *a clear indication of just how good this classic dish tastes.*

Ingredients:

Serves 4
Saltimbocca

- 8 escalopes of veal
- 16 slices of prosciutto
- 8 large sage leaves
- butter
- 1 tbsp olive oil

- •300 ml dry Marsala or dry white wine
- •250 g sautéed spinach

- 1 clove garlic, thinly sliced
- 250 gm baby spinach leaves

Serve with:

roasted rosemary potatoes

Preparation

1. Season veal escalopes to taste with sea salt and freshly ground black pepper. Trim prosciutto slices to size of escalopes, then place over escalopes to almost cover, and weave toothpicks through sage to secure.
2. Heat butter and olive oil in a large frying pan and pan-fry escalopes (prosciutto-side down first), in batches, for 1 minute or until golden. Turn and cook for another 1 minute or until golden, then transfer escalopes to a plate, remove toothpicks and cover to keep warm. Add Marsala to pan and boil over high heat until reduced by half, then strain sauce through a fine sieve into a jug.
3. Meanwhile, for sautéed spinach, place butter and garlic in a saucepan, stir over medium heat until butter melts and garlic is soft. Add washed but still-wet spinach leaves and stir over medium heat until just wilted. Add 1 tbsp of sauce and season to taste.

4. Serve Saltimbocca alla Romana with sautéed spinach and roasted rosemary potatoes to the side, and sauce drizzled over the dish. ENJOY!

67. Veal Escalopes in Lemon Sauce (Scaloppine al limone)

Ingredients

Serves 4

- 400 gr (14.10 oz) Veal Escalopes
- 1 ½ Glass White Wine
- 60 gr (2.11 oz) Butter
- Juice of 2 Lemons
- Fresh Chopped Parsley
- Whole grain Flour
- Extra Virgin Olive Oil
- Sea Salt and Black Pepper

Preparation

1. Lightly dust the escalopes with whole grain flour. Heat olive oil in a frying pan and let it heat. Place the escalopes into the pan, add salt and a pinch of black pepper. Cook for 2 to 3 minutes each side until well gilded then turn over the escalopes and season this side as well with salt and black pepper and remove the excess olive oil.
2. Replace the pan over the heat and add butter, pour in the lemon juice and let it evaporate. Pour in the white wine and let it cook for another 2 minutes. Once your escalopes are ready, transfer to a serving dish, pour the sauce over them, sprinkle with fresh chopped parsley, lemon zest strips and serve. ENJOY!

© Natalie Mitchell

68. Wiener Schnitzel… the classic veal dish

Ingredients:

Serves 4

- 4 veal cutlets
- Sea salt
- Whole grain flour
- 1 egg, whisked together with 2 tablespoons coconut milk or water
- Whole grain dry bread crumbs
- Extra Virgin olive Oil

Preparation

1. Pound the meat well, slash at a number of places at the edges and salt lightly. Turn the schnitzels one after another in the whole grain flour, in the egg mixture and finally in the whole grain bread crumbs, pressing the crumbs into the meat well and then shaking off any excess.
2. Heat a generous amount of olive oil in a suitable pan and fry the schnitzels on both sides until golden brown while swinging the pan slightly. Remove the meat from the pan and drain well.
3. Traditionally, the Wiener Schnitzel is served with potatoes, a green salad or potato salad.
4. The essential extra is a lemon wedge, which one squeezes over the golden brown, crisp coating or anchovies.

© Natalie Mitchell

69. Rack of Lamb

Ingredients

Serves 4

- 1/2 cup whole grain fresh bread crumbs
- 2 tablespoons minced garlic
- 2 tablespoons chopped fresh rosemary
- 1/4 teaspoon black pepper
- 2 tablespoons olive oil
- 1 (7 bone) rack of lamb, trimmed
- 1 teaspoon sea salt
- 1 teaspoon black pepper
- 2 tablespoons olive oil
- 1 tablespoon Dijon mustard

Preparation

1. Preheat your oven to 450 degrees F (230 degrees C). Move oven rack to the center position. In a large bowl, combine whole grain bread crumbs, garlic, rosemary, 1 teaspoon salt and 1/4 teaspoon pepper. Toss in 2 tablespoons olive oil to moisten mixture.

© Natalie Mitchell

Set aside.

2. Season the rack all over with salt and pepper. Heat 2 tablespoons olive oil in a large heavy oven proof skillet over high heat. Sear rack of lamb for 1 to 2 minutes on all sides. Set aside for a few minutes. Brush rack of lamb with the mustard. Roll in the bread crumb mixture until evenly coated. Cover the ends of the bones with foil to prevent charring.

3. Arrange the rack bone side down in the skillet. Roast the lamb in preheated oven for 12 to 18 minutes, depending on the degree of doneness you want. With a meat thermometer, take a reading in the center of the meat after 10 to 12 minutes and remove the meat, or let it cook longer, to your taste.

4. Let it rest for 5 to 7 minutes, loosely covered, before carving between the ribs.

70. Ginger Me up Chicken! Honey & Ginger Organic Chicken Breasts

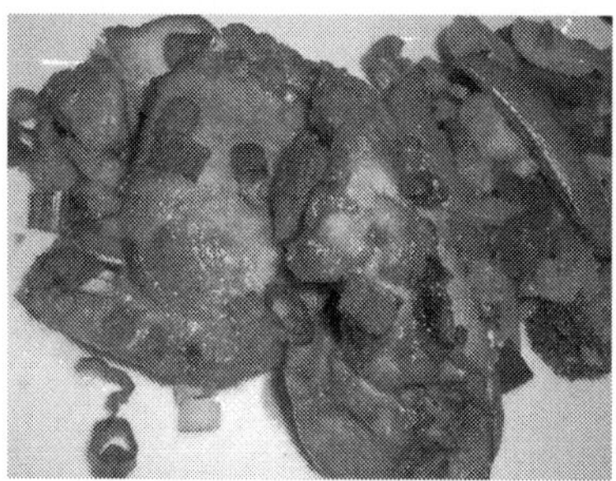

Ingredients:

Serves: 4

- 4 large boneless skinless organic chicken breasts
- 2 tablespoons honey
- 1-2 tablespoon Dijon mustard
- 4 tablespoons filter water
- 2-3 teaspoons ground ginger or 1 tablespoon freshly ground

ginger root
- 2-4 garlic cloves, peeled & crushed
- sea salt, to taste
- fresh ground black pepper, to taste
- 1/2-1 teaspoon cayenne pepper (optional)
- spring onion

Preparation

1. Preheat the oven to 180C or 350°F.
2. Select a sturdy oven dish - preferably non-stick.
3. Place the chicken breasts into the baking dish.
4. Mix the honey, mustard, water, ginger & crushed garlic (and cayenne pepper if using) together in a measuring jug.
5. Pour over the chicken breasts, easing them up slightly so the mixture runs underneath them.
6. Season with salt and freshly ground black pepper to taste and bake in the oven for 45 to 60 minutes.
7. Serve one chicken breast per person with some of the cooking sauce drizzled over the top of the chicken.
8. Garnish with chopped spring onion & serve with a medley of steamed vegetables
9. To pan fry, heat up a frying pan and add the chicken breasts - dry fry them briefly to give them a bit of color and add the cooking sauce, mix well and cook for about 20- 30 minutes over a medium heat. ENJOY!

71. Walnut and Rosemary Oven-Fried Chicken

Ingredients

Serves 4

- 1/4 cup coconut milk
- 2 tablespoons Dijon mustard
- 4 (6-ounce) chicken cutlets
- 1/3 cup whole wheat bread crumbs
- 1/3 cup finely chopped walnuts
- 3/4 teaspoon minced fresh rosemary
- 1/4 teaspoon sea salt
- 1/4 teaspoon freshly ground black pepper
- Olive oil
- Rosemary leaves (optional)

Preparation

1. Preheat oven to 425°.

2. Combine coconut milk and mustard in a shallow dish, stirring with a whisk. Add chicken to coconut milk mixture, turning to coat.

3. Heat a small skillet over medium-high heat. Add bread crumbs to pan; cook 3 minutes or until golden, stirring frequently. Combine bread crumbs, nuts, and next 4 ingredients (through pepper) in a shallow dish. Remove chicken from coconut milk mixture; discard

© Natalie Mitchell

coconut milk mixture. Dredge chicken in bread crumbs mixture.

4. Arrange a wire rack on a large baking sheet; brush rack with olive oil. Arrange chicken on rack. Bake at 425° for 12 minutes or until chicken is done. Garnish with rosemary leaves, if desired. ENJOY!

72. Roasted sweet potatoes as a side dish

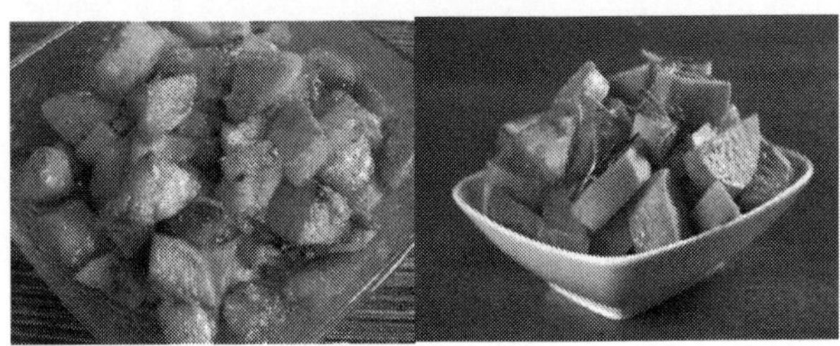

Ingredients

Serves: 6

- 2 large sweet potatoes, peeled and sliced into chunks
- 1 onion, peeled and sliced (optional)
- 2 tablespoons of olive oil
- sea salt
- fresh thyme leaves

Preparation

Prep: 15min › Cook:40min › Ready in:55min

- Heat oven to 200 degrees C.
- Toss the sweet potatoes with olive oil in a baking dish. Sprinkle over some sea salt. Cover and bake for half an hour, then remove cover and allow to crisp up for 10 - 20 minutes.

• Sprinkle over some fresh thyme leaves before serving.

73. Garlic Mushrooms as a side dish

Ingredients:
Serves 4

- 60 ml Extra virgin olive oil
- 500 g Mushrooms, thinly sliced
- 3 clove Garlic, minced
- 60 ml Dry sherry
- 1 tbsp Fresh lemon juice
- Pinch of dried chili flakes
- Sea salt and pepper to taste
- 1 tbsp Parsley, chopped

Preparation

1. Heat a skillet over medium-high heat. Pour in olive oil and swirl to coat the bottom. Add in sliced mushrooms and minced garlic. Cook, stirring frequently, for about 2 minutes.
2. Reduce the heat to medium. Drizzle in the sherry and lemon juice. Season with chili flakes, salt and pepper. Stir to combine. Cook until the mushrooms are softened. Stir in chopped parsley.

Stir to combine and dish off.

74. Roasted Chickpeas as a side dish

Ingredients:

- 3/4 tsp Cumin seeds
- 3/4 tsp Coriander seeds
- 350 g Cooked chickpeas, drained
- 1 tbsp Extra-virgin olive oil
- Pinch of cayenne pepper
- Sea salt

Preparation

1. Preheat oven to 200C/400F. Toast cumin seeds and coriander seeds in small skillet over medium heat until beginning to brown, about 2 minutes. Cool. Transfer to spice mill and process until finely ground.
2. Place chickpeas, olive oil, pinch of cayenne, and ground spices in medium bowl. Sprinkle with salt, then toss to coat evenly. Transfer to small-rimmed baking sheet. Roast in oven until lightly browned and crunchy, stirring occasionally, about 35 minutes.
3. Can be made 4 hours ahead. Let stand at room temperature. Reheat in 200C/400F oven until warm, about 5 minutes, before serving.

HEALTHY deserts!

75. "Better than Sex" Gourmet Dark Chocolate Cake

You'll notice that instead of sugar I'm using a natural herb sweetener called Stevia, which is widely available for purchase.

Ingredients

- 6 tsp Stevia or 12 packets
- 2& ¾ cups whole wheat flour
- ¾ cup cocoa (I use and recommend Special Dark Cocoa)
- 1 & ½ teaspoons baking powder
- 1 & ½ teaspoons baking soda
- 1 teaspoon sea salt
- 2 large free range eggs
- 1 cup coconut milk
- ½ cup olive oil
- 2 teaspoons vanilla
- 1 cup boiling water
- One Bowl Dark Chocolate Frosting (Below)

© Natalie Mitchell

Preparation

1. Preheat oven to 350° F. Grease and flour two 9-inch cake rounds or one 13x9x2-inch baking pan.
2. In a large mixing bowl, stir together the first six ingredients (Stevia through salt); add eggs, coconut milk, olive oil and vanilla; beat on medium speed for 2 minutes.
3. Stir in boiling water (batter will be thin); pour into prepared pan(s) and bake in a preheated 350° F oven for 35-40 minutes or until a toothpick inserted in center comes out clean.
4. If baking cake rounds, allow rounds to cool slightly before turning out onto wire racks to cool completely. If using rectangular baking pan, allow cake to cool completely before icing. ENJOY!

76. Coconut Creme Brulee

Ingredients
Serves 6

- 1 quart coconut cream
- 1 vanilla bean, split and scraped
- 6 tsp Stevia or 12 packets, divided
- 6 large egg yolks

© Natalie Mitchell

- 2 quarts hot water

Preparation

1. Preheat the oven to 325 degrees F.

2. Place the coconut cream, vanilla bean and its pulp into a medium saucepan set over medium-high heat and bring to a boil. Remove from the heat, cover and allow to sit for 15 minutes. Remove the vanilla bean and reserve for another use.

3. In a medium bowl, whisk together 6 tsp or 12 packets of Stevia and the egg yolks until well blended and it just starts to lighten in color. Add the coconut cream a little at a time, stirring continually. Pour the liquid into 6 (7 to 8-ounce) ramekins. Place the ramekins into a large cake pan or roasting pan. Pour enough hot water into the pan to come halfway up the sides of the ramekins. Bake just until the creme brulee is set, but still trembling in the center, approximately 40 to 45 minutes. Remove the ramekins from the roasting pan and refrigerate for at least 2 hours and up to 3 days.

4. Remove the creme brulee from the refrigerator for at least 30 minutes prior to browning on top. Divide the remaining Stevia equally among the 6 dishes and spread evenly on top. Using a torch, melt the Stevia and form a crispy top.

5. Allow the creme brulee to sit for at least 5 minutes before serving. ENJOY!

77. Marzipan Cake

© Natalie Mitchell

Ingredients:

Serves: 8-10

- 6 ounces marzipan
- 12 tablespoons unsalted butter, at room temp
- 1/4 teaspoon almond extract
- 5 eggs, at room temp
- 3/4 cup whole grain flour, plus some
- whole grain flour, for dusting
- 1 1/4 teaspoons baking powder
- 1/4 teaspoon sea salt
- 6 tsp Stevia or 12 packets

Preparation

1. Preheat oven to 350 degrees. Butter a loaf pan and dust with whole grain flour. Tap out the excess flour.
2. In a food processor pulverize together the Stevia and marzipan until the mixture is in fine pieces. Transfer the mixture to a large bowl.
3. Add the butter and almonds extract and mix until light and fluffy, about 1-2 minutes.
4. Add the eggs one at a time, beating well after each addition until thoroughly combined.
5. Sift together the whole grain flour, baking powder, and sea salt over the egg mixture and beat in just until thoroughly blended.
6. Pour the butter into the prepared pan.

© Natalie Mitchell

7. Bake until a toothpick inserted into the center comes out clean and the top springs back when lightly pressed - about 1 hour 15 minute
8. Transfer the pan to a wire rack and let cool for 15 minutes, then run a knife blade around the edge of the cake and invert onto the rack.
9. Lift off the pan and cool the cake upright on the rack for at least 30 minutes before serving.

78. Marzipan

Marzipan is a smooth almond candy used to make candy centers, form figurines, and cover cakes. This is a great all-purpose marzipan recipe that comes together quickly and requires just three ingredients. I like it because it has a lovely smooth texture and light almond taste. If you want to boost the almond flavor, add 1/2-1 tsp of almond extract to taste.
A note on ingredients: you can buy the almond paste, or use this almond paste recipe to make your own.

Prep Time: 5 minutes

Total Time: 5 minutes

Yield: 1.5 lbs marzipan

Ingredients:

- 1 lb almond paste
- 12 tsp powdered Stevia
- 2 large egg whites, lightly beaten

Preparation

1. Coarsely chop up the almond paste with a knife until it is in small quarter-size chunks, and place the almond paste in the bowl of a large stand mixer.

2. Add the powdered Stevia to the mixing bowl and mix them together on low speed with the paddle attachment until the almond paste has broken down and everything has a fine, sandy texture.

3. With the mixer running on low, slowly add the egg whites until everything comes together in a ball in the mixer. You may find that you do not need to add all of the egg whites.

4. Once the marzipan has formed a ball, take it out of the mixer, dust a workstation with powdered cane sugar, and knead the marzipan until it is completely smooth and has a nice, pliable texture.

5. You can use the marzipan immediately, or wrap it up for later use. To store it, wrap it tightly with plastic wrap and then place it in a zip-top plastic bag. Marzipan will keep for 3 months in the refrigerator or up to 6 months in the freezer. Make sure to bring marzipan to room temperature before using it. ENJOY!

79. Ganache Glazed Marzipan Cake with Cognac Soaked Apricots

We all need a few cakes in our repertoire to rely on for special occasions, and this marzipan cake is perfect for important birthdays, anniversaries and other significant events. It is elegant, sophisticated and actually improves in texture and flavor if made one or two days in advance. This recipe features almond paste in the batter for flavor and moistness, minced apricots soaked in cognac and folded into the cake, and dark chocolate shavings. The top is covered with a layer of marzipan and then glazed with chocolate ganache.

Ingredients

Have Ready:

- 2 batches (about 4 cups) Dark Chocolate Ganache, soft and spreadable consistency,
- 4 ounces marzipan,

Cake:

- 1 cup minced dried apricots
- ½ cup cognac
- ¾ cup plus 1 tablespoon whole grain flour
- 1½ cups toasted, blanched, sliced almonds
- ¼ teaspoon sea salt
- 2 ounce bulk piece of dark chocolate

© Natalie Mitchell

- ½ cup plus 2 tablespoons (1¼ sticks) unsalted butter, at room temperature, cut into pieces
- 6½ ounces almond paste, crumbled into pieces
- 5 tsp Stevia or 10 packets
- 1 teaspoon vanilla extract
- 1 teaspoon almond extract
- 5 large eggs, at room temperature

Syrup:

- 1/4 tsp Stevia
- 1 tablespoon water
- 1 tablespoon cognac

Preparation

1. **For the Cake:** Combine apricots and cognac in a small saucepan and bring to a boil over medium heat; remove from heat and let sit 10 minutes. Alternately, combine in microwaveable bowl and heat on high power for 1 to 2 minutes or until very hot. Remove from microwave and let sit 10 minutes. Set aside. In either case, take care to not allow the liquor to ignite.
2. Position rack in middle of oven. Preheat oven to 325°F. Coat two 8-inch by 2-inch round cake pans with nonstick olive oil spray, line bottoms with parchment rounds, then spray parchment.
3. Place whole grain flour, almonds and sea salt in bowl of food processor fitted with a metal blade. Process until almonds are ground to a very fine meal; set aside. Grate the dark chocolate using the largest holes on a hand box grater; set aside.
4. Beat butter in standing mixer until creamy with flat paddle on medium-high speed, about 1 minute. Add the almond paste and beat until combined. Add Stevia gradually and continue to beat, about 3 minutes at medium-high speed, until very light and fluffy. Beat in the vanilla and almond extracts. Add organic eggs one at a time, beating well after each addition, scraping down the bowl once or twice. Add whole grain flour mixture and pulse the mixer on and off taking care not to over mix. Fold in shaved dark chocolate and apricots with any liquid with a few broad strokes. Divide butter

© Natalie Mitchell

evenly in pans and smooth tops with offset spatula.

5. Bake for about 20 to 25 minutes or until a toothpick shows a few moist crumbs when removed. The cake will be tinged with light golden brown around the top and edges and will have begun to come away from the sides of the pan. Cool pans on racks for 5 minutes. Unmold, peel off parchment, and place directly on racks to cool completely. Trim layers to be level, if necessary. Layers are ready to fill and glaze. Alternatively, place layers on cardboards and double wrap in plastic wrap; store at room temperature if assembling within 24 hours.

6. **For the Syrup:** Combine water and Stevia in a small pot. Stir to wet Stevia. Place over medium heat and bring to a simmer. Cook until Stevia dissolves, swirling pot once or twice. Remove from heat, cool to room temperature and stir in cognac.

7. **For the Assembly**: Have all components ready to use. Place one cake layer, bottom side down, on a cardboard round of the same size and place on cake turntable. Brush with half the syrup, then spread a layer of ganache evenly over cake. Top with second cake layer, bottom side up, brush with remaining syrup. Roll out marzipan on work surface lightly dusted with confectioners' sugar or cornstarch to a thickness of ¼-inch. Using cake pan as a guide, cut out an 8-inch circle. Place marzipan circle on top of cake. Cover top and sides of cake with a crumb coat of ganache; chill until firm, about 1 hour. Place cake on rack set over a clean pan. Heat remaining ganache until fluid, but not hot. Pour the liquid ganache over center of cake; it will spread out and begin to drip down sides. Gently facilitate this process with an icing spatula, to help cover the sides, but try not to touch the top of the cake. Any excess ganache that drips down to pan can be re-used. Chill briefly to set ganache, about 1 hour or up to 1 day.

For the Cake Decoration: Place cake on display plate. You can make a simple flower as you can see in the picture with some extra sliced blanched almonds and a bit of apricot for the center, or, you can go wild and make **Marzipan Roses** and/or **Apricot Roses**. Cake may be served immediately or refrigerated in airtight container up to 2 days. Bring to room temperature before serving. ENJOY!

80. Quinoa cookies with Rye Flakes and Flaxseed

These cookies are made using **nutrient-dense quinoa**, a complete protein, rich in **iron**, **minerals** and **amino acids**, **rye flakes** and **flaxseed**. You can experiment by replacing rye flakes with oats or quinoa flakes or a mix of two. Dark chocolate chips can also be added for a richer, moister taste. And of course you can always frost them with dark chocolate. Enjoy them as a wholesome breakfast or as a tasty snack any time you like.

Ingredients:

- 150 g Rye flakes
- 150 g Cooked quinoa
- 2 tbsp Flax seed
- 4 tsp Stevia

- 2 tbsp Vanilla protein powder
- ½ tsp Baking soda
- 2 tsp Baking powder
- 90 ml Coconut oil, melted
- 70 ml Maple syrup
- 1 tsp Vanilla extract
- 2-3 tbsp Coconut milk

Preparation

1. Melt the coconut oil over low heat. Set aside to cool. Roughly blend rye flakes into powder. Preheat the oven to 180C/350F.
2. Whisk together the blended rye flakes, cooked quinoa, flaxseed, Stevia, vanilla protein powder, baking soda, and baking powder in a large mixing bowl.
3. Stir in melted coconut oil, maple syrup, vanilla extract and coconut milk. Mix to combine. Shape the dough into inch balls and flatten each into a round circle with the palm of your hand. Place them on the parchment-lined baking trays. Bake for 10 minutes until golden brown. ENJOY!

Common vegetables do contain the protein that you need, and they're complete proteins as well.

According to official sources **we need only 2.5 to 11% of our calories from protein** and common vegetables easily supply that amount. Vegetables average around 22% protein, beans 28%, and grains 13%.

Professional estimates suggest we need as little as 2.5% of our calories from protein. The U.S. government's recommendation is 5-11%, based on various factors.

The World Health Organization recommends a similar amount. It's probably safe to assume that the official recommendations are padded with generous safety margins, to cover people who need more protein than average.

In general, **plant proteins** have **no cholesterol** and fat (saturated fats) as opposed to proteins from **animal sources**. That's why if you compare a person who is taking proteins from plants to someone who consumes proteins from animal sources, you can expect the latter to be more likely to develop diseases related to the **heart**, **blood pressure**, etc. and also to be more at risk of increased amounts of **fibrin** floating in the blood that can eventually cover more and more cancer cells making it impossible for white cells to recognize and kill them.

Plant proteins also have more Beta-carotene, dietary fiber, Vitamin C, Vitamin E, Folate, Iron, Magnesium and Calcium, etc.

To reduce the production of mucus in the body as much as possible I recommend you make sure you avoid consuming mucus-producing **dairy products** (milk, cheese, yogurt of any kind, cream and ice cream). This avoidance of dairy products applies to goat dairy products as well. Organic Butter is the exception in that it is ok to consume as it is lactose free and about 80-82% fat (higher fat butters are available if you look for them), 17% water and only contains about 1% milk solids (protein).
Note: Organic is an important component to butter being ok because the fat is where the hormones and toxins that the animal was exposed to will reside in a non-organic product.

I promised earlier to explain in more detail about the effects of dairy products on the human body.

Eating and drinking dairy products causes the body to produce mucus, especially in the gastro-intestinal tract. **In the human colon**, beta-casomorphin-7 an exorphin derived from the **breakdown of dairy products, stimulates mucus production** from the MUC5AC gene. This gene has been linked to **mucus hypersecretion** in the pulmonary tracts.

Cow's milk, cheese, yogurts of any kind, cream, ice cream and goat dairy products as well as fibrin (animal protein like red meat) are notorious as the most **cancer-assisting foods** we can consume.

Casein, the protein component in milk, is a very thick and coarse substance and is used to make one of the strongest glues known to man. There is **300%** more casein in cows' milk than in human milk. It can be said that cow's milk is unsuitable for the human body.

The **casein** in cows' milk can **clog** and **irritate** the body's **entire respiratory system**. Dairy products are implicated in almost all respiratory problems. Hay fever, asthma, bronchitis, sinusitis, colds, runny noses and ear infections can all be caused by the consumption of dairy products. Dairy products are also the leading cause of allergies.

"There is compelling evidence, now published in top scientific journals and some of which is decades old, showing that cows' milk is associated, possibly even causally, with a wide variety of serious human ailments including various cancers, cardiovascular diseases, diabetes and an array of allergy-related diseases. And, this food contains no nutrients that cannot be better obtained from other far more nutritious and tasty foods." Dr. Colin Campbell

"Inclusion of milk will only reduce your diet's nutritional value and safety. Most of the people on the planet live very healthfully without cow's milk. You can too." Robert M. Kradjian M.D

"I no longer recommend dairy products...there was a time when cow's milk was considered very desirable. But research along with clinical experience has forced doctors and nutritionists to rethink this recommendation" Dr. Benjamin Spock

According to Dr. Julian Whitaker in his 'Health & Healing' newsletter in an article entitled 'Tomorrow's Medicine Today' (October 1998 Vol. 8, No. 10) the notion that milk is healthy for you is "udder" nonsense. While eating fruits, vegetables and whole grains has been documented to lower the risk of heart attack, high

© Natalie Mitchell

blood pressure and cancer, the widely touted health benefits of dairy products are questionable at best. In fact, ***dairy products*** *are clearly linked as a* ***cause*** *of* ***osteoporosis, heart disease****,* ***obesity, cancer, allergies and diabetes****. He argues that dairy products are anything but "health" foods.*

"Dairy products are the leading cause of food allergy, often revealed by constipation, diarrhea, and fatigue. Many cases of asthma and sinus infections are reported to be relieved and even eliminated by cutting out dairy." Natural Health, July, 1994, Frank Oski, M.D., Chief of Pediatrics at Johns Hopkins Medical School

In my practice quite often I saw people with **acne.** I recommended that they avoid all dairy products at least for 3 months and in all cases it made a huge difference.

Removing milk and dairy products (apart from butter in small quantities) could be the most effective thing you can do to clear up your skin as well as improving your health generally.

A 2007 study carried out by Harvard School of Public Health found that there was a clear link between those who **drank milk regularly** and those who suffered with **acne**.
If you are a big fan of dairy products and love drinking milk by itself or with cereals, I strongly recommend you replace dairy products with equally delicious non-dairy alternatives such as the following all of which I find quite acceptable as a substitute:

- **Almond Milk,**
- **Almond-Coconut Milk (my favorite),**
- **Brown Rice Milk,**
- **Hazelnut Milk,**
- **Quinoa Milk,**
- **Oat Milk and others made of natural cereals and nuts.**

Be careful to avoid any form of Soy Milk.

I suggest you experiment with two or three different non-dairy milks until you find one that you love.

Chapter 5

CANCER CELL FIGHTING CURRY DISHES

For some of you it is well-known information and for the others it will be useful to find out about the **cancer fighting properties** of herbs that are widely used in curry dishes. Before we explore that, I would like to share this fascinating story with you:

Woman Stuns Researchers by Overcoming Cancer with Turmeric Spice

By Anthony Gucciardi

"While expensive cancer drugs linked to premature death and mega-tumors are pushed by many mainstream doctors as the only option outside of chemotherapy, a growing number of informed individuals are consistently opting to instead utilize natural methods that are known to conquer cancer cells and effectively negate the disease — without harsh side effects.

One such person, Vicky Stewart of Britain, chose such a path when she refused mainstream medical cancer treatments and instead began consuming powerful turmeric spice.

Despite excessive warnings from MD's who insisted that Vicky would surely not recover using super foods that are commonly touted as 'ineffective medicine' by pharma-backed doctors, Stewart found amazing success by altering her lifestyle and taking in extra amounts of super foods like turmeric each day.

Stewart recalls to The Telegraph how her doctor repeatedly voiced concern over switching to a healthy diet full of turmeric to fight the cancer (one of many turmeric health benefits), telling her that it would do virtually nothing: "The doctors absolutely will not say that the diet is going to do anything to help the cancer in any way."

Four years later with absolutely no mainstream treatments, she is still **cancer free** with no signs of it coming back. At the age of 44, Stewart is now the center of a major research project led by scientists who are fascinated by what she has done.

© Natalie Mitchell

Research Shows Turmeric Spice is a Natural Cancer Fighter

While it is indeed fascinating, it should come as no surprise that Vicky healed herself naturally using turmeric and other lifestyle changes. In fact, copious amounts of research highlight the anti-cancer properties of turmeric (in many cases due to it's active compound **curcumin**), and countless individuals have used it to aid themselves in the fight against many diseases.

Not only has peer-reviewed research by the UCLA shown that turmeric can naturally block the growth of cancer cells, but in more than 9 studies it was revealed that turmeric can reduce tumor size by a whopping 81%. And this is just the tip of the iceberg.

So why is it so fascinating that a spice that has been used for thousands upon thousands of years by many South Asian and Middle Eastern countries as a 'heal-all' substance can actually stop cancer naturally?

As Stewart explains, turmeric has a unique ability (along with other great super foods) to essentially cause cancer to regress in a number of ways. As she puts it, it essentially caused the cancer cells to 'commit suicide'. Stewart explains to The Telegraph: "Turmeric kind of makes cancer cells commit suicide and ginger and garlic are great to cook with."

"No cancer has been found that is not affected by curcumin" **(MD Anderson Cancer Center, Texas)**

"**Curcumin** has many serious fans in the fight to beat cancer - UCLA, the MD Anderson Cancer Center, the Emory School of Medicine and Tufts to name but four important American Cancer Centers. Why? It is a powerful antioxidant that is also anti-viral and anti-bacterial; plus it seems to have great potential to fight cancer, especially colorectal cancer."

Cumin is another spice commonly used in curry. Cumin contains some unique phytochemicals, such as *phthalides* and *polyacetylenes,* which show cancer-protective activity and anti-inflammatory properties.

Cumin has been seen to effectively *decrease the incidence of chemically induced tumors of the stomach, colon, and cervix.* Its cancer-preventive activity can be explained by its significant antioxidant activity and the ability of cumin to **modulate the metabolism of carcinogens**. Cumin seeds are known to induce the activity of glutathione-S-transferase, a protective enzyme that helps eliminate cancer-causing substances.

Hot Chili Peppers Make Cancer Cells Commit Suicide

"**Hot chili peppers** again used in most curry spices not only fire up your taste buds, they also put turn up the heat on **cancer cells**, forcing them to self-destruct. A study in the Sept. 4, 2002 issue of the *Journal of the National Cancer Institute* reports that natural substances found in chili peppers kill cancer cells by starving them of oxygen. Researchers tested two compounds in hot chili peppers—capsaicin and a related compound called resiniferatoxin— on human skin cancer cells. Both compounds belong to a group of naturally occurring phytochemicals called vanilloids. The majority of the skin cancer cells exposed to either of the two substances died." The World's Healthiest Foods

As you will notice all my curry recipes include **coconut milk** or **coconut cream**. Some people will add dairy products which I highly recommend you to avoid for the reasons we discussed above. I would like to introduce you to a few well-known benefits of the coconut milk and cream.

Coconut milk helps control weight and keeps blood sugar level under a check. Also, it helps you feel full faster and hence very beneficial for people who are trying to **lose weight**. If you feel full, you tend to eat less. Moreover, it also reduces your **bad cholesterol** and is a great cure for **arthritis** and **joint pains**. Coconut milk has some beauty benefits too. It **moisturizes** your skin and nourishes it from within making it look beautiful and soft, I think Ladies will find this part beneficial too.

More coconut milk benefits:

Decreases the risk of joint inflammation:
Selenium is an important antioxidant. It controls the free radicals (cancer killing properties) and thereby helps in relieving the symptoms of arthritis. It is observed that people with low levels of selenium may suffer from rheumatoid arthritis.

Helps to fight cancer and lower high blood pressure:
People who are concerned about their blood pressure will not face any problem consuming foods containing potassium. Potassium helps in lowering blood pressure levels in the body as well as by being alkalizing cancer-fighting mineral.

Helps in maintaining healthy immune system:
Coconut milk helps in warding off colds and coughs by keeping the immune system healthy. It supplies vitamin C to the body which boosts the immune system.

Promotes the health of prostate gland:
Zinc plays a vital role in promoting the health of prostate gland. A preliminary study showed that it slows down the activities of cancer cells.

81. Thai Yellow Curry with potatoes

This curry chicken recipe is my family's favorite. It's a classic yellow curry made with chunks of chicken and potatoes, and tastes like one of those wonderful curry dishes you can find in the marketplaces and streets of Bangkok. The use of curry powder helps the dish come together quickly and easily. If you can, make your own using my recipe, or look for a good Madras curry powder at your local Asian or Indian food store - a Madras blend works well with Thai flavors, and will give you far better results than your average supermarket curry powder. ENJOY!

Ingredients:

Serves: 4 +

- 1 lb chicken breast or thigh, chopped into small chunks, or whole chicken pieces
- 2-3 potatoes, chopped into chunks
- optional: 1-2 medium ripe tomatoes, chopped into chunks
- 1/4 cup fresh coriander for garnish
- 2 Tbsp Thai curry powder or 3 Tbsp. Madras curry powder or regular curry powder
- 1 bay leaf

- optional: 1 cinnamon stick
- 1/2 to 1 tsp. chili flakes or cayenne pepper, to taste
- 2 shallots or 1/2 cup purple onion, diced
- 4-5 cloves garlic, minced
- 1 thumb-size piece galangal or ginger, grated
- 1/2 cup organic chicken stock or broth
- 1+1/2 Tbsp. sweet tomato puree
- 1 can thick coconut milk
- 2-3 Tbsp. fish sauce
- optional: 1/4 tsp. Stevia
- 2-3 Tbsp. olive oil for stir-frying
    - 1bay leaf

82. Thai Green Curry Chicken

This Thai Green Curry Chicken recipe features chunks of tender chicken simmered in a homemade green curry sauce along with healthy vegetables (zucchini and ripe red bell pepper). The result is a gourmet-style Thai green curry that is very aromatic and beautiful to serve (great for entertaining!). The key to good green curry is in not only using the right ingredients, but knowing when to add them. Because this curry is made the same as in Thailand (on your stovetop), I recommend using only smaller pieces or cuts of chicken, allowing for faster cooking and the freshest possible taste. ENJOY!

Ingredients:

Serves: 2 to 3

GREEN CURRY PASTE:

- 4 small green Thai chilies, or substitute 1 to 2 jalapeno peppers
- 1/4 cup shallot or purple onion, diced
- 4 cloves garlic, minced
- 1 thumb-size piece galangal or ginger, grated
- 1 stalk fresh minced lemongrass or 3 Tbsp. frozen or bottled prepared lemongrass
- 1/2 tsp. ground coriander
- 1/2 tsp. ground cumin
- 3/4 to 1 tsp. shrimp paste
- 1 (loose) cup fresh coriander/cilantro leaves and stems, chopped
- 1/2 tsp. ground white pepper (can be purchased at some supermarkets, or at Asian food stores)
- 3 Tbsp. fish sauce
- 1/4 tsp. Stevia
- 2 Tbsp. lime juice

CURRY INGREDIENTS:

- 1 to 1.5 lbs. (about 0.7 kg) boneless chicken thigh or breast, cut into chunks
- 1 can coconut milk
- 1 tsp. grated lime zest
- 1 zucchini, sliced lengthwise several times, then cut into chunks
- Generous handful fresh basil
- 2 Tbsp. coconut oil

Preparation

1. Place all the "green curry paste" ingredients together in a food processor, and process to a paste. If necessary, add a few Tbsp. of

the coconut milk to help blend ingredients. Set aside.

2. Prepare the lime leaves by tearing the leaf away from either side of the stem. Discard the central stem. Then, using scissors, cut leaves into thin strips. Set aside.
3. Warm a wok or large frying pan over medium-high heat. Add the oil and swirl around, then add the green curry paste.
4. Stir-fry briefly to release the fragrance (30 seconds to 1 minute), then add 3/4 of the coconut milk, reserving 2-3 Tbsp. per serving portion for later.
5. Add the chicken, stirring to incorporate. When the curry sauce comes to a boil, reduce heat to medium or medium-low, until you get a nice simmer.
6. Cover and allow to simmer 3-5 more minutes, or until chicken is cooked through. Stir occasionally.
7. Add zucchini, plus the strips of lime leaf (or lime zest), stirring well to incorporate. Simmer another 2-3 minutes, or until vegetables are softened but still firm and colorful.
8. Do a taste-test for salt, adding 1-2 Tbsp. fish sauce if not salty enough. If you'd prefer a sweeter curry, add a little more sugar. If too salty, add a squeeze of lime or lemon juice. If too spicy, add more coconut milk. Note that this curry should be a balance of salty, spicy, sweet and sour, plus bitter (the bitter is found in the fresh basil garnish).
9. Serve this curry in bowls with Thai jasmine rice on the side, allowing guests to add their own. Top each portion with fresh basil, then drizzle over 2-3 Tbsp. coconut milk, and ENJOY!

83. Keralan fish curry

© Natalie Mitchell

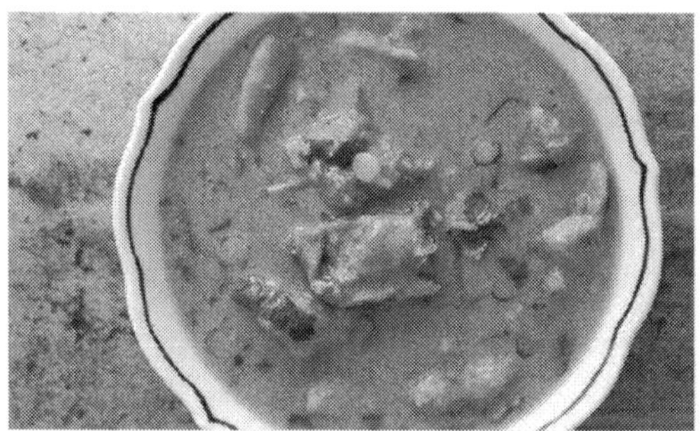

Creamy, rich and packed with spices, this tray baked curry is fresh and super-delicious. *Serve in the middle of the table and let your guests help themselves, and serve with clove-spiked rice, warm chapatis and poppadoms on the side for a really epic curry*

Ingredients
Serves 4-6

- 3 medium onions
- 4 cloves of garlic
- 5 cm piece of fresh ginger
- 2 fresh red chilies, deseeded
- 1 large bunch of fresh coriander, leaves picked
- 1 red pepper, deseeded
- olive oil
- 2 teaspoons brown mustard seeds
- 2 teaspoons fenugreek seeds
- 2 teaspoons fennel seeds
- 1 handful of curry leaves
- 1 x 1.5 kg side of salmon, scaled and pin-boned, skin on
- sea salt
- freshly ground black pepper
- olive oil
- 300 g ripe cherry tomatoes

- 28 peeled tiger prawns
- 2 x 400 g tins light coconut milk
- 4 lemons

Preparation

1. Preheat the oven to 160°C/325°F/gas
2. Peel and finely slice the onions, garlic and ginger. Finely slice the chilies and coriander stalks, then slice the peppers. Place your largest roasting tray on the hob over a medium heat and add a good splash of olive oil, the spices and curry leaves.
3. Fry for 2 minutes, then add the chopped veg, garlic and coriander stalks. Cook for about 15 minutes, or until soft and golden, stirring occasionally.
4. Place the salmon into the tray, skin side down. Season and drizzle with olive oil, then carefully turn the salmon skin side up and place the tray in the oven for around 20 minutes, or until the salmon is almost cooked through. Meanwhile, quarter the tomatoes and butterfly the prawns by carefully running a sharp knife down the back of each one and flattening them out.
5. Remove the tray from the oven and preheat the grill to full temperature. Carefully peel the skin off the salmon and place onto a piece of tin foil. Stir the tomatoes, prawns, coconut milk and the zest and juice from 1 lemon into the tray and gently simmer on the hob over a medium to low heat until the prawns are cooked through.
6. Meanwhile, place the skin under the grill for 2 - 3 minutes or until lovely and crisp – the skin can turn quickly so keep a close eye on it.
7. When done, carefully remove the crispy skin from under the grill and set aside to cool. Use a large spoon to break the salmon into big chunks. Season the sauce to taste with salt, pepper and a squeeze of lemon juice, then snap up and scatter over the crispy salmon skin, sprinkle with the reserved coriander leaves and serve with lots of lemon wedges for squeezing over. ENJOY!

84. Thai Yellow Vegetable Curry

(Vegan/gluten-free!)

This Vegetarian Thai Yellow Curry is authentic, homemade vegan Thai food at its best! Note that here I have dispensed with making a curry paste; instead, all the minced herbs and dry spices are added directly to the curry pot - a great time-saver if you're in a hurry! And unlike a lot of other yellow curry recipes out there, I don't use curry powder, preferring to add the individual spices for a superior-tasting curry. Serve with your choice of plain jasmine rice, coconut, or whole grain Thai coconut rice for a delicious, healthy, and nutritious vegan dinner. Wonderful for a fall or winter meal. ENJOY!

Ingredients:

- 2 shallots, chopped, or 1/3 cup chopped purple onion
- 1 thumb-size piece of ginger or Thai ginger/galangal, grated
- 4 cloves garlic, minced
- 1-2 hot yellow chilies, minced, or 1-2 red chilies, or 1/2 to 1 tsp. dried crushed red chili (chili flakes) - adjust to your preferred spiciness
- 1 tsp. ground coriander
- 2 tsp. ground cumin
- 3/4 tsp. ground turmeric
- 1/3 tsp. ground white pepper (available in the spice section)

© Natalie Mitchell

- 2 bay leaves
- 1/2 cup organic chicken stock
- 1 to 1/2 cups canned chickpeas (drained)
- 1 carrot, sliced
- 2-3 cups peeled squash or pumpkin, cubed
- 1 potato, cubed
- Optional: 1 cup cubed yam or sweet potato
- 1 14 ounce can coconut milk (full fat)
- 3 Tbsp. fish sauce
- 3 Tbsp. fresh lime juice
- 1/4 tsp. Stevia
- 2 Tbsp. tomato puree
- 1/2 tsp. whole cumin seed
- 1/4 cup fresh Thai basil (or sweet basil)
- 2 Tbsp. coconut oil

Preparation

1. Heat a wok, large frying pan or pot over medium-high heat. Drizzle in the oil and swirl around, then add the shallots, ginger, garlic, and chili. Stir-fry 1-2 minutes. While stir-frying, add the dry spices: coriander, ground cumin, turmeric, white pepper, and bay leaves.
2. Add stock plus the chickpeas, carrot, squash, potato, and yam (if using), stirring well. Add coconut milk and bring to a gentle boil.
3. Reduce heat to medium-low and simmer 10 to 12 minutes (for a thicker curry, do not cover). While simmering, add the soy sauce, lime juice, brown sugar, and ketchup. Finally, add the whole cumin seed. Continue simmering until vegetables are cooked to your liking.
4. Taste-test the curry, adding more soy sauce if you prefer it saltier/more flavorful. If too salty or sweet for your liking, add more lime juice. Add more sugar if you find it too sour. More chili can be added for more spice.
5. Transfer to a serving dish and top with plenty of fresh basil. Serve with plenty of Thai jasmine rice. Also excellent with my Thai Coconut Rice or Thai Brown Coconut Rice. ENJOY!

85. Roasted vegetable Vindaloo with golden chicken skewers

Ingredients
Serves 4

For the paste:

- 1 whole bulb of garlic, cloves separated and peeled
- 1 heaped tablespoon turmeric
- 1 heaped tablespoon garam masala
- 2 heaped tablespoons raisins
- 1 level teaspoon of sea salt
- 1 level teaspoon of ground cumin
- 1 heaped teaspoon fennel seeds
- 2 dried red chilies
- a bunch of fresh coriander, leaves picked and stalks chopped
- 1 red onion, peeled and roughly chopped
- 200 ml white wine vinegar

- 2 tablespoons olive oil

For the chicken skewers:

- 4 x 150 g skinless free-range chicken breast
- olive oil

- 1 lemon

For the curry:

- 1 kg large ripe tomatoes
- sea salt
- freshly ground pepper
- 1 cauliflower, broken into florets, stalk sliced, leaves removed
- 3red onions, peeled and roughly sliced
- 1x 400 g tin of chickpeas
- 500 ml organic chicken or vegetable stock
- 500 g mixed peas, broad beans and sweet corn
- 1 x 200 g bag of baby spinach

Preparation

Vindaloo *is a famous curry from Goa but has European roots. That part of India was, for many hundreds of years, actually under Portuguese control. It was the Portuguese who introduced vinegar to Goa and put the 'vin' (vinegar) in vindaloo ('loo' was the garlic). With this recipe, you're creating a wonderful standout vegetable curry but then adding a meat portion for any non- veggie people at the table. It's a great curry for a mixed dinner party – everyone's happy.*

1. Preheat your oven to 200°C/400°F/gas 6.
2. Put all the paste ingredients except the coriander leaves into a liquidizer and zap until smooth, then scrape the paste out into a bowl. Roughly chop the tomatoes and add to the liquidizer, season well, then blitz again until smooth and put aside for later.
3. In a large casserole-type pan, toss the cauliflower florets and red onions with half the curry paste. Add 600ml of water, and roast in the hot oven for 40 minutes, stirring halfway through.
4. Meanwhile, cut the chicken into finger-sized strips, toss them in the bowl with the remaining curry paste, cover and pop into the fridge. After 40 minutes, carefully move the hot pan from the oven to the hob.
5. Drain and add the chickpeas, along with the stock and blitzed

tomatoes and simmer on a medium heat for about 30 minutes, or until the consistency you like.

6. Meanwhile, preheat a large griddle pan over a high heat. Thread the chicken pieces on to 6 or 8 metal or wooden skewers. Drizzle with a little oil, season from a height, and cook on the screaming hot griddle for around 10 to 12 minutes, turning each one every now and again, until golden, sizzly and cooked through. Squeeze over some lemon juice and give the pan a good shake, scraping the bottom of the pan for around 30 seconds to get all the intense flavor. Transfer everything to a plate and set aside.
7. Go back to your curry and mash a few times to thicken up the sauce. Add the delicate veggies (peas, beans, corn and spinach) for the last 3 minutes of cooking, then have a taste and adjust the seasoning to taste.
8. Serve with basmati rice, the chicken skewers and anything else you fancy. ENJOY!

86. Seafood curry

This is a cracker of a prawn, mussel and fish curry with noodles, is full of goodness and easy to put together.

Ingredients

Serves 4

- 400 ml light coconut milk
- 200 g large, raw prawns
- 4 small fresh red mullet fillets
- 2 fresh sea bream fillets
- 2 handfuls fresh, live mussels
- medium egg noodles, cooked, to serve

For the curry paste

- 6 spring onions, washed and trimmed
- 3 hot red chilies, deseeded (2 finely chopped and 1 finely sliced)
- 2 cloves garlic
- thumb-sized piece ginger, finely chopped
- stalks lemongrass, trimmed and finely chopped
- zest and juice of 2 limes
- large bunch fresh coriander, stalks removed and finely chopped, and leaves reserved to garnish
- olive oil

Preparation

1. Make the curry paste. Put the onions, chopped red chilies, garlic, ginger, lemongrass, lime zest and juice, and coriander stalks into a processor. Whizz to a paste, season, then whizz again with a little olive oil, to loosen as necessary.
2. Get a large pan nice and hot, and add the paste. Allow to cook down for a couple of minutes, stirring. Add the coconut milk and stir well. Bring to the boil, then reduce the heat to a simmer. Add the prawns, red mullet and bream fillet pieces, cover with a lid and allow to simmer for 2–3 minutes. Next, add the mussels, cover with a lid, and cook for another 2–3 minutes, until all the shells are open. Discard any that remain shut.
3. Serve on some cooked egg noodles. Scatter with the reserved coriander leaves and the sliced red chili. ENJOY!

87. Thai Scallop and Shrimp Curry

This Thai scallop and shrimp curry will impress your family as well as your guests. The scallops and shrimp are simmered in a flavorful Thai curry and white wine sauce just until tender and served up with jasmine rice or a loaf of crusty French bread. Eggplant or okra is added for a delicious compliment to the seafood. This is a true gourmet Thai dish you'll enjoy making, and because of the tenderness of the scallops and shrimp, it cooks up quickly and easily. If you're interested in wine pairings, I would suggest a crisp white wine or a nice bottle of Shiraz. ENJOY!

SERVES 2-3 with rice

Ingredients:

- 1/2 lb. fresh or frozen scallops
- 2-3 cups raw fresh or frozen medium to large shrimp
- 10-12 okra (available at Asian stores and markets) or 1+1/2 cups chopped eggplant
- 3 cloves garlic, minced
- 1/2 shallot or 3 tbsp. minced onion
- 1 red chili, minced with seeds removed or 1/8 tsp. chili flakes
- 3+1/2 tsp. ground coriander seed
- 1/3 tsp. whole cumin seed
- 1/2 cup dry white wine

- 1+1/4 cups organic chicken stock
- 1/2 cup coconut milk
- 3 tsp. fish sauce
- 3 tsp. cornstarch dissolved in 2 tbsp water
- handful fresh coriander/cilantro or fresh basil
- 2 Tbsp coconut oil

Preparation

1. Thaw scallops and shrimp if frozen and rinse both well. Cut caps off the ends of the okra and slice in half lengthwise. If using eggplant, chop into large chunks.
2. Heat a large non-stick frying pan or wok over medium-high heat. Add oil and swirl around, then add garlic, shallot/onion and chili. Stir-fry 1 minute.
3. Add ground coriander and cumin seed and continue stir-frying 1 minute.
4. Add red wine and gently boil on medium-high heat 5 minutes.
5. Add organic chicken stock plus the okra or eggplant. Bring back to a gentle boil for 8-10 minutes or until vegetables have softened (okra may take a few minutes longer depending on firmness). Stir occasionally and do not cover.
6. Push vegetables to the outside of the pan and add scallops and shrimp. Bring back to gentle boil for 5 more minutes.
7. Add fish sauce and 1/2 cup of coconut milk plus cornstarch/water mixture. Stir gently for 1-2 minutes until sauce thickens.
8. Reduce heat to low and taste-test for flavor, adding more fish sauce until flavorful enough. Add up to 1/4 cup more coconut milk if you'd like it creamier or if it's too spicy for your taste. More chili can be added for more heat.
9. Top with fresh coriander or basil and serve with plenty of Thai jasmine rice and ENJOY!

88. The best Aloo Gobi

Ingredients

- 1 small head cauliflower, or ½ a big one, cut into large florets
- 1 splash olive oil
- 1 tablespoon black mustard seeds
- 1 large pinch asafoetida
- 12 curry leaves, pulled off their stalk
- ½ teaspoon ground turmeric
- 4 medium-sized potatoes, peeled and cut into chunks
- 1 big handful frozen peas
- 3 colored chilies, seeded and chopped
- 1 small bunch fresh coriander
- coconut shavings

Preparation

1. Bring a pot of salted water to the boil and add your cauliflower. Bring back to the boil for 1 minute, then remove the florets with a slotted spoon and leave in a colander. Keep the cauliflower water to one side.
2. Heat a wide pan big enough to hold all the ingredients at once. Add a good splash of olive oil and when it's hot, add the mustard seeds, the asafoetida, the curry leaves and turmeric. Fry for a few seconds then add the diced potatoes, just enough of the cauliflower

water to cover them and some salt. Cover with a lid and simmer gently until the potatoes are just cooked. Add the peas, chilies and cauliflower florets, stir and replace the lid. Cook over a gentle heat until everything is cooked and soft, and the liquid has reduced. Taste and season well with salt and pepper, sprinkle with loads of chopped coriander and some coconut shavings and serve. ENJOY!

89. Brussel sprouts in curry sauce

Ingredients:

Serves 4

- 1/2 kg or 1 lb (approximately) of Brussels sprouts
- 2 tbsps olive oil
- 5-6 curry leaves
- 1/2 tsp mustard seeds
- 2 green chilies chopped fine
- 2" piece ginger grated
- 1/2 tsp turmeric powder
- 1 tsp coriander powder
- 1 tsp cumin powder
- 1 tsp red chili powder (use less for less spicy)
sea salt to taste
- Fresh chopped coriander to garnish

Preparation

1. Wash the Brussels sprouts and pat dry. Cut the 'stem' off each one and peel off the top few leaves. Wash again if required. Cut each Brussels sprout into half lengthwise and then into quarters.
2. Set up a wok on medium heat. When hot, add the olive oil.
3. When the oil is hot, add the mustard seeds, green chilies, curry leaves and fry till the seeds stop spluttering.
4. Now add the ginger and sauté for a minute.
5. Add the Brussels sprouts and then the turmeric, coriander, cumin, red chili powder and sea salt to taste. Mix well. Sprinkle with a little water.
6. Cook for 7-8 minutes or until the sprouts are done. If the water dries up before the Brussels sprouts are cooked, feel free to sprinkle more water as required. Stir gently but often to keep the dish from burning. Do not cover the wok as you could end up overcooking the Brussels sprouts and they will lose their pretty color (and turn grayish!) and their nutrients.
7. When cooked, garnish the dish with fresh chopped coriander and serve with hot Indian flatbread. ENJOY!

90. Southern Indian vegetable curry with curry leaves

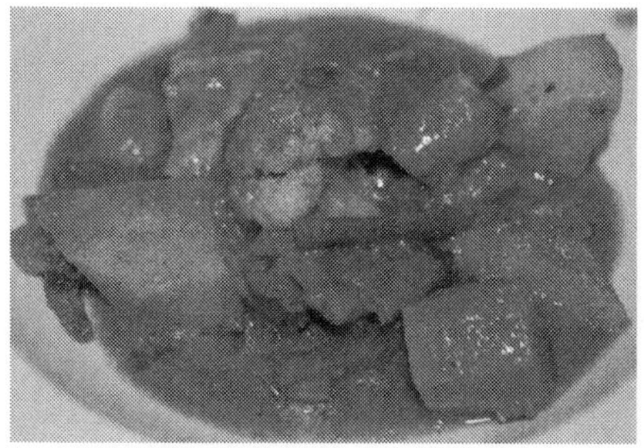

Ingredients

- 2 tablespoons olive oil
- 1 teaspoon mustard seeds
- 2 fresh green chilies, deseeded and chopped
- 1 bunch curry leaves
- 2 onions, peeled and shredded

- ½ teaspoon ground coriander
- 1 pinch ground cumin seeds
- ½ teaspoon garam masala
- ¼ teaspoon turmeric
- ¼ teaspoon chili powder
- 6 ripe tomatoes, chopped
- 2 sweet potatoes, peeled and cubed
- 2 potatoes, peeled and cubed
- 1 aubergine, cubed
- 100 ml coconut milk
- 1 handful French beans
- 1 handful peas
- 1 handful okra, sliced
- sea salt
- freshly ground black pepper

Preparation

1. Heat the oil in a pan and fry the mustard seeds for 2 to 3 minutes or until they start to pop.
2. Add the chilies, curry leaves, onions, coriander, cumin seeds, garam masala, turmeric, and chili powder. Stir and cook over a medium heat until the onion is soft. Stir in the chopped tomatoes. Add your potatoes and aubergine to the sauce. Pour in the coconut milk and cook until the potato is soft and cooked through. Throw in the beans, peas and okra. Season and cook for a few more minutes until tender, then serve with some nice basmati rice. ENJOY!

91. Green curry, crispy chicken, kimchee slaw, rice noodles

Ingredients

For the chicken

- 8 organic chicken thighs, skin on and bone in
- 2 tablespoons sesame seeds
- 2 large tablespoons runny honey

For the kimchee slaw

- 1 small bunch radishes
- 1 red onion
- ½ Chinese cabbage
- 1 small bunch fresh coriander
- 1 fresh red chili
- 1 fresh green chili

For the curry sauce

- 2 cm piece fresh ginger
- 2 limes
- sesame oil
- 2 cm piece fresh ginger
- 2 fresh red chilies
- a few fresh lime leaves, optional
- 1 bunch fresh coriander

© Natalie Mitchell

- 4 cloves garlic
- 1 stick lemongrass
- 1 small bunch spring onions
- sesame oil
- 300 ml organic chicken stock
- 200 g fine green beans
- 400 ml light coconut milk
- lime juice

For the noodles
- 250 g rice noodles
- 1 lime

For the seasonings
- olive oil
- sea salt
- black pepper

For the garnishes
- prawn crackers
- chili sauce
- 1 lime
- ½ romaine lettuce
- a few sprigs fresh coriander

Preparation

1. Put 1 large and 1 smaller frying pan on a high heat. Put the thin slicer disc attachment into the food processor. Tip the chicken thighs into the largest frying pan, skin side down. Drizzle with olive oil, add a pinch of salt & pepper and leave to cook, turning every minute or so for 18 to 20 minutes, or until cooked through. Wash the radishes well. Peel and halve the red onion. Shred the radishes, red onion and Chinese cabbage in the food processor. Tip into a serving bowl. Add the bunch of coriander and the chilies (stalks removed) to the processor and whiz. Peel

© Natalie Mitchell

and crush in the ginger, then tip into the bowl.

2. Put some greaseproof paper on top of the chicken then place the smaller frying pan on top of that, with something heavy like a pestle & mortar in it to weight it down. The heat from the smaller pan will get the chicken cooking on both sides and make it dead crispy.
3. Put the slicer attachment into the food processor. Peel the ginger and put it into the food processor with the chilies (stalks removed), lime leaves and most of the coriander. Crush in 4 unpeeled cloves of garlic. Halve the lemongrass and discard the outer leaves, trim the spring onions, and add both to the processor. Zap to a paste, adding a good drizzle of sesame oil and a good few lugs of olive oil as you go.
4. Move the top pan to a medium heat and get rid of the greaseproof paper. Carefully drain away the fat and turn the chicken pieces skin side up. Add 2 tablespoons of sesame seeds to the empty frying pan and leave to toast until golden, tossing occasionally, then put into a small bowl and take the pan off the heat.
5. Squeeze in the juice from both limes, and add a pinch of salt and a splash of sesame oil. Really scrunch together with your hands. Taste to check the balance. Put a large saucepan on a medium heat, for the curry sauce.
6. Carefully drain the fat again, then wipe the pan with kitchen paper and reduce the heat. Add 2 tablespoons of curry paste from the food processor, toss to coat and glaze the chicken, then turn the chicken over and carry on cooking to make it sticky and delicious. Fill and boil the kettle.
7. Tip the rest of the curry paste into the hot saucepan and stir in the chicken stock. Trim the green beans and add. Turn up the heat under the saucepan. Shake the tin of coconut milk then add and stir in. Bring to the boil, then turn down and leave to tick away.
8. Put the noodles into the empty frying pan with a pinch of salt and cover with boiled water. Leave for a few minutes and as soon as the noodles are soft enough to eat, quickly drain, then rinse under cold water and return to the frying pan. Drizzle over some sesame oil and a good squeeze of lime juice. Add a pinch of salt

and toss.

9. Check the chicken is cooked through then add 2 tablespoons of honey and toss, flipping the chicken skin side down again.
10. Pile some prawn crackers on a serving board with a good pool of chili sauce. Cut the lime into wedges, put some on the side and squeeze one of them over. Click off the lettuce leaves, wash and spin dry. Put into a bowl and add the coriander. Take to the table. Taste and correct the seasoning with lime juice, cook for another minute or so if you want a thicker sauce then take straight to the table.
11. Divide the noodles between 4 bowls. Put the chicken on a platter and let everyone layer up noodles, chicken, bean sprouts, kimchee slaw, and sauce. Finish with a pinch of toasted sesame seeds. ENJOY!

92. Easy Thai Coconut Curry Chicken

This sumptuous Coconut Curry Chicken recipe is cooked entirely from scratch, yet is very easy to make. It comes paired with sweet potato or yam for just a touch of sweetness in an otherwise savory Thai curry. You won't find any curry powder in this recipe - that's because I'm using the original spices that go into curry powder (without the other additives you'll find in most commercial brands). And there's no need to make a separate curry paste either - the sauce is cooked up right in the pan for an easy, everyday curry perfect for both family and guests alike. ENJOY!

SERVES 4-5 with rice

Ingredients:

- 1 to 1.5 lbs. (0.6 kg) organic chicken pieces or boneless breast or thigh, cut into chunks
- yam or sweet potato, up to 2.5 cups, chopped into chunks
- 3 Tbsp. dry flaked unsweetened coconut (baking type)
- 3/4 cup organic chicken stock
- 1 can (14 ounces) coconut milk
- 2 shallots or 1/4 cup purple onion, finely chopped
- 1 thumb-size piece galangal or ginger, grated or minced
- 4 cloves garlic, minced
- 1-2 fresh red chilies, minced, or 1/2 to 3/4 tsp. dried crushed chili from the spice aisle (chili flakes)
- 3 Tbsp. fish sauce
- 1 Tbsp. cooked tomato puree
- 3/4 tsp. ground turmeric
- 1 Tbsp. ground coriander
- 1/2 Tbsp. ground cumin
- 1/2 tsp. whole cumin seeds
- 1 bay leaf
- 1-2 lime leaves, or substitute 1 Tbsp. lime juice
- 1/4 tsp. Stevia
- 2-3 Tbsp. coconut oil
- 1/4 cup fresh coriander

Preparation

1. Heat a wok or large frying pan over medium-high heat. Add the flaked coconut, 'dry frying' it by stirring until fragrant and lightly toasted to a light golden-brown. Transfer to a bowl to cool.

2. Return pan to heat. Add 2 Tbsp. oil plus shallots/onion, ginger, garlic and chili. Stir-fry 1-2 minutes.
3. While stir-frying, add the following: turmeric, coriander, and 2 types cumin. Stir spices in, adding a little more oil if needed.
4. Add stock plus 3/4 can of coconut milk. Add the bay leaf and lime leaves or lime juice. Also add the fish sauce, tomato puree, and 1/2 tsp. brown sugar, stirring everything together well.
5. Add chicken and bring to a gentle boil, then reduce to a simmer (medium-low). Simmer 20 minutes for whole chicken pieces or 10 minutes for boneless chicken. Stir occasionally.
6. Add the sweet potato or yam plus 1/2 the toasted coconut. Continue simmering 10 more minutes, or until potato/yam has softened enough to easily pierce with a fork and chicken is cooked. Stir occasionally.
7. Reduce heat to minimum. Add remaining coconut milk and stir to dissolve into the curry sauce. Taste-test for salt and spice, adding more fish sauce if not salty or flavorful enough, or more chili for a spicier curry. Add more brown sugar if you prefer it sweeter. Portion out into bowls and top with fresh coriander plus a final sprinkling of toasted coconut. Pair with rice and ENJOY!

93. Chicken Tikka Masala

© Natalie Mitchell

Once you've marinated your chicken in all those amazing spices, this tikka masala's super fast!

Ingredients

- ½ fresh red chili, deseeded
- 1 clove of garlic, peeled
- 15 g fresh ginger
- 1 tablespoon olive oil
- 1 pinch paprika
- ½ tablespoon garam masala
- 1 teaspoon tomato puree
- 3 sprigs of fresh coriander, leaves picked and chopped, stalks reserved
- 400 g higher-welfare chicken breast, preferably free-range or organic, diced into 2.5cm pieces
- 1 small onion, peeled and sliced
- ½ ripe red pepper, deseeded and sliced
- ½ ripe green pepper, deseeded and sliced
- 1 pinch ground cinnamon
- 1 pinch ground coriander
- 1 pinch turmeric
- 400 g ripe plum tomatoes
- 150 ml coconut cream

Preparation

(Note: the marinade will need to be prepared the day before so the chicken can marinate overnight.)

For the marinade

1. Zap the chili, garlic, ginger and olive oil in the food processor. Add the paprika, garam masala and tomato puree, plus the coriander stalks, and blitz again to form a paste. Place the chicken pieces in a large bowl, coat them with the marinade and leave in the fridge overnight.
2. The next day: In a little olive oil, on a medium heat, fry the onion, peppers and spices in a large saucepan. Cook gently for 10 minutes then add the tin of tomatoes and coconut cream. Add the chicken pieces and simmer gently for 15 to 20 minutes until cooked. Just before serving, stir through the coconut cream and chopped coriander leaves.
3. Serve with fluffy basmati boiled rice and a mixed leaf salad. ENJOY!

94. Lamb Curry

Serves 4-6 people

Ingredients:

- 1 kg boneless lamb shoulder or stewing lamb, cut into 1 and a 1/2" chunks
- 4 tbsps olive oil
- 2 large onions sliced thin
- 2 tbsps garlic paste
- 1 tbsp ginger paste
- 2 tsps coriander powder
- 1 tsp cumin powder
- 1/2 tsp turmeric powder
- 1/2 tsp red chili powder
- 2 tsps garam masala powder
- 150 ml coconut cream
- Sea salt to taste
- Chopped coriander to garnish

Preparation:

1. Heat the olive oil in a heavy bottomed pan, on medium heat.
2. When hot, add the onions. Sauté till the onions begin to turn a pale golden brown in color. Now remove from the oil with a slotted spoon and drain on paper towels. Turn off heat.
3. Grind the onions into a smooth paste (adding very little to no water) in a food processor. Once done, remove into a separate container.
4. Now grind garlic and ginger pastes with coconut cream in the food processor, into a smooth paste. Remove into a separate container and keep aside for later use.
5. Heat the oil left over from frying the onions again and add the onion paste. Sauté for 2-3 minutes.
6. Now add all the powered spices. Mix well.
7. Sauté the resulting masala (onion spice mixture) until the oil begins to separate from it. This can take up to 10 minutes to happen.
8. Now add the lamb pieces to the masala, season with sea salt to taste and stir to fully coat the lamb pieces with the

masala. Sauté till the lamb is browned well.

9. Add 1/2 a cup of hot water to the pan, stir to mix well, simmer the heat and cover the pan. Cook till the lamb is tender. You will need to keep checking on the lamb as it cooks and adding more water if all the water dries up. Stir often to prevent burning. The dish should have a fairly thick gravy when done.
10. When the lamb is cooked, garnish with chopped coriander and serve with hot Chapatis (Indian flatbread), Naans (tandoor-baked Indian flatbread) or basmati boiled rice.
11. Tip: Use a pressure cooker to cook Lamb Curry and it will be done in half the time it takes to cook in an open pot!

Chapter 6

Recipes for Your Defensive Army of Enzymes to kill Cancer Cells and improve digestion

In order to break down food efficiently and effectively, your body needs a sufficient supply of digestive enzymes. Some of these digestive enzymes come from the pancreas, others are produced in the stomach, while still others are secreted by the salivary glands and glands in the small intestines. Raw foods also contain natural enzymes that make their own digestion easier, but the more foods are refined, the more digestive enzymes your body must produce on its own to assimilate them properly.

The major reason enzyme levels become depleted in the body is that we eat mostly processed, undernourished, irradiated and cooked food full of sugars and empty carbohydrates like white flour, etc. Big increases of soy food consumption are playing a great role too. I have a full chapter about how soy foods impact our health in my book **"How To Kill Cancer Cells".** You will be surprised to see how much soy and soybean oil and soy lecithin is sneaked into the food we buy. Unfortunately unless you carefully read the whole list of ingredients - which is usually printed in such small type that a lot of people have difficulty reading it - most of us are unaware that we are eating food products containing soy. I would strongly recommend that you carefully read the list of ingredients of each product you consider buying when doing your food shopping. It's only an investment of time the first time you do it; subsequently you will know what the healthy choices are for you the next time.

Our digestive system was designed to process **raw food**. Raw food, when it is picked **ripe and organic**, has enzymes in it that help break down that food in the upper stomach where it sits for about 30 to 45 minutes. The enzymes in the food predigest that food. Then in the lower stomach the pancreas, when healthy and functioning as it should, excretes more enzymes. Dairy products damage very much the health of the pancreas.

When we eat cooked, undernourished, irradiated and processed foods, most of the enzymes have been killed and the food does not predigest in the upper stomach. So when it reaches the lower stomach *two things happen.* The pancreas must make **extra enzymes** to try and break down the food.

And often food is only partially digested due to poor pancreas function and also to the cold drinks with ice that a lot of people consume these days while eating.

The pancreas, after decades of overworking, eventually is no longer able to produce an adequate supply of enzymes. So you develop **low levels** of all types of enzymes, and your body then *cannot* naturally kill cancer cells using enzymes.

You will be surprised but, in addition, food that is not completely digested all very often makes its way into our bloodstream. This happens especially when people have leaky gut syndrome from **candida** overgrowth. This partially digest food is treated as a toxin, and the immune system has to get rid of it. This puts an additional strain on the already overworked immune system.

Studies have found that the immune system treats the ingestion of cooked food as a toxic poison, causing a jump in white blood cells in an attempt to get rid of it as fast as possible.

*"Fresh **Papaya** is a good **source of enzymes**. You have the papaya melons as the source of the enzyme Papain. The damasking effect of these enzymes against the pericellular layer of the malignant cell is something very concrete in the immunology of cancer. Now I*

prefer, rather than advising the use of papaya tablets, that the individual seeking these enzymes get them directly from the fresh papaya fruit. You have nothing to lose by eating fresh papaya melons."- **Dr. Krebs, Jr.**

95. Shrimp, Papaya and Arugula Salad

Ingredients

Serves 4

- 1 papaya (small or medium)
- 20 shrimp (small, or 12 large chopped roughly)
- 1/4 tsp pumpkin seeds, 1/4 tbs sunflower seeds
- 1/4 tsp tarragon (dried)
- 1/8 tsp sea salt
- 1/8 tsp ground white pepper
- bunch of **arugula** (about 3 oz., washed and dried)
- 1/4 cup **olive oil**

Preparation

1. Prepare grill. Toss shrimp in bowl with 1 Tbsp. oil. Transfer to grill and cook, turning, until firm, about 4-5 minutes. Transfer cooked shrimp to a large salad bowl.
2. Half papaya, remove black seeds, half again and cut it into cubes, add arugula, pumpkin seeds, sunflower seeds, tarragon, season with pepper and sea salt. Enjoy!

96. Papaya and long beans Salad

Ingredients
Serves 2

- 1/2 papaya - finely shredded into long strands
- 4 garlic cloves
- 3 small red or green chilies
- 4-5 Tbsp lemon juice
- 10-15 long beans - chopped
- 2 Tbsp unsalted peanuts - roasted
- 1/4 Tbsp sea salt

Preparation

1. In a mortar, lightly pound the garlic, add the chilies and lightly pound again.
2. Add lemon juice, roasted peanuts, long beans and slightly bruise them.
3. Add the shredded papaya, lightly pound and stir until all the

ingredients have blended together.

4. Arrange on a serving dish and garnish with crushed peanuts. ENJOY!

Dietary sources of all kinds of enzymes are good, and the consumption of at least 70% fresh foods vs. 30% cooked foods helps **ensure a supply of healthy enzymes** for the body (cooking at temperatures above 116°F destroys enzymes in the food). Fresh foods generally contain all the enzymes required for their own digestion, easing the burden on the digestive system. However, certain foods are more easily digested when cooked because heat breaks down starch (potatoes, for example). Cooking softens cellulose, making foods easier to chew and this, in turn, makes nutrients more available. However, **juicing** as we discussed above, also breaks down cellulose and frees the nutrients while retaining the **enzymes** that would be destroyed by cooking.

97. Avocado and Papaya Salad with Lime Dressing

Ingredients

Serves 2

- 2 ripe papayas
- 2 avocados
- 2 limes, juiced
- 1 tablespoon honey
- 1/4 teaspoon sea salt

- 1/4 teaspoon freshly cracked black pepper
- 4 cups mixed baby lettuce greens

Preparation

1. Combine the lime juice, honey, sea salt and pepper; blend until smooth.

2. Peel the papayas and cut them in half. Using a spoon, remove the seeds; discard seeds.

3. Slice the papaya halves into thin wedges. Cut the avocados in half and remove the pits. Slice the flesh into thin strips.

4. Arrange the fruit slices on salad plates, alternating between papaya and avocado.

5. Combine the greens and dressing in a bowl and toss well to coat.

6. Mound a portion of the greens in the center of each plate. Drizzle with a few drops of dressing. ENJOY!

98. Spinach, bean sprouts and boiled egg salad

Ingredients:

Serves 2

© Natalie Mitchell

- 1 cup olive oil
- 2 tablespoons finely chopped onion
- 2 tablespoons lime juice
- 1 package (10 ounces) fresh spinach
- 1 cup bean sprouts
- 1 red onions
- 2 hard-cooked eggs, sliced
- 3 apricot kernels
- sea salt

Preparation

1. In a serving bowl, toss the spinach, bean sprouts, and cut red onions. Drizzle with olive oil mixed with lime juice.
2. Garnish with egg slices and apricot kernels. Add sea salt according to your taste.
3. Serve immediately.

Unsprouted seeds or beans contain enzyme inhibitors, which can be neutralized by cooking. However, soaking or sprouting the seeds and beans also removes the enzyme inhibitors and **sprouts have a high concentration of vegetable enzymes and other nutrients**. Therefore, it is a good idea to soak your grains and beans in water for a minimum of 12 hours before eating them. Soaked grains and beans are called "pre-sprouts" and are much more digestible because the enzyme inhibitors have been deactivated. Allowing the seeds to sprout for three days allows the synthesis of new proteins, plus there is a dramatic increase in the vitamins and essential fatty acids within the sprouts.

99. Curried Lentil Salad

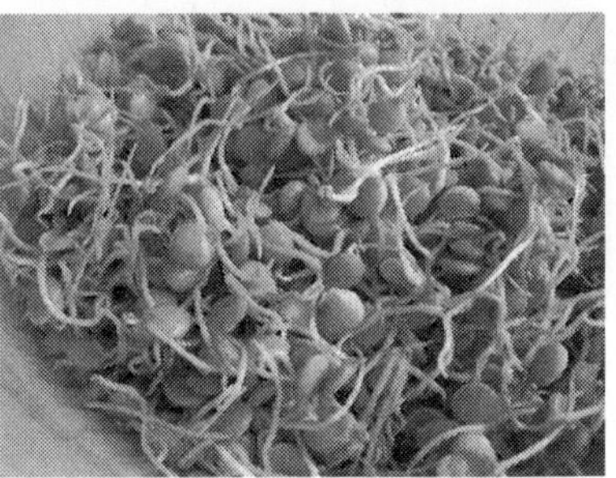

Ingredients:

- 2 Cups sprouted lentils
- 1/2 Cup onion, chopped
- 2 tsp Braggs Liquid Aminos
- 1 Tbsp fresh lemon juice
- 1 clove garlic, minced
- 1 tsp curry powder

Preparation

1. In a small bowl, mix the liquid aminos, lemon juice, garlic and curry powder.
2. In a separate mixing bowl, combine lentils and onions.
3. Pour dressing over the lentils and toss well.

This salad also makes a tasty filling for an avocado

100. Sprouted Hummus

Ingredients

- 1 Cup mixed crunchy sprouts
- 1 Tbsp tahini
- 1 Tbsp fresh lemon juice
- 1 Tbsp olive oil
- 1 clove garlic, minced
- 1 tsp ground cumin
- salt & pepper to taste

101. Black Bean Dip

Ingredients

- 3 Cups sprouted black beans
- 1 medium onion
- 1 tsp cumin
- 1/4 tsp cayenne
- 1 clove garlic
- Chopped parsley

Preparation

1. Using a food processor or high-powered blender, combine all ingredients until well mixed and smooth. Add chopped parsley.

2. Blend all ingredients in a food processor until smooth. ENJOY!

Take a look at a list of common legumes. I bet more than one of these will surprise you:

- Alfalfa
- Black beans
- Carob
- Clover
- Cowpeas (black-eyed peas)
- Garbanzo beans (chickpeas)
- Lentils
- Mung beans
- Peas
- Peanuts

Cooking food thoroughly kills bacteria and viruses, which is why with raw foods, cleanliness with food handling becomes very important. The temperature of food and beverages also makes a difference to digestion. Warm food relaxes the stomach and aids digestion. **Cold food** and **beverages** contract the muscles of the stomach, **hindering proper digestion**.

As mentioned earlier, it's quite dangerous for our digestive system to have cold drinks consumed with meals. **Drink water or organic fruits and vegetable juices between meals and stop 15 min before the meal and start drinking again 30-35 min after the meal.** Beverages interfere with digestion because the **digestive liquid** and **enzymes** get carried **out** with the beverage rather than staying in the stomach. Also, drinking beverages might wash down food that has **not been properly broken** down through chewing and mixing with saliva in the mouth. This is certainly a way to create an environment to encourage colon cancer.

Lightly steaming vegetables warms and softens them while retaining most of their enzymes and nutrients.

Chapter 7

ENERGY BOOSTING, ALKALIZING JUICES RECIPES

The **best** and the **quickest way** you can **alkalize** and increase your energy and then maintain the alkalinity your body requires will be for you to make the life sustaining decision to only eat the foods your body's tissues and cells require to keep you free from a lot of nasty diseases. In reality this means you will consistently eat, on a daily basis, fresh, preferably organic vegetables, a variety of non-acidic fruits and other natural foods that contain plenty of **alkalizing minerals** and **antioxidant vitamins.**

I also recommend that you include alkaline beverages in your diet to achieve perfect alkalinity. This will mean that you make a point of drinking fresh fruit & vegetable juices that you can get at your local health or grocery store. The regular consumption of these kinds of juices, many of which are quite delicious – and others that will grow on you (no pun intended!) - will further reduce the time it takes you to reach and maintain the level of alkalinity your body needs to stay healthy.

Before we take a detailed look at the additional alkalizing food charts and tables later in the chapter which will guide you in what to select for your everyday alkalizing nutrients and minerals, I want to stay on the subject of alkalizing beverages and introduce to you a **SUPER ALKALINE juice or pill supplement** which you may have heard of and which is commonly **known as "Wheatgrass".**

I can't emphasize enough to you how beneficial this juice is to our bodies. You can take it via **shots of fresh wheatgrass juice** on its own, as a friend of mine does, or mixed into a cocktail of your fruit or vegetable juice choices according to your taste preferences - which is my personal preference.

Next, I will go into detail with you about the benefits of this important juice which I recommend be taken every day when you feel unwell or you have an acidic pH test result and otherwise 2-3 times a week for good health support for your system.

WONDERFUL WHEATGRASS IS ONE OF THE BEST ALKALINITY SOURCES FOR OUR BODIES

*"When we **love**, we always strive to become **better** than we are. When we strive **to become better** than we are, everything around us **becomes better too**."*

Paulo Coelho, the Alchemist

WHEATGRASS…THE SUPERJUICE!

Wheatgrass should become recognized by you as a rather powerful and increasingly available tool for your body as it possesses the amazing ability to literally cleanse the blood, organs and gastrointestinal tract within the body of **debris** and built-up **toxins**; it **increases the red blood-cell count** and it also lowers blood pressure by dilating the blood pathways throughout the body.

Wheatgrass also stimulates the body's **metabolism** and **enzyme systems** by enriching blood cells in the body.

Wheatgrass fights tumors and neutralizes toxins.

Recent studies have shown that wheatgrass juice has a powerful tumor-fighting ability without introducing into the body the usual toxicity effect of drugs that inhibit cell-destroying agents. The many active compounds found in wheatgrass juice cleanse the blood and neutralize and digest toxins in our cells.

The enzymes and amino acids found in wheatgrass can protect us from carcinogens like no other food or medicine. **If taken two or three times a week, it strengthens our cells**, **detoxifies** the **liver** and bloodstream, and chemically neutralizes environmental pollutants.

Wheatgrass juice also greatly restores alkalinity to the blood. The juice's abundance of **alkaline minerals** helps **reduce over-acidity** in the blood if taken regularly. It can be used successfully to treat peptic ulcers, ulcerative colitis, constipation, diarrhea, and other complaints of the gastrointestinal tract.

What makes Wheatgrass so special? Wheatgrass is a **concentrated** source of many nutrients, especially **Beta-carotene (Vitamin A), Calcium, Iron, Vitamin K, Vitamin C, Vitamin B12, Folic acid, Vitamin B6** and other trace nutrients.

Research strongly suggests the reason this super juice works so well in the human body is that Wheatgrass has a significant structural similarity to our own blood. It contains **70% living chlorophyll,** chlorophyll being the basis of all plant life. Please note it is important that your fresh wheatgrass shot needs to be consumed within two hours of purchase to avoid the benefit of the living chlorophyll degrading!

Science has proven that chlorophyll **arrests growth** and **development** of unfriendly bacteria and helps to destroy **free radicals**. **Chlorophyll (wheatgrass juice)** has a nearly identical chemical structure to **hemoglobin (red blood cells),** which is the body's **critical oxygen** and **iron-carrying** blood protein. **Dr. Birscher**, a research scientist, called chlorophyll "**Concentrated**

Sun Power." He says chlorophyll **increases** function of the **heart,** and positively affects the **vascular system**, the **uterus**, the **intestine** and the **lungs**. According to **Dr. Birscher**, nature uses chlorophyll as a **body cleanser**, **rebuilder** and **neutralizer of toxins**.

Dr. Yoshihide Hagiwara, president of the Hagiwara Institute of Health in Japan, is a leading advocate for the use of wheatgrass as **food** and **medicine**. He reasons that since chlorophyll is soluble in fat particles, and fat particles are absorbed directly into the blood via the lymphatic system, chlorophyll can also be absorbed in this way. In other words, when the "blood" of plants is absorbed in humans it is transformed into human blood, which transports nutrients to **every cell of the body**.

Wheatgrass offers the benefits of a liquid oxygen transfusion since the juice contains liquid oxygen. **Oxygen** is vital to many body processes: it stimulates **digestion** (the oxidation of food), promotes **clearer thinking** (the brain utilizes 25% of the body's oxygen supply), and protects the blood against anaerobic bacteria.

Interestingly, Wheatgrass has been found to return grey hair to its natural color again and **greatly increases energy levels**, when consumed daily.

A note of caution: Please do not cook it! We can only get the benefits of the many enzymes found in wheatgrass by eating it fresh and uncooked. Cooking destroys **100 percent** of the **enzymes** that are so vital for us in food.

The power of Wheatgrass can also:

- **Neutralize toxic substances** like cadmium, nicotine, strontium, mercury, and polyvinyl chloride.

- **Lessen the effects of radiation**. Onc enzyme found in wheatgrass, SOD, lessens the effects of radiation and acts as an anti-inflammatory compound that may **prevent cellular damage** following **heart attacks** or exposure to irritants.

Detoxification is the process of reducing the **"body burden"** by **eliminating toxins** that have been building for years or even decades. Because of the presence of **chlorophyll,** wheatgrass juice will cause detoxification to take place. If your body has stored toxins, it will Detox your body. Not surprisingly, this will yield really positive benefits for your body

A word of caution: If you Detox too quickly, it is possible to have side effects that cause you to **temporarily** feel worse. When toxins re-enter the bloodstream, they can trigger an immune response that is termed a "healing crisis". This is a natural process, but can be uncomfortable and may include symptoms such as a headache (particularly for high sugar consumers), flu-like feelings, diarrhea or fatigue. I would recommend you start with a small amount of juice (1 oz.) every third day and work your way up to avoid this experience. Please note it is necessary to drink plenty of water when detoxing, approximately 2 liters a day.

If the Detox reaction is noticeable to you, recognize it as a positive sign, consider reducing your juice consumption temporarily and be confident that it will pass. In a short period of time (less than 1 week for most people, 1 month in rare circumstances) your body will be cleansed and you will experience the **mental clarity** and physical **rejuvenation** that comes with supplementing your food with **wheatgrass juice.**

Suggested Dosage:

For normal health maintenance -1 to 2 oz. daily;
For therapeutic dosage - 3 to 5 oz. daily;
In health crisis – 6 to 10 oz. daily.

Recommended duration period for an intake over four ounces a day is 60 days following which a “maintenance” level of two ounces a day intake will be more than satisfactory.

Wheatgrass juice is best taken on an empty stomach at least 15 minutes before a meal. For those who can't take it straight, do mix it with fruit or vegetable juices according to your own taste.

You may be surprised to learn that it's also very important not to drink any cold water or other drinks with your meals; you should stop drinking 15 min before a meal and refrain from drinking for 30-45 min after a meal. Why? Liquids dilute stomach juices and reduce the quality of digestion, sending poorly digested food particles into the colon.

I do so want to make sure you enjoy your more alkaline food and beverage nutrition selections every day, so while on the subject of beverages, here are several of my favorite combinations of the Super Alkaline Fresh Vegetables and Fresh Fruit Juices which I recommend you to enjoy at least two or three times a week and which will improve your overall health and sexual energy and rebuild your body's natural defensive capabilities.

You do not actually have to go to a juice bar to do this – you can also start making and drinking **fresh juices from organic and ripe fruits and vegetables** in your own kitchen with a juicer and play around with the proportions of ingredients according to your **own taste preferences**. As you noticed above I emphasized using only ripe and organic fruits and vegetables. This is so important - in order for a fruit or vegetable to optimally ripen, it must remain attached to the branch on the tree or bush as it ripens. This allows nutrients to be continuously fed into the fruit during the ripening process while on the tree or bush. Staying attached to the plant or bush also permits the fruit or vegetable and its plant to receive the correct amount of UV rays from the sun which make photosynthesis occur throughout the plant. Once you pluck the fruit or vegetable, it's no longer receiving nutrients, and the ripening process designed by nature stops. The fact is that often the fruits and vegetables available at your local grocery store are not naturally ripened. Unripen fruits and vegetables can be rather acidic and so create acidity in the body, which is opposite to naturally ripe fruits and vegetables, which are alkaline.

I hope you enjoy some of my favorite **fresh juice** recipes **below that are not only healthy but delicious at any time of day** and then you may enjoy involving your own creativity and imagination to create your own recipes using vegetables and fruits from the alkalinity charts in my book.

Sample these Delicious Fresh Vegetable Juice mixes – and please do try to confirm before you buy that your fruit and veggies are from **organic suppliers**. You will have fun and enjoy experimenting to find the best ratios of vegetables and fruits in each juice mix according to your own tastes.

1. Apple
Asparagus
Fennel
Garlic
Pumpkin

2. Bok Choy
Ginger root
Butternut Squash
Celery
Chia Seeds (1 half tsp in powder form to have the best absorption)
Fresh Wheatgrass shot (1 – 2 oz)
(You can use wheatgrass powder if fresh wheatgrass juice is not accessible.)

2. Jicama
Leek
Garlic
Peas
Sweet Potatoes
Chia Seeds (1 half tsp in powder form)
Fresh Wheatgrass shot (1 – 2 oz)

3. Apple - chew the seeds
Turnip
Spirulina
Ginseng
Chia Seeds (1 half tsp in powder form)
Fresh Wheatgrass shot (1 – 2 oz)

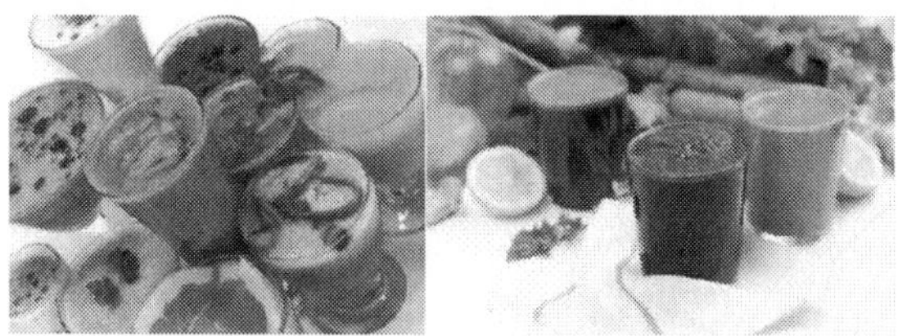

4. Squash
Spirulina
Brussels sprouts
Broccoli

© Natalie Mitchell

Chia Seeds (1 half tsp in powder form)
Fresh Wheatgrass shot (1 – 2 oz)

5. Fennel
   Carrots
   Apricot seeds (kernels) – 2-3 pieces
   Alfalfa
   Bamboo
   Chia Seeds (1 half tsp in powder form)
   Fresh Wheatgrass shot (1 – 2 oz)

6. Apple
   Carrot
   Celery
   Ginger
   Spinach
   Chia Seeds (1 half tsp in powder form to have the best absorption)
   Fresh Wheatgrass shot (1 – 2 oz)
   (You can use wheatgrass powder if fresh wheatgrass juice is not accessible.)

7. Kale
   Cucumber
   Garlic
   Alfalfa
   Celeriac
   Chia Seeds (1 half tsp in powder form)
   Fresh Wheatgrass shot (1 – 2 oz)

© Natalie Mitchell

8. Apple - chew the seeds
   Pumpkin
   Spirulina
   Ginseng
   Chia Seeds (1 half tsp in powder form)
   Fresh Wheatgrass shot (1 – 2 oz)

9. Alfalfa grass
   Spirulina
   Brussels sprouts
   Broccoli
   Chia Seeds (1 half tsp in powder form)
   Fresh Wheatgrass shot (1 – 2 oz)

10. Kale
   Carrots
   Apricot seeds (kernels) – 2-3 pieces
   Alfalfa
   Bamboo
   Chia Seeds (1 half tsp in powder form)
   Fresh Wheatgrass shot (1 – 2 oz)

You have to enjoy the taste if you are going to slurp these healthy juices frequently. Please feel free to play with quantities and ingredients according to your personal taste and preferences. Don't be put off by the color of some of these juice mixes; some of the most delicious juices are rather unappetizing from a color standpoint.

Here are some of my favorite fresh, SUPER ALKALINE (ripe please!) **fruit juices (organic sources)**:

1. Papaya
Blueberries
Bananas
Goji Berries
Chia Seeds (1 half tsp in powder form)

© Natalie Mitchell

Fresh Wheatgrass shot (1 – 2 oz)

2. Banana
   Coconut water
   Apple
   Goji berries
   Chia Seeds (1 half tsp in powder form)
   Fresh Wheatgrass shot (1 – 2 oz)

3. Pomegranate
Goji Berries
Mango
Coconut Milk
Cashew nuts
Papaya
Chia Seeds (1 half tsp in powder form)
Fresh Wheatgrass shot (1 – 2 oz)

4. Grapes
Guava
Papaya
Lime juice
Chia Seeds (1 half tsp in powder form)
Fresh Wheatgrass shot (1 – 2 oz)

5. Papaya
   Mango
   Lime
   Blackberries
   Chia Seeds (1 half tsp in powder form)
   Fresh Wheatgrass shot (1 – 2 oz)

6. Banana
   Papaya
   Coconut water
   Apple
   Goji berries
   Chia Seeds (1 half tsp in powder form)
   Fresh Wheatgrass shot (1 – 2 oz)

7. Pomegranate
   Mango
   Cranberry
   Blackberries
   Goji berries
   Chia Seeds (1 half tsp in powder form)
   Fresh Wheatgrass shot (1 – 2 oz)

© Natalie Mitchell

For you to have more fun creating your own fruit recipes you will find a table of fruits and vegetables at the end of the book were as an addition you can find out the average mineral and vitamin content they should contain.

Chapter 8

Herbs and Vegetables -

Anti-Inflammatory with Cancer Preventative properties

Inflammation causes is a huge topic these days as recent research indicates that there is no longer any doubt that inflammation produces a cascade of events responsible for most chronic diseases including **cancer**. Often medical doctors prescribe drug treatment and there are times when this is what is needed. There are also instances when alternatives are appropriate and I would like you to be well equipped with information about herbs and vegetables that have **anti-inflammatory properties**. Some of them are widely available and you can include them in your diet as preventative as well as enjoying their delicious taste. Many herbs can work on inflammation in a multi-faceted holistic and balanced way and you don't get the side effects like from drugs.

Turmeric (*Curcuma longa*) 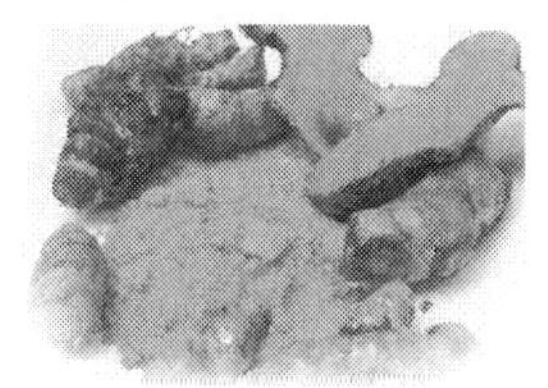	Over the past several years, numerous studies have emerged on the benefits of Turmeric and on its anti-cancerous properties. Curcumin, which is present in Turmeric (Curcuma Longa), is a powerful antioxidant. Turmeric is also a powerful anti-inflammatory and is very

© Natalie Mitchell

	effective in treating all kinds of inflammatory diseases as well as arthritis, tendinitis, injuries, etc. The plant is also a powerful blood purifier and is highly effective in reducing excessive cholesterol. Turmeric is very safe and has been used in Chinese medicine for more than 4,000 years.
Ginger: (Zingiber officinalis) 	Ginger has a long history of use as an anti-inflammatory and many of its constituents have been identified as having anti-inflammatory properties. Ginger has been shown to be more effective against bacterial staph infections than antibiotics. It can kill cancer cells. Its anti-inflammatory effects are already famous. It can resolve brain inflammations and ease or cure a variety of gut problems, such as ulcerative colitis and acid reflux. And ginger can even alleviate the effects of gamma radiation. It has also been indicated for arthritis, fevers, headaches, toothaches, coughs, bronchitis, osteoarthritis, rheumatoid arthritis, to ease tendonitis, lower

	cholesterol and blood pressure and aid in preventing internal blood clots.
Garlic 	Medical scientists, who have new evidence of its potency against cancer and heart disease, are now rediscovering garlic, recognized for its healing powers in ancient times. Sulphides, which are found in garlic in large amounts, stop the growth of tumors and inhibit carcinogens. According to the National Cancer Institute, garlic lies among the top of the list of foods ingested as a potential weapon against many types of cancer. Garlic is a natural, potent antibiotic, antiviral and antifungal herb. A study done at Boston University School of Medicine conducted tests in which garlic proved to be as effective as an antibiotic in killing 14 types of bacteria in reoccurring infections. Garlic has also been shown in some studies to decrease high blood sugar, boost metabolism, inhibit growth and formation of cancer cells, prevent inflammation, and alleviate allergies and asthma.

Cardamom 	The study, published in the April-June 2005 issue of "Asian Pacific Journal of Cancer Prevention," found cancer cell reproduction was diminished and apoptosis -- programmed cell death -- was increased in response to supplementation with three doses of 0.5 percent cardamom extract per day for eight weeks. Additionally, cardamom has anti-inflammatory effects, as observed by the inhibition of cyclooxygenase 2, also known as COX2 -- a pro-inflammatory enzyme.
Cayenne 	Cayenne pepper has anti-inflammatory, antioxidant, antiseptic, diuretic, analgesic, expectorant, and diaphoretic properties. According to an article published in the "Indian Journal of Cancer" in Jan-March 2010, there are other substance in chili peppers and cayenne, known collectively as capsaicinoids, that offer anticancer benefits. Capsaicin appears to induce cancer cell death by blocking several proteins and interrupting

	signaling pathways required for cancer cell growth survival and proliferation.
Chives 	Chives help inhibit the growth of tumors and cancer. The small onions have been found helpful in the treatment of esophageal, stomach, prostrate and gastrointestinal tract cancers. Selenium in the small onion helps to protect cells from the effects of toxins and free radicals. Like most plants in the allium group, chives have antibiotic properties. The natural antibacterial and antiviral agents in the vegetable work with vitamin C to destroy harmful microbes. This makes the plant an excellent natural defense against the common cold, flu and certain yeast infections.
Nutmeg 	Nutmeg which is made by grinding the seeds produced by the nutmeg tree offers help for those fighting cancer battles with certain forms of leukemia. A recent medical study has shown that nutmeg extract causes cancer cells to

	self-destruct in leukemia patients. Nutmeg is known to have anti-inflammatory properties and can be used to treat joint and muscle pain.
Cilantro 	Cilantro or, more commonly, coriander is a potent herb that has anti-cancer properties. The prevalent anti-oxidants in cilantro are beta-carotene, quercetin and rutin. This herb, normally used in chelation therapy for people suffering from lead poisoning, helps remove free radicals by getting rid of the heavy metals in your body. Dr. Yoshiaki Omura from the Heart Disease Research Foundation, New York, NY, USA, has actually found that fresh cilantro removes heavy metals – and with it the free radicals too – from the body in less than 2 weeks.
Cinnamon 	Cinnamon is a common and flavorful spice that contains polyphenols. The polyphenol compounds help reduce cancer risk by preventing damage to healthy cells. Cinnamon, which is made from the dried tree bark of Asian cinnamon trees, has also shown

	evidence of having the ability to stop the cancer cell growth of melanoma.
Cloves	Cloves are a common spice often used around Thanksgiving and Christmas for adding flavor to Holiday dinner recipes, and the same spice that flavors your Christmas ham will also reduce your cancer risk by protecting your skin cells from malignant melanomas.
Black Pepper	Angiogenesis is a physiological process enabling the growth of new blood vessels from pre-existing ones. A vital mechanism for wound healing, angiogenesis is also a key process involved in tumor growth and progression. Several previous studies suggest that piperine, an alkaloid compound found abundantly in black pepper, has diverse physiological actions including the ability to kill cancer cells.
Basil	Basil is well known for its medicinal value. Apart from having anti-inflammatory, blood pressure lowering, and nervous system stimulating properties,

	this popular herb has been found to have chemo-protective potential for colon cancer. In fact, a study found that basil played a significant role in reducing colon tumors in experimental animals. In cell culture and animal studies basil has been found to exhibit antimicrobial, anti-inflammatory, anti-diabetic, antioxidant and anti-cancer activity.
Parsley 	Parsley is rich in antioxidants like vitamin C, beta-carotene and quercetin, and also contains less well known flavonoids like apigenin, luteolin and chrysoeroil. Apigenin research studies have associated it with a decreased risk of pancreatic cancer, leukemia, cervical and ovarian cancer. Apigenin has also been shown to interfere with cancer cell proliferation, exhibiting strong anti-tumor properties. Not only does apigenin possesses remarkable anti-cancer properties, it's also a powerful anti-inflammatory and antioxidant. Chrysoeroil has also been studied for

	its potential anti-cancer benefits, particularly with regards to preventing breast cancer.
Chamomile	Recent and on-going research has identified chamomile's specific anti-inflammatory, anti-bacterial, anti-allergenic and sedative properties, validating its long-held reputation. Most evaluations of tumor growth inhibition by chamomile involve studies with apigenin, which is one of the bioactive constituents of chamomile. Studies on preclinical models of skin, prostate, breast and ovarian cancer have shown promising growth inhibitory effects.
Rosemary	Rosmarinic acid, a natural polyphenolic antioxidant found in rosemary, has been found to have anti-bacterial, anti-inflammatory, and anti-oxidant functions. Rosemary contains proven anti-inflammatory properties that can reduce the risk of colon cancer.
Stinging Nettle	In ancient Greek times, the stinging nettle was used mainly as a diuretic and laxative. Now the plant is used for many cures; illnesses include

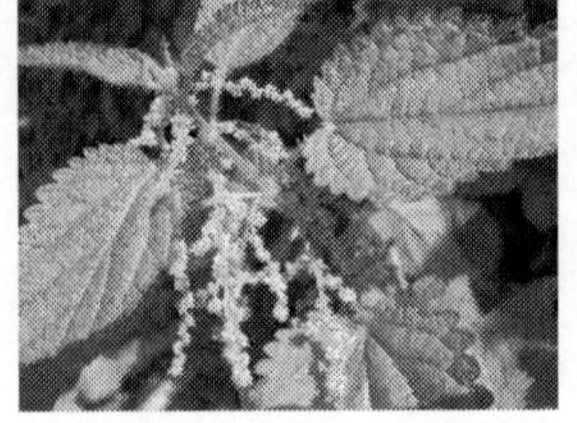	**cancer** and **diabetes**. Stinging Nettle has **anti-inflammatory properties** and treats illness of the urinary track. The stinging nettle is a **blood purifier** and thus cleans eczema internally. It is the best blood purifier available and has an influence over the pancreas. Stinging nettle also assists in **lowering blood sugar**. Nettle has been studied extensively and has shown promise in treating Alzheimer's disease, arthritis, asthma, bladder infections, bronchitis, bursitis, gingivitis, gout, hives, kidney stones, laryngitis, multiple sclerosis, PMS, prostate enlargement, sciatica, and tendinitis!

The best, as you know, is always to enjoy everything in moderation. Sometimes people, having discovered for example what a great preventative and healing power garlic has, start consuming it every day, which is quite dangerous. As well as having healing power, like everything else garlic can become a poison when taken in high doses. When you nourish your precious body with a variety of different fruits, vegetables, good carbs and good fat then your cells have plenty of good quality building material to operate and regenerate with. It will not take long for you to see the difference in your health!

Boost your Brain

For many of us, we live in hectic environments with lots of stress as well as time limitations so much so that it can be hard to find time to even think about providing good nutrition for our bodies and brain. As a result many people have high acidity in their system without realizing it, minerals and vitamin deficiency which can result or slowly encourage some dangerous disease, which otherwise could be prevented by the body.

One of the very important parts of our body - our brain - consists of about 100 billion brain cells called **neurons** that drive our thinking, learning, feeling and states of being. To do their best work, neurons need good fats, protein, complex carbohydrates, micronutrients - vitamins, minerals and phytonutrients - and water. Your quality of thinking and the health of your brain depend dramatically on the quality of food you provide for it!
Good quality food provides proper functioning for our brain as about one-fifth of the oxygen, nutrients and energy consumed by a person go directly to the brain, which is primarily composed of fat and water.
Proper nutrition enhances neurogenesis, the process of generating new brain cells.

Your brain cells actually need twice as much energy as the other cells in your body.
Neurons are constantly communicating with each other and have a high demand for energy because they're always in a state of metabolic activity. Even during your sleep, neurons are still at work repairing and rebuilding their worn out structural components.
They are manufacturing enzymes and neurotransmitters that must be transported out to the very ends of their nerve branches some that can be several inches, or feet, away.

It would be useful for you as well to understand the difference between high-glycemic-index foods, which are mainly processed carbohydrates like everything made from white flower, white rice, white sugar, etc. These processed foods spike the level of your blood sugar quite dramatically, which can lead to diabetes, heart disease, cancer, obesity, etc.

Diets rich in high-glycemic-index foods have been linked to an increased risk for diabetes, heart disease and overweight and there is preliminary work linking high-glycemic diets to age-related macular degeneration, ovulatory infertility and colorectal cancer.

One of the most important factors that determine a food's glycemic index is how much it has been processed. Milling and grinding **removes** the **fiber-rich outer bran** and the **vitamin- and mineral-rich inner germ**, leaving mostly the starchy endosperm.

Eating **whole grains, beans, legumes, fruits and vegetables**—all foods with a **low glycemic index**—is indisputably good for many aspects of health as well as very important food for your brain. The quality of your thinking, sharpness of your brain, memory capacity, the level of your energy, sexual health, the strength of your immune system and of course the shape of your body depends very much on the quality of the food you are providing for it! You will be very excited and quite surprised to see how all unwanted fat will be gently melting as soon as you provide your body with good fats, good carbs, plenty of vegetables, legumes and fruits.
The choice is YOURS as it is your body and you are the only One who chooses what to feed it with! You can treat it to what it wants or not!

Chapter 9

Know the Antioxidants with Cancer Cells Killing Properties

You already know a lot about the power of antioxidants and now I would like to introduce you a super cancer-killing antioxidant found in the sea!

Ecklonia Cava is a brown algae (seaweed) that grows off the coast of Japan and Korea proven **100 times more powerful than any land-based antioxidants**. Over 15 years of research and nearly 40 million USD worth of clinical studies back it up. It's the only **FDA-approved Ecklonia Cava marine algae** extract on the market. It works in your body for 12 hours compared to land based Antioxidants that work only for 30 minutes. *Ecklonia cava* is a potent antioxidant that has the ability to pass through the **blood-brain barrier**, which means it can reach the brain.

During the 19th century a French doctor named René Quinton discovered that sea water is 98% identical to blood. It makes sense that the latest and potentially most-beneficial, most well-researched, life-changing nutrient has come from the sea. Ecklonia

Cava Extract's (ECE) benefits are countless and the research results are staggering.

100 Times Stronger & 2400% Longer Than Green Tea!

The potency of an antioxidant is often determined by its molecular structure, which is made up of rings. Most antioxidants have **three connected rings**. Ecklonia Cava has up to **eight interconnected rings**, making its free-radical scavenging ability 10X-100X times more powerful than other antioxidants.

Up To 12 Hours Of Antioxidant Protection!

Fat-soluble ocean nutrients like Ecklonia Cava stay in the body for an extended period of time. The half-life of Ecklonia Cava is up to 12 hours, compared to 30 minutes for water-soluble, land-based polyphenols like green tea. That means that you have up to 12 full hours of antioxidant protection roaming your body and **eliminating free radicals**.

Millions On Research

Dr. Haengwoo Lee and his team spent over 32 million dollars on research, from in vitro to animal and human studies. The results are in and they are quite extraordinary. The benefits of Ecklonia Cava are many.

Research Conducted:

- Cardiovascular health including cholesterol, blood pressure, blood flow & vascular flexibility.
- Brain function related to blood flow & oxygen supply, memory, alertness, relaxation & response to stress
- Inflammation, cartilage protection, comparison to popular inflammation medications & nerve pain
- Sexual performance & comparison to popular sexual performance drugs
- Weight management & lipid metabolism
- Nerve pain
- Allergies

- Sugar spikes & pancreas support
- Sleeplessness

The Blood-Brain Barrier and Sex Enhancement

Because it is fat-soluble, Ecklonia Cava also has the ability to cross the blood-brain barrier. This allows antioxidants to work in ways that traditional water-soluble antioxidants **cannot.** Ecklonia Cava can penetrate deep into the fatty tissues of the body where much of the **acidifying toxicity hides**.

Ecklonia cava is not only superior to all land based antioxidants, it may be the king in the sea too. Also known as a sea polyphenol, Ecklonia's super powers emanate from its unique molecular structure that acts as a master switch, activating key genes, such as Nrf2, that turn on a universal network of anti-oxidant and anti-inflammatory processes to defend your body against a broad array of "cellular assassins".

The result is improved brain, heart, breast, prostate, joints and overall health, with a stronger immune system and greater physical and sexual vitality.

You might be wondering where you can find Ecklonia Cava. The good news is that it is actually available from quite a few suppliers:

© Natalie Mitchell

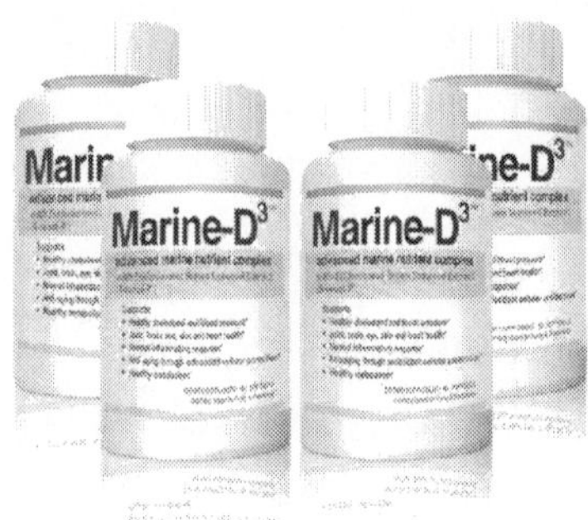

20 Common Foods With the Most Antioxidants

Rank	Food item	Serving size	Total antiox idant capacity per serving size
1	Small Red Bean (dried)	Half cup	13,727
2	Ripe Wild blueberry	1 cup	13,427
3	Red kidney bean (dried)	Half cup	13,259
4	Pinto bean	Half cup	11,864
5	Ripe Blueberry (cultivated)	1 cup	9,019
6	Ripe Cranberry	1 cup (whole)	8,983
7	Artichoke (cooked)	1 cup (hearts)	7,904
8	Ripe Blackberry	1 cup	7,701
9	Ripe Prune	Half cup	7,291
10	Ripe Raspberry	1 cup	6,058
11	Ripe Strawberry	1 cup	5,938
12	Red Delicious apple	1 whole	5,900
13	Granny Smith apple	1 whole	5,381
14	Pecan	1 ounce	5,095
15	Ripe Sweet cherry	1 cup	4,873

16	Ripe Black plum	1 whole	4,844
17	Russet potato (cooked)	1 whole	4,649
18	Black bean (dried)	Half cup	4,181
19	Ripe Plum	1 whole	4,118
20	Gala apple	1 whole	3,903

Another Super Strong Antioxidant from Mother Nature

We have available from Mother Nature another **Super Strong Antioxidant**: **"Chia Seeds"** that you might like to consider adding to your meals. Chia Seeds are an excellent source of omega three fatty acids. Chia seeds great for reducing inflammation in the arteries and keeping blood pumping, according to (among others) a study out of the University of Maryland Medical Center. Chia seeds are also rich in protein, fiber, iron, zinc combining to boost stamina and circulation.

Chia is an astonishingly powerful **natural seed**. In 2008, a study by the Department of Foods and Nutrition, Purdue University, Indiana, USA reported that Chia contained, among other things, **significant amounts of antioxidants**.

Chia's army of antioxidants include flavonol aglycones: quercetin, kaempferol, and myricetin; and flavonol glycosides: **chlorogenic acid** and **caffeic acid.** These antioxidants have significant value to **human health.**

There are also reports saying that the **black Chia seeds** may contain 12%-15% more antioxidants that the **white seeds**. A study by the US-based Nutritional Science Research Institute performed a study on Chia seeds.

"... Chia seeds as one of the most powerful, whole food antioxidant we know."

Antioxidants contained in Chia seeds

Quercetin, one of Chia's **powerful antioxidants**, has been at the top of recent health news. Early this year, a study by researchers at the University of South Carolina's Arnold School of Public Health shows that *quercetin* significantly **boosted energy**, endurance and fitness in healthy men and women who were not involved in some type of daily physical training. This means that this antioxidant's fatigue-fighting properties could help average adults who battle fatigue and stress daily.

Quercetin, kaempferol, and *myricetin* are **antioxidants** that could protect against a host of chronic diseases like **ischemic heart disease**, cerebrovascular disease, **lung cancer**, **prostate cancer**, asthma, and **diabetes**.

Chlorogenic Acid, another of Chia's **antioxidants**, has been found by a study to possess **anti-cancer properties** and could be used to prevent growth of certain **brain tumors**. It could also slow the release of glucose into the bloodstream after a meal, and is a compound of interest for reducing the risk of developing Type 2 Diabetes. *Chlorogenic acids* do other things too: help the flow of bile, thus reducing bile stagnation and promoting **liver** and **gallbladder health**. It could also help to reduce cardiovascular risks. The body easily absorbs its nutritional benefits if it is sourced from natural, whole foods.

Caffeic acid, another antioxidant in Chia, may be used as a component to contribute to the prevention of the following: colitis, a condition that could lead to colon cancer, cardiovascular disease,

certain cancers, mitosis (cell division) and inflammation. It may also be used in the healthy maintenance of the **immune system.**

The most important antioxidants contained in Chia seeds are **chlorgenic acid** and **caffeic acid.** These are antioxidants that play a major role in **cancer prevention** and fighting **free radicals**.

Omega-3s

Chia seeds are the highest plant source of omega-3s. Omega-3s are healthy fatty acids that are needed for normal body and **brain functioning**, hormonal balance and the **absorption** of essential vitamins. Chia seeds consist of approximately 60 to 65% omega-3s, making them a potent **anti-inflammatory food**. Furthermore, since Chia seeds are a whole food and rich in antioxidants, they maintain freshness longer than most other sources of omega-3s such as fish oils and hemp seeds.

Recommended Doses:

Chia seeds are unique in that there is no recommended dosage or evidence of risks from possibly eating too much. The amount used varies among individuals, how they feel and their needs. Adults consuming Chia for general nutrition and health purposes, such as increased energy, might typically consume 2 tbsp. per day. Personally, I like to sprinkle a flat teaspoonful of ground chia seeds on my oat porridge or organic cereal in the morning.

100 grams (3.5oz.) of Omega^3 Chia is:

- a source of **Magnesium** equivalent to 53 ounces of Broccoli
- a source of **Iron** equivalent to 10 ounces of Spinach
- a source of **Folate** equivalent to 2 ounces of Asparagus
- a source of **Fiber** equivalent to 4 ounces of Bran

- a source of **Calcium** equivalent to 23 ounces of sesame seed
- a source of **Potassium** equivalent to 6 ounces of Bananas
- a source of **Antioxidants** equivalent to 10 ounces of Blueberries
- a source of **Omega3** Fatty Acids equivalent to 28 ounces of Atlantic Salmon

The above information shows you how rich Chia Seeds are in **alkalizing minerals** and full of **antioxidants** that can play a crucial role for you at this particular moment when you are actively seeking to get healthier, helping to quickly assist in providing an alkalizing effect for your system. Chia seeds will also be important generally in the future to help you to continue staying healthy.

Have fun cooking healthy foods for you and your love ones and ENJOY every minute of your precious life!

Table 1

Best Alkalizing Fruits with Mineral and Vitamin content

Fruits	Amount	Minerals Contained	Vitamins Contained
Apple	One medium apple with skin contains 0.47 grams of protein, 95 calories, and 4.4 grams of dietary fiber.	Potassium - 195 mg Calcium - 11 mg Phosphorus - 20 mg Magnesium - 9 mg Manganese - 0.064 mg Iron - 0.22 mg Sodium - 2 mg Copper - 0.049 mg Zinc - 0.07 mg Also contains a trace amount of other minerals.	Vitamin A - 98 IU Vitamin B1 (thiamine) - 0.031 mg Vitamin B2 (riboflavin) - 0.047 mg Niacin - 0.166 mg Folate - 5 mcg Pantothenic Acid - 0.111 mg Vitamin B6 - 0.075 mg Vitamin C - 8.4 mg Vitamin E - 0.33 mg Vitamin K - 4 mcg Contains some other vitamins in small amounts.
Avocado	One medium avocado contains 4.02 grams of protein, 322 calories and 13.5 grams of fiber.	Potassium - 975 mg Phosphorus - 105 mg Magnesium - 58 mg Calcium - 24 mg Sodium - 14 mg Iron - 1.11 mg Selenium 0.8 mcg Manganese - 0.285 mg Copper - 0.382 mg Zinc - 1.29 mg Also contains small amounts of other minerals.	Vitamin A - 293 IU Vitamin C - 20.1 mg Vitamin B1 (thiamine) - 0.135 mg Vitamin B2 (riboflavin) - 0.261 mg Niacin - 3.493 mg Folate - 163 mcg Pantothenic Acid - 2.792 mg Vitamin B6 - .517 mg Vitamin E - 4.16 mg Vitamin K - 42.2 mcg Contains some other vitamins in small amounts.
Banana	One medium banana	Potassium - 422 mg	Vitamin A - 76 IU Vitamin B1

	contains 1.29 grams of protein, 105 calories and 3.1 grams of dietary fiber.	Phosphorus - 26 mg Magnesium - 32 mg Calcium - 6 mg Sodium - 1 mg Iron - 0.31 mg Selenium 1.2 mcg Manganese - 0.319 mg Copper - 0.092 mg Zinc - 0.18 mg Also contains small amounts of other minerals.	(thiamine) - 0.037 mg Vitamin B2 (riboflavin) - 0.086 mg Niacin - 0.785 mg Folate - 24 mcg Pantothenic Acid - 0.394 mg Vitamin B6 - 0.433 mg Vitamin C - 10.3 mg Vitamin E - 0.12 mg Vitamin K - 0.6 mcg Contains some other vitamins in small amounts.
Blackberries	One cup of blackberries contains 2 grams of protein, 62 calories and 7.6 grams of dietary fiber.	Potassium - 233 mg Phosphorus - 32 mg Magnesium - 29 mg Calcium - 42 mg Sodium - 1 mg Iron - 0.89 mg Selenium 0.6 mcg Manganese - 0.93 mg Copper - 0.238 mg Zinc - 0.76 mg Also contains small amounts of other minerals.	Vitamin A - 308 IU Vitamin B1 (thiamine) - 0.029 mg Vitamin B2 (riboflavin) - 0.037 mg Niacin - 0.93 mg Folate - 36 mcg Pantothenic Acid - 0.397 mg Vitamin B6 - 0.043 mg Vitamin C - 30.2 mg Vitamin E - 1.68 mg Vitamin K - 28.5 mcg Contains some other vitamins in small amounts.
Blackcurrants	One cup of blackcurrants contains 1.57 grams of protein and 71 calories.	Potassium - 361 mg Phosphorus - 66 mg Magnesium - 27 mg Calcium - 62 mg Sodium - 2 mg Iron - 1.72 mg Manganese - 0.287 mg Copper - 0.096 mg Zinc - 0.3 mg Also contains small amounts of	Vitamin A - 258 IU Vitamin B1 (thiamine) - 0.056 mg Vitamin B2 (riboflavin) - 0.056 mg Niacin - 0.336 mg Pantothenic Acid - 0.446 mg Vitamin B6 - 0.074 mg Vitamin C - 202.7 mg Vitamin E - 1.12 mg

		other minerals.	Contains some other vitamins in small amounts.
Blueberries	One cup of blueberries contains 1.1 grams of protein, 84 calories and 3.6 grams of dietary fiber.	Potassium - 114 mg Phosphorus - 18 mg Magnesium - 9 mg Calcium - 9 mg Sodium - 1 mg Iron - 0.41 mg Selenium 0.1 mcg Manganese - 0.497 mg Zinc - 0.24 mg Also contains small amounts of other minerals.	Vitamin A - 217 IU Vitamin B1 (thiamine) - 0.055 mg Vitamin B2 (riboflavin) - 0.061 mg Niacin - 0.08 mg Folate - 9 mcg Pantothenic Acid - 0.184 mg Vitamin B6 - 0.077 mg Vitamin C - 14.4 mg Vitamin E - 2.29 mg Vitamin K - 28.6 mcg Contains some other vitamins in small amounts.
Boysenberries	One cup of frozen boysenberries contains 1.45 grams of protein, 66 calories and 7 grams of dietary fiber.	Potassium - 183 mg Phosphorus - 36 mg Magnesium - 21 mg Calcium - 36 mg Sodium - 1 mg Iron - 1.12 mg Selenium 0.3 mcg Manganese - 0.722 mg Copper - 0.106 mg Zinc - 0.29 mg Also contains small amounts of other minerals.	Vitamin A - 88 IU Vitamin B1 (thiamine) - 0.07 mg Vitamin B2 (riboflavin) - 0.049 mg Niacin - 1.012 mg Folate - 83 mcg Pantothenic Acid - 0.33 mg Vitamin B6 - 0.074 mg Vitamin C - 4.1 mg Vitamin E - 1.15 mg Vitamin K - 10.3 mcg Contains some other vitamins in small amounts.
Breadfruit	One cup of fresh breadfruit contains 2.35 grams of protein, 227 calories and 10.8 grams of dietary fiber.	Potassium - 1078 mg Phosphorus - 66 mg Magnesium - 55 mg Calcium - 37 mg Sodium - 4 mg Iron - 1.19 mg Selenium 1.3	Vitamin B1 (thiamine) - 0.242 mg Vitamin B2 (riboflavin) - 0.066 mg Niacin - 1.98 mg Folate - 31 mcg Pantothenic Acid - 1.05 mg

		mcg Manganese - 0.132 mg Copper - 0.185 mg Zinc - 0.26 mg Also contains small amounts of other minerals.	Vitamin B6 - 0.22 mg Vitamin C - 63.8 mg Vitamin E - 0.22 mg Vitamin K - 1.1 mcg Contains some other vitamins in small amounts.
Cantaloupe	One medium wedge (slice) of cantaloupe contains 0.58 grams of protein, 23 calories and 0.6 grams of dietary fiber.	Potassium - 184 mg Phosphorus - 10 mg Magnesium - 8 mg Calcium - 6 mg Sodium - 11 mg Iron - 0.14 mg Selenium 0.3 mcg Manganese - 0.028 mg Copper - 0.028 mg Zinc - 0.12 mg Also contains small amounts of other minerals.	Vitamin A - 2334 IU Vitamin B1 (thiamine) - 0.028 mg Vitamin B2 (riboflavin) - 0.013 mg Niacin - 0.506 mg Folate - 14 mcg Pantothenic Acid - 0.072 mg Vitamin B6 - 0.05 mg Vitamin C - 25.3 mg Vitamin E - 0.03 mg Vitamin K - 1.7 mcg Contains some other vitamins in small amounts.
Cherimoya	One cup of diced, fresh cherimoya contains 2.51 grams of protein, 120 calories and 4.8 grams of dietary fiber.	Potassium - 459 mg Phosphorus - 42 mg Magnesium - 27 mg Calcium - 16 mg Sodium - 11 mg Iron - 0.43 mg Manganese - 0.149 mg Copper - 0.11 mg Zinc - 0.26 mg Also contains small amounts of other minerals.	Vitamin B1 (thiamine) - 0.162 mg Vitamin B2 (riboflavin) - 0.21 mg Niacin - 1.03 mg Folate - 37 mcg Pantothenic Acid - 0.552 mg Vitamin B6 - 0.411 mg Vitamin C - 20.2 mg Vitamin A - 8 IU Vitamin E - 0.43 mg Contains some other vitamins in small amounts.
Cherries	One cup of fresh cherries, with pits, contains 1.46 grams of	Potassium - 306 mg Phosphorus - 29 mg Magnesium - 15	Vitamin A - 88 IU Vitamin B1 (thiamine) - 0.037 mg Vitamin B2

© Natalie Mitchell

	protein, 87 calories and 2.9 grams of dietary fiber.	mg Calcium - 18 mg Iron - 0.5 mg Zinc - 0.1 mg Manganese - 0.097 mg Copper - 0.083 mg Also contains small amounts of other minerals.	(riboflavin) - 0.046 mg Niacin - 0.213 mg Folate - 6 mcg Pantothenic Acid - 0.275 mg Vitamin B6 - 0.068 mg Vitamin C - 9.7 mg Vitamin E - 0.1 mg Vitamin K - 2.9 mcg Contains some other vitamins in small amounts.
Chinese pear	One Chinese (Asian) pear, about 3 inches in diameter, contains 1.38 grams of protein, 116 calories and 9.9 grams of dietary fiber.	Potassium - 333 mg Phosphorus - 30 mg Magnesium - 22 mg Calcium - 11 mg Selenium 0.3 mcg Manganese - 0.165 mg Copper - 0.138 mg Zinc - 0.06 mg Also contains small amounts of other minerals.	Vitamin B1 (thiamine) - 0.025 mg Vitamin B2 (riboflavin) - 0.028 mg Niacin - 0.602 mg Folate - 22 mcg Pantothenic Acid - 0.193 mg Vitamin B6 - 0.06 mg Vitamin C - 10.4 mg Vitamin E - 0.33 mg Vitamin K - 12.4 mcg Contains some other vitamins in small amounts.
Cranberries	One cup of cranberries contains 0.39 grams of protein, 46 calories and 4.6 grams of dietary fiber.	Potassium - 85 mg Phosphorus - 13 mg Magnesium - 6 mg Calcium - 8 mg Sodium - 2 mg Iron - 0.25 mg Selenium 0.1 mcg Manganese - 0.36 mg Copper - 0.061 mg Zinc - 0.1 mg Also contains small amounts of other minerals.	Vitamin A - 60 IU Vitamin B1 (thiamine) - 0.012 mg Vitamin B2 (riboflavin) - 0.02 mg Niacin - 0.101 mg Folate - 1 mcg Pantothenic Acid - 0.295 mg Vitamin B6 - 0.057 mg Vitamin C - 13.3 mg Vitamin E - 1.2 mg Vitamin K - 5.1 mcg Contains some other vitamins in small amounts.
Figs	One large,	Potassium - 148	Vitamin A - 91 IU

	fresh fig contains 0.48 grams of protein, 47 calories and 1.9 grams of dietary fiber.	mg Phosphorus - 9 mg Magnesium - 11 mg Calcium - 22 mg Sodium - 1 mg Iron - 0.24 mg Selenium 0.1 mcg Manganese - 0.082 mg Copper - 0.045 mg Zinc - 0.1 mg Also contains small amounts of other minerals.	Vitamin B1 (thiamine) - 0.038 mg Vitamin B2 (riboflavin) - 0.032 mg Niacin - 0.256 mg Folate - 4 mcg Pantothenic Acid - 0.192 mg Vitamin B6 - 0.072 mg Vitamin C - 1.3 mg Vitamin E - 0.07 mg Vitamin K - 3 mcg Contains some other vitamins in small amounts.
Gooseberries	One cup of gooseberries contains 1.32 grams of protein, 66 calories and over 6.5 grams of dietary fiber.	Potassium - 297 mg Phosphorus - 40 mg Magnesium - 15 mg Calcium - 38 mg Sodium - 2 mg Iron - 0.47 mg Selenium 0.9 mcg Manganese - 0.216 mg Copper - 0.105 mg Zinc - 0.18 mg Also contains small amounts of other minerals.	Vitamin A - 435 IU Vitamin B1 (thiamine) - 0.06 mg Vitamin B2 (riboflavin) - 0.045 mg Niacin - 0.45 mg Folate - 9 mcg Pantothenic Acid - 0.429 mg Vitamin B6 - 0.12 mg Vitamin C - 41.5 mg Vitamin E - 0.56 mg Contains some other vitamins in small amounts.
Grapes	One cup of grapes contains 1.09 gram of protein, 104 calories and 1.4 grams of dietary fiber.	Potassium - 288 mg Phosphorus - 30 mg Magnesium - 11 mg Calcium - 15 mg Sodium - 3 mg Iron - 0.54 mg Selenium 0.2 mcg Manganese - 0.107 mg Copper - 0.192 mg Zinc - 0.11 mg Also contains small amounts of	Vitamin A - 100 IU Vitamin B1 (thiamine) - 0.104 mg Vitamin B2 (riboflavin) - 0.106 mg Niacin - 0.284 mg Folate - 3 mcg Pantothenic Acid - 0.076 mg Vitamin B6 - 0.13 mg Vitamin C - 16.3 mg Vitamin E - 0.29 mg Vitamin K - 22 mcg

		other minerals.	Contains some other vitamins in small amounts.
Guava	One cup of fresh guava contains 4.21 grams of protein, 112 calories and 8.9 grams of dietary fiber.	Potassium - 688 mg Phosphorus - 66 mg Magnesium - 36 mg Calcium - 30 mg Sodium - 3 mg Iron - 0.43 mg Selenium 1 mcg Manganese - 0.247 mg Copper - 0.38 mg Zinc - 0.38 mg Also contains small amounts of other minerals.	Vitamin A - 1030 IU Vitamin B1 (thiamine) - 0.111 mg Vitamin B2 (riboflavin) - 0.066 mg Niacin - 1.789 mg Folate - 81 mcg Pantothenic Acid - 0.744 mg Vitamin B6 - 0.181 mg Vitamin C - 376.7 mg Vitamin E - 1.2 mg Vitamin K - 4.3 mcg Contains some other vitamins in small amounts.
Lemon	One lemon without peel contains 0.92 grams protein, 24 calories and 2.4 grams of dietary fiber.	Potassium - 116 mg Phosphorus - 13 mg Magnesium - 7 mg Calcium - 22 mg Sodium - 2 mg Iron - 0.5 mg Selenium 0.3 mcg Manganese - 0.025 mg Copper - 0.031 mg Zinc - 0.05 mg Also contains small amounts of other minerals.	Vitamin A - 18 IU Vitamin B1 (thiamine) - 0.034 mg Vitamin B2 (riboflavin) - 0.017 mg Niacin - 0.084 mg Folate - 9 mcg Pantothenic Acid - 0.16 mg Vitamin B6 - 0.067 mg Vitamin C - 44.5 mg Vitamin E - 0.13 mg Contains some other vitamins in small amounts.
Lime	One lime contains 0.47 grams of protein, 20 calories and 1.9 grams of dietary fiber.	Potassium - 68 mg Phosphorus - 12 mg Magnesium - 4 mg Calcium - 22 mg Sodium - 1 mg Iron - 0.4 mg Selenium 0.3 mcg Manganese - 0.005 mg	Vitamin A - 34 IU Vitamin B1 (thiamine) - 0.02 mg Vitamin B2 (riboflavin) - 0.013 mg Niacin - 0.134 mg Folate - 5 mcg Pantothenic Acid - 0.145 mg Vitamin B6 - 0.029 mg

		Copper - 0.044 mg Zinc - 0.07 mg Also contains small amounts of other minerals.	Vitamin C - 19.5 mg Vitamin E - 0.15 mg Vitamin K - 0.4 mcg Contains some other vitamins in small amounts.
Loganberries	One cup of frozen loganberries contains 2.23 grams of protein, 81 calories and 7.8 grams of dietary fiber.	Potassium - 213 mg Phosphorus - 38 mg Magnesium - 31 mg Calcium - 38 mg Sodium - 1 mg Iron - 0.94 mg Selenium 0.3 mcg Manganese - 1.833 mg Copper - 0.172 mg Zinc - 0.5 mg Also contains small amounts of other minerals.	Vitamin A - 51 IU Vitamin B1 (thiamine) - 0.074 mg Vitamin B2 (riboflavin) - 0.05 mg Niacin - 1.235 mg Folate - 38 mcg Pantothenic Acid - 0.359 mg Vitamin B6 - 0.096 mg Vitamin C - 22.5 mg Vitamin E - 1.28 mg Vitamin K - 11.5 mcg Contains some other vitamins in small amounts.
Lychee	One cup of fresh lychees contains 1.58 grams of protein, 125 calories and 2.5 grams of dietary fiber.	Potassium - 325 mg Phosphorus - 59 mg Magnesium - 19 mg Calcium - 10 mg Sodium - 2 mg Iron - 0.59 mg Selenium 1.1 mcg Manganese - 0.104 mg Copper - 0.281 mg Zinc - 0.13 mg Also contains small amounts of other minerals.	Vitamin B1 (thiamine) - 0.021 mg Vitamin B2 (riboflavin) - 0.123 mg Niacin - 1.146 mg Folate - 27 mcg Vitamin B6 - 0.19 mg Vitamin C - 135.8 mg Vitamin E - 0.13 mg Vitamin K - 0.08 mcg Contains some other vitamins in small amounts.
Mango	One mango without peel contains 1.06 grams of protein, 135 calories and 3.7 grams of	Potassium - 323 mg Phosphorus - 23 mg Magnesium - 19 mg Calcium - 21 mg	Vitamin A - 1584 IU Vitamin B1 (thiamine) - 0.12 mg Vitamin B2 (riboflavin) - 0.118 mg

© Natalie Mitchell

	dietary fiber.	Sodium - 4 mg Iron - 0.27 mg Selenium 1.2 mcg Manganese - 0.056 mg Copper - 0.228 mg Zinc - 0.08 mg Also contains small amounts of other minerals.	Niacin - 1.209 mg Folate - 29 mcg Pantothenic Acid - 0.331 mg Vitamin B6 - 0.227 mg Vitamin C - 57.3 mg Vitamin E - 2.32 mg Vitamin K - 8.7 mcg Contains some other vitamins in small amounts.
Mulberries	One cup of fresh mulberries contains 2.02 grams of protein and 2.4 grams of dietary fiber.	Potassium - 272 mg Phosphorus - 53 mg Magnesium - 25 mg Calcium - 55 mg Sodium - 14 mg Iron - 2.59 mg Selenium 0.8 mcg Copper - 0.084 mg Zinc - 0.17 mg Also contains small amounts of other minerals.	Vitamin A - 35 IU Vitamin B1 (thiamine) - 0.041 mg Vitamin B2 (riboflavin) - 0.141 mg Niacin - 0.868 mg Folate - 8 mcg Vitamin B6 - 0.07 mg Vitamin C - 51 mg Vitamin E - 1.22 mg Vitamin K - 10.9 mcg Contains some other vitamins in small amounts.
Nectarine	One cup of sliced fresh nectarine contains 1.52 grams of protein, 63 calories and 2.4 grams of dietary fiber.	Potassium - 287 mg Phosphorus - 37 mg Magnesium - 13 mg Calcium - 9 mg Iron - 0.4 mg Manganese - 0.077 mg Copper - 0.123 mg Zinc - 0.24 mg Also contains small amounts of other minerals.	Vitamin A - 475 IU Vitamin B1 (thiamine) - 0.049 mg Vitamin B2 (riboflavin) - 0.039 mg Niacin - 1.609 mg Folate - 7 mcg Pantothenic Acid - 0.265 mg Vitamin B6 - 0.036 mg Vitamin C - 7.7 mg Vitamin E - 1.1 mg Vitamin K - 3.1 mcg Contains some other vitamins in small amounts.
Olives	One tablespoon of ripe olives contains 0.07	Potassium - 1 mg Calcium - 7 mg Sodium - 73 mg	Vitamin A - 34 IU Niacin - 0.003 mg Pantothenic Acid - 0.001 mg

© Natalie Mitchell

	grams of protein, 10 calories and 0.3 grams of dietary fiber.	Iron - 0.28 mg Selenium 0.1 mcg Manganese - 0.002 mg Copper - 0.021 mg Zinc - 0.02 mg Also contains small amounts of other minerals.	Vitamin B6 - 0.001 mg Vitamin C - 0.1 mg Vitamin E - 0.14 mg Vitamin K - 0.1 mcg Contains some other vitamins in small amounts.
Papaya	One cup of cubed fresh papaya contains 0.85 grams of protein, 55 calories and 2.5 grams of dietary fiber.	Potassium - 360 mg Phosphorus - 7 mg Magnesium - 14 mg Calcium - 34 mg Sodium - 4 mg Iron - 0.14 mg Selenium 0.8 mcg Zinc - 0.1 mg Manganese - 0.015 mg Copper - 0.022 mg Also contains small amounts of other minerals.	Vitamin A - 1532 IU Vitamin B1 (thiamine) - 0.038 mg Vitamin B2 (riboflavin) - 0.045 mg Niacin - 0.473 mg Folate - 53 mcg Pantothenic Acid - 0.305 mg Vitamin B6 - 0.027 mg Vitamin C - 86.5 mg Vitamin E - 1.02 mg Vitamin K - 3.6 mcg Contains some other vitamins in small amounts.
Passion fruit	One cup of fresh passion fruit contains 5.19 grams of protein, 229 calories and 24.5 grams of dietary fiber.	Potassium - 821 mg Phosphorus - 160 mg Magnesium - 68 mg Calcium - 28 mg Sodium - 66 mg Iron - 3.78 mg Selenium 1.4 mcg Copper - 0.203 mg Zinc - 0.24 mg Also contains small amounts of other minerals.	Vitamin A - 3002 IU Vitamin B2 (riboflavin) - 0.307 mg Niacin - 3.54 mg Folate - 33 mcg Vitamin B6 - 0.236 mg Vitamin C - 70.8 mg Vitamin E - 0.05 mg Vitamin K - 1.7 mcg Contains some other vitamins in small amounts.
Peach	One medium peach (with skin) contains 1.36 grams of protein, 58 calories and 2.2 grams	Potassium - 285 mg Phosphorus - 30 mg Magnesium - 14 mg Calcium - 9 mg	Vitamin A - 489 IU Vitamin B1 (thiamine) - 0.036 mg Vitamin B2 (riboflavin) - 0.047 mg

	dietary fiber.	Iron - 0.38 mg Selenium 0.1 mcg Manganese - 0.091 mg Copper - 0.102 mg Zinc - 0.26 mg Also contains small amounts of other minerals.	Niacin - 1.209 mg Folate - 6 mcg Pantothenic Acid - 0.229 mg Vitamin B6 - 0.037 mg Vitamin C - 9.9 mg Vitamin E - 1.09 mg Vitamin K - 3.9 mcg Contains some other vitamins in small amounts.
Pear	One medium pear contains 0.68 grams of protein, 103 calories and 5.5 grams dietary fiber.	Potassium - 212 mg Phosphorus - 20 mg Magnesium - 12 mg Calcium -16 mg Sodium - 2 mg Iron - 0.3 mg Selenium 0.2 mcg Manganese - 0.087 mg Copper - 0.146 mg Zinc - 0.18 mg Also contains small amounts of other minerals.	Vitamin A - 41 IU Vitamin B1 (thiamine) - 0.021 mg Vitamin B2 (riboflavin) - 0.045 mg Niacin - 0.279 mg Folate - 12 mcg Pantothenic Acid - 0.085 mg Vitamin B6 - 0.05 mg Vitamin C - 7.5 mg Vitamin E - 0.21 mg Vitamin K - 8 mcg Contains some other vitamins in small amounts.
Persimmon	One fresh persimmon contains 0.2 grams of protein and 32 calories.	Potassium - 78 mg Phosphorus - 6 mg Calcium - 7 mg Iron - 0.62 mg Also contains small amounts of other minerals.	Vitamin C - 16.5 mg Contains some other vitamins in small amounts.
Plum	One cup of sliced, fresh plums contains 1.15 grams of protein, 76 calories and 2.3 grams dietary fiber.	Potassium - 259 mg Phosphorus - 26 mg Magnesium - 12 mg Calcium - 10 mg Iron - 0.28 mg Manganese - 0.086 mg Copper - 0.094 mg Zinc - 0.17 mg Also contains	Vitamin A - 569 IU Vitamin B1 (thiamine) - 0.046 mg Vitamin B2 (riboflavin) - 0.043 mg Niacin - 0.688 mg Folate - 8 mcg Pantothenic Acid - 0.223 mg Vitamin B6 - 0.048 mg Vitamin C - 15.7

		small amounts of other minerals.	mg Vitamin E - 0.43 mg Vitamin K - 10.6 mcg Contains some other vitamins in small amounts.
Pomegranate	One fresh pomegranate contains 4.71 grams of protein, 234 calories and 11.3 grams dietary fiber.	Potassium - 666 mg Phosphorus - 102 mg Magnesium - 34 mg Calcium - 28 mg Sodium - 8 mg Iron - 0.85 mg Selenium 1.4 mcg Manganese - 0.336 mg Copper - 0.446 mg Zinc - 0.99 mg Also contains small amounts of other minerals.	Vitamin B1 (thiamine) - 0.189 mg Vitamin B2 (riboflavin) - 0.149 mg Niacin - 0.826 mg Folate - 107 mcg Pantothenic Acid - 1.063 mg Vitamin B6 - 0.211 mg Vitamin C - 28.8 mg Vitamin E - 1.69 mg Vitamin K - 46.2 mcg Contains some other vitamins in small amounts.
Prickly Pear	One cup of raw prickly pears contains 1.09 grams of protein, 61 calories and 5.4 grams dietary fiber.	Potassium - 328 mg Phosphorus - 36 mg Magnesium - 127 mg Calcium - 83 mg Sodium - 7 mg Iron - 0.45 mg Selenium 0.9 mcg Copper - 0.119 mg Zinc - 0.18 mg Also contains small amounts of other minerals.	Vitamin A - 64 IU Vitamin B1 (thiamine) - 0.021 mg Vitamin B2 (riboflavin) - 0.089 mg Niacin - 0.685 mg Vitamin B6 - 0.089 mg Folate - 9 mcg Vitamin C - 20.9 mg Contains some other vitamins in small amounts.
Star fruit aka Carambola	One cup of fresh star fruit contains 1.37 grams of protein, 41 calories and 3.7 grams dietary fiber.	Potassium - 176 mg Phosphorus - 16 mg Magnesium - 13 mg Calcium - 4 mg Sodium - 3 mg Iron - 0.11 mg Selenium 0.8	Vitamin A - 81 IU Vitamin B1 (thiamine) - 0.018 mg Vitamin B2 (riboflavin) - 0.021 mg Niacin - 0.484 mg Folate - 16 mcg Pantothenic Acid -

		mcg Manganese - 0.049 mg Copper - 0.181 mg Zinc - 0.16 mg Also contains small amounts of other minerals.	0.516 mg Vitamin B6 - 0.022 mg Vitamin C - 45.4 mg Vitamin E - 0.2 mg Contains some other vitamins in small amounts.
Watermelon	I medium wedge (slice) of watermelon (about 2 cups edible portion) contains 1.74 grams of protein, 86 calories and 1.1 grams of dietary fiber.	Potassium - 320 mg Phosphorus - 31 mg Magnesium - 29 mg Calcium - 20 mg Sodium - 3 mg Iron - 0.69 mg Selenium 1.1 mcg Manganese - 0.109 mg Copper - 0.12 mg Zinc - 0.29 mg Also contains small amounts of other minerals.	Vitamin A - 1627 IU Vitamin B1 (thiamine) - 0.094 mg Vitamin B2 (riboflavin) - 0.06 mg Niacin - 0.509 mg Folate - 9 mcg Pantothenic Acid - 0.632 mg Vitamin B6 - 0.129 mg Vitamin C - 23.2 mg Vitamin E - 0.14 mg Vitamin K - 0.3 mcg Contains some other vitamins in small amounts.

© Natalie Mitchell

Table 2

Best Alkalizing and Fat -Burning Nuts, Seeds and Grains

Nut/Seed	Protein/Fiber	Minerals	Vitamins
Almonds	1 ounce (23 whole nuts) of raw almonds contains 6.02 grams protein, 163 calories and 3.5 grams of dietary fiber.	Potassium - 200 mg Phosphorus - 137 mg Calcium - 75 mg Magnesium - 76 mg Iron - 1.05 mg Selenium - 0.7 mcg Zinc - 0.87 mg Manganese - 0.648 mg Copper - 0.282 mg Also contains a small amount of other minerals.	Vitamin B1 (thiamine) - 0.06 mg Vitamin B2 (riboflavin) - 0.287 mg Niacin - 0.96 mg Folate - 14 mcg Pantothenic Acid - 0.133 mg Vitamin B6 - 0.041 mg Vitamin E - 7.43 mg Contains some other vitamins in small amounts.
Amaranth	100 grams of cooked amaranth contain 3.8 grams protein, 102 calories and 2.1 grams dietary fiber.	Potassium - 135 mg Phosphorus - 148 mg Calcium - 47 mg Magnesium - 65 mg Iron - 2.1 mg Sodium - 6 mg Manganese - 0.854 mg Zinc - 0.86 mg Copper - 0.149 mg Selenium - 5.5 mcg Also contains trace amounts of other minerals.	Vitamin B1 (thiamine) - 0.015 mg Vitamin B2 (riboflavin) - 0.022 mg Niacin - 0.235 mg Vitamin B6 - 0.113 mg Folate - 22 mcg Vitamin E - 0.19 mg Contains some other vitamins in small amounts.
Barley (Pearled)	100 grams of cooked, pearled barley contain 2.26 grams protein, 123 calories and	Potassium - 93 mg Phosphorus - 54 mg Calcium - 11 mg Magnesium - 22 mg Iron - 1.33 mg	Vitamin B1 (thiamine) - 0.083 mg Vitamin B2 (riboflavin) - 0.062 mg Niacin - 2.063 mg Pantothenic Acid -

© Natalie Mitchell

	3.8 grams dietary fiber.	Sodium - 3 mg Manganese - 0.259 mg Zinc - 0.82 mg Copper - 0.105 mg Selenium - 8.6 mcg Also contains trace amounts of other minerals.	0.135 mg Vitamin B6 - 0.115 mg Folate - 16 mcg Vitamin A - 7 IU Vitamin E - 0.01 mg Vitamin K - 0.8 mcg Contains some other vitamins in small amounts.
Brazil Nuts	1 ounce (6 whole nuts) contains 4.06 grams of protein, 186 calories and 2.1 grams of fiber.	Potassium - 187 mg Phosphorus - 206 mg Calcium - 45 mg Magnesium - 107 mg Iron - 0.69 mg Sodium - 1 mg Manganese - 0.347 mg Zinc - 1.15 mg Copper - 0.494 mg Selenium - 543.5 mcg Also contains trace amounts of other minerals.	Vitamin C - 0.2 mg Vitamin B1 (thiamine) - 0.175 mg Vitamin B2 (riboflavin) - 0.01 mg Niacin - 0.084 mg Pantothenic Acid - 0.052 mg Vitamin B6 - 0.029 mg Folate - 6 mcg Vitamin E - 1.62 mg Contains some other vitamins in small amounts.
Buckwheat	100 grams of buckwheat contain 13.25 grams protein, 343 calories and 10 grams dietary fiber.	Potassium - 460 mg Phosphorus - 347 mg Calcium - 18 mg Magnesium - 231 mg Iron - 2.2 mg Sodium - 1 mg Manganese - 1.3 mg Zinc - 2.4 mg Copper - 1.1 mg Selenium - 8.3 mcg Also contains trace amounts of other minerals.	Vitamin B1 (thiamine) - 0.101 mg Vitamin B2 (riboflavin) - 0.425 mg Niacin - 7.02 mg Pantothenic Acid - 1.233 mg Vitamin B6 - 0.21 mg Folate - 30 mcg Contains some other vitamins in small amounts.
Cashews	One ounce of raw, unsalted cashew nuts contains 5.17 grams of protein, 157 calories and 0.94 grams of	Potassium - 187 mg Phosphorus - 168 mg Calcium - 10 mg Magnesium - 83 mg Iron - 1.89 mg	Vitamin C - 0.1 mg Vitamin B1 (thiamine) - 0.12 mg Vitamin B2 (riboflavin) - 0.016 mg Niacin - 0.301 mg

© Natalie Mitchell

	fiber.	Sodium - 3 mg Manganese - 0.469 mg Zinc - 1.64 mg Copper - 0.622 mg Selenium - 5.6 mcg Also contains trace amounts of other minerals.	Pantothenic Acid - 0.245 mg Vitamin B6 - 0.118 mg Folate - 7 mcg Vitamin E - 0.26 mg Vitamin K - 9.7 mcg Contains some other vitamins in small amounts.
Chestnuts	Ten (10) roasted kernels with no salt added contain 2.66 grams protein, 206 calories and 4.3 grams fiber. (Note: chestnuts must be boiled or roasted before eating due to the high levels of tannic acid.)	Potassium - 497 mg Phosphorus - 90 mg Calcium - 24 mg Magnesium - 28 mg Iron - 0.76 mg Sodium - 2 mg Manganese - 0.991 mg Zinc - 0.48 mg Copper - 0.426 mg Selenium - 1 mcg Also contains trace amounts of other minerals.	Vitamin C - 21.8 mg Vitamin B1 (thiamine) - 0.204 mg Vitamin B2 (riboflavin) - 0.147 mg Niacin - 1.127 mg Pantothenic Acid - 0.465 mg Vitamin B6 - 0.417 mg Folate - 59 mcg Vitamin A - 20 IU Vitamin E - 0.42 mg Vitamin K - 6.6 mcg Contains some other vitamins in small amounts.
Coconut	One cup of raw, shredded coconut contains 2.66 grams of protein, 283 calories and 7.2 grams of dietary fiber.	Potassium - 285 mg Phosphorus - 90 mg Calcium - 11 mg Magnesium - 26 mg Iron - 1.94 mg Sodium - 16 mg Manganese - 1.2 mg Zinc - 0.88 mg Copper - 0.348 mg Selenium - 8.1 mcg Also contains trace amounts of other minerals.	Vitamin C - 2.6 mg Vitamin B1 (thiamine) - 0.053 mg Vitamin B2 (riboflavin) - 0.016 mg Niacin - 0.432 mg Pantothenic Acid - 0.24 mg Vitamin B6 - 0.043 mg Folate - 21 mcg Vitamin E - 0.19 mg Vitamin K - 0.2 mcg Contains some other vitamins in small amounts.
Flax Seed	One tablespoon of raw flax seeds contains 1.88	Potassium - 84 mg Phosphorus - 66 mg Calcium - 26 mg	Vitamin C 0.1 mg Vitamin B1 (thiamine) - 0.169 mg Vitamin B2

	grams of protein, 55 calories and 2.8 grams of dietary fiber.	Magnesium - 40 mg Iron - 0.59 mg Sodium - 3 mg Manganese - 0.256 mg Zinc - 0.45 mg Copper - 0.126 mg Selenium - 2.6 mcg Also contains trace amounts of other minerals.	(riboflavin) - 0.017 mg Niacin - 0.317 mg Pantothenic Acid - 0.101 mg Vitamin B6 - 0.049 mg Folate - 9 mcg Vitamin E - 0.03 mg Vitamin K - 0.4 mcg Contains some other vitamins in small amounts.
Hazelnuts	One ounce (21 whole kernels) of hazelnuts contains 4.24 grams of protein, 178 calories and 2.7 grams of dietary fiber.	Potassium - 193 mg Phosphorus - 82 mg Calcium - 32 mg Magnesium - 46 mg Iron - 1.33 mg Manganese - 1.751 mg Zinc - 0.69 mg Copper - 0.489 mg Selenium - 0.7 mcg Also contains trace amounts of other minerals.	Vitamin C - 1.8 mg Vitamin B1 (thiamine) - 0.182 mg Vitamin B2 (riboflavin) - 0.032 mg Niacin - 0.51 mg Pantothenic Acid - 0.26 mg Vitamin B6 - 0.16 mg Folate - 32 mcg Vitamin A - 6 IU Vitamin E - 4.26 mg Vitamin K - 4 mcg Contains some other vitamins in small amounts.
Macadamias	One once (10-12 kernels) of raw macadamia nuts contains 2.24 grams protein, 204 calories and 2.4 grams fiber.	Potassium - 104 mg Phosphorus - 53 mg Calcium - 24 mg Magnesium - 37 mg Iron - 1.05 mg Sodium - 1 mg Manganese - 1.171 mg Zinc - 0.37 mg Copper - 0.214 mg Selenium - 1 mcg Also contains trace amounts of other minerals.	Vitamin C - 0.3 mg Vitamin B1 (thiamine) - 0.339 mg Vitamin B2 (riboflavin) - 0.046 mg Niacin - 0.701 mg Pantothenic Acid - 0.215 mg Vitamin B6 - 0.078 mg Folate - 3 mcg Vitamin E - 0.15 mg Contains some other vitamins in small amounts.
Millet	100 grams of cooked millet contain 3.51	Potassium - 62 mg Phosphorus -	Vitamin B1 (thiamine) - 0.106 mg

	grams protein, 119 calories and 1.3 grams dietary fiber.	100 mg Calcium - 3 mg Magnesium - 44 mg Iron - 0.63 mg Sodium - 2 mg Manganese - 0.272 mg Zinc - 0.91 mg Copper - 0.161 mg Selenium - 0.9 mcg Also contains trace amounts of other minerals.	Vitamin B2 (riboflavin) - 0.082 mg Niacin - 1.33 mg Pantothenic Acid - 0.171 mg Vitamin B6 - 0.108 mg Folate - 19 mcg Vitamin A - 3 IU Vitamin E - 0.02 mg Vitamin K - 0.3 mcg Contains some other vitamins in small amounts.
Oats	100 grams of oats contain grams 16.89 protein, 389 calories and 10.6 grams dietary fiber.	Potassium - 429 mg Phosphorus - 523 mg Calcium - 54 mg Magnesium - 177 mg Iron - 4.72 mg Sodium - 2 mg Manganese - 4.916 mg Zinc - 3.97 mg Copper - 0.626 mg Also contains trace amounts of other minerals.	Vitamin B1 (thiamine) - 0.763 mg Vitamin B2 (riboflavin) - 0.139 mg Niacin - 0.961 mg Pantothenic Acid - 1.349 mg Vitamin B6 - 0.119 mg Folate - 56 mcg Contains some other vitamins in small amounts.
Peanuts	One ounce of dry roasted peanuts contains 6.71 grams of protein, 166 calories and 2.3 grams of dietary fiber.	Potassium -187 mg Phosphorus - 101 mg Calcium - 15 mg Magnesium - 50 mg Iron - 0.64 mg Sodium - 2 mg Manganese - 0.591 mg Zinc - 0.94 mg Copper - 0.190 mg Selenium - 2.1 mcg Also contains trace amounts of other minerals.	Vitamin B1 (thiamine) - 0.124 mg Vitamin B2 (riboflavin) - 0.028 mg Niacin - 3.834 mg Pantothenic Acid - 0.395 mg Vitamin B6 - 0.073 mg Folate - 41 mcg Vitamin E - 1.96 mg Contains some other vitamins in small amounts.
Pecans	One ounce (19 halves) of raw pecans contains 2.6	Potassium - 116 mg Phosphorus - 79 mg	Vitamin C - 0.3 mg Vitamin B1 (thiamine) - 0.187 mg

	grams protein, 196 calories and 2.7 grams fiber.	Calcium - 20 mg Magnesium - 34 mg Iron - 0.72 mg Manganese - 1.276 mg Zinc - 1.28 mg Copper - 0.34 mg Selenium - 1.1 mcg Also contains trace amounts of other minerals.	Vitamin B2 (riboflavin) - 0.01 mg Niacin - 0.331 mg Pantothenic Acid - 0.245 mg Vitamin B6 - 0.06 mg Folate - 6 mcg Vitamin A - 16 IU Vitamin E - 0.4 mg Vitamin K - 1 mcg Contains some other vitamins in small amounts.
Pine Nuts / Pignolias	One ounce of pine nuts (167 kernels) contains 3.88 grams of protein, 191 calories and 1.0 grams of dietary fiber.	Potassium - 169 mg Phosphorus - 163 mg Calcium - 5 mg Magnesium - 71 mg Iron - 1.57 mg Sodium - 1 mg Manganese - 2.495 mg Zinc - 1.83 mg Copper - 0.375 mg Selenium - 0.2 mcg Also contains trace amounts of other minerals.	Vitamin C - 0.2 mg Vitamin B1 (thiamine) - 0.103 mg Vitamin B2 (riboflavin) - 0.064 mg Niacin - 1.244 mg Pantothenic Acid - 0.089 mg Vitamin B6 - 0.027 mg Folate - 10 mcg Vitamin A - 8 IU Vitamin E - 2.65 mg Vitamin K - 15.3 mcg Contains some other vitamins in small amounts.
Pistachios	One ounce of dry roasted pistachio nuts (no salt) (49 kernels) contains 6.05 grams of protein, 162 calories and 2.9 grams of dietary fiber.	Potassium - 295 mg Phosphorus - 137 mg Calcium - 31 mg Magnesium - 34 mg Iron - 1.19 mg Sodium - 3 mg Manganese - 0.361 mg Zinc - 0.65 mg Copper - 0.376 mg Selenium - 2.6 mcg Also contains trace amounts of other minerals.	Vitamin C - 0.7 mg Vitamin B1 (thiamine) - 0.238 mg Vitamin B2 (riboflavin) - 0.045 mg Niacin - 0.404 mg Pantothenic Acid - 0.145 mg Vitamin B6 - 0.361 mg Folate - 14 mcg Vitamin A - 74 IU Vitamin E - 0.55 mg Vitamin K - 3.7 mcg Contains some other vitamins in small amounts.

Pumpkin Seeds	One ounce of roasted pumpkin or squash seed kernels (no salt) contains 8.46 grams of protein, 163 calories and 1.8 grams of dietary fiber.	Potassium - 223 mg Phosphorus - 333 mg Calcium - 15 mg Magnesium - 156 mg Iron - 2.29 mg Sodium - 5 mg Manganese - 1.273 mg Zinc - 2.17 mg Copper - 0.361 mg Selenium - 2.7 mcg Also contains trace amounts of other minerals.	Vitamin C - 0.5 mg Vitamin B1 (thiamine) - 0.02 mg Vitamin B2 (riboflavin) - 0.043 mg Niacin - 1.256 mg Pantothenic Acid - 0.162 mg Vitamin B6 - 0.028 mg Folate - 16 mcg Vitamin A - 2 IU Vitamin E - 0.16 mg Vitamin K - 1.3 mcg Contains some other vitamins in small amounts.
Quinoa	100 grams of cooked quinoa contain 4.4 grams protein, 120 calories and 2.8 grams dietary fiber.	Potassium - 172 mg Phosphorus - 152 mg Calcium - 17 mg Magnesium - 64 mg Iron - 1.49 mg Sodium - 7 mg Manganese - 0.631 mg Zinc - 1.09 mg Copper - 0.192 mg Selenium - 2.8 mcg Also contains trace amounts of other minerals.	Vitamin B1 (thiamine) - 0.107 mg Vitamin B2 (riboflavin) - 0.11 mg Niacin - 0.412 mg Vitamin B6 - 0.123 mg Folate - 42 mcg Vitamin A - 5 IU Vitamin E - 0.63 mg Contains some other vitamins in small amounts.
Rice - Brown	100 grams of cooked brown rice contain 2.32 grams of protein, 112 calories and 1.8 grams of dietary fiber.	Potassium - 79 mg Phosphorus - 77 mg Calcium - 10 mg Magnesium - 44 mg Iron - 0.53 mg Sodium - 1 mg Manganese - 1.097 mg Zinc - 0.62 mg Copper - 0.081 mg Also contains trace amounts of other minerals.	Vitamin B1 (thiamine) - 0.102 mg Vitamin B2 (riboflavin) - 0.012 mg Niacin - 1.33 mg Pantothenic Acid - 0.392 mg Vitamin B6 - 0.149 mg Folate - 4 mcg Contains some other vitamins in small amounts.

Rice - Wild	100 grams of cooked wild rice contain 3.99 grams of protein, 101 calories and 1.8 grams of dietary fiber	Potassium - 101 mg Phosphorus - 82 mg Calcium - 3 mg Magnesium - 32 mg Iron - 0.6 mg Sodium - 3 mg Manganese - 0.282 mg Zinc - 1.34 mg Copper - 0.121 mg Selenium - 0.8 mcg Also contains trace amounts of other minerals.	Vitamin B1 (thiamine) - 0.052 mg Vitamin B2 (riboflavin) - 0.087 mg Niacin - 1.287 mg Pantothenic Acid - 0.154 mg Vitamin B6 - 0.135 mg Folate - 26 mcg Vitamin A - 3 IU Vitamin E - 0.24 mg Vitamin K - 0.5 mcg Contains some other vitamins in small amounts.
Rye	100 grams of rye contain 10.34 grams protein, 338 calories and 14.6 grams dietary fiber.	Potassium - 510 mg Phosphorus - 332 mg Calcium - 24 mg Magnesium - 110 mg Iron - 2.63 mg Sodium - 2 mg Manganese - 2.577 mg Zinc - 2.65 mg Copper - 0.367 mg Selenium - 13.9 mcg Also contains trace amounts of other minerals.	Vitamin B1 (thiamine) - 0.316 mg Vitamin B2 (riboflavin) - 0.251 mg Niacin - 4.27 mg Pantothenic Acid - 1.456 mg Vitamin B6 - 0.294 mg Folate - 38 mcg Vitamin A - 11 IU Vitamin E - 0.85 mg Vitamin K - 5.9 mcg Contains some other vitamins in small amounts.
Sesame Seeds	One tablespoon of dried sesame seeds (no salt) contains 1.6 grams of protein, 52 calories and 1.1 grams of dietary fiber.	Potassium - 42 mg Phosphorus - 57 mg Calcium - 88 mg Magnesium - 32 mg Iron - 1.31 mg Sodium - 1 mg Manganese - 0.221 mg Zinc - 0.7 mg Copper - 0.367 mg Selenium - 3.1 mcg Also contains trace amounts of other minerals.	Vitamin B1 (thiamine) - 0.071 mg Vitamin B2 (riboflavin) - 0.022 mg Niacin - 0.406 mg Pantothenic Acid - 0.005 mg Vitamin B6 - 0.071 mg Folate - 9 mcg Vitamin A - 1 IU Vitamin E - 0.02 mg Contains some other vitamins in small amounts.

© Natalie Mitchell

Spelt	100 grams of cooked, spelt contain 5.5 grams protein, 127 calories and 3.9 grams dietary fiber.	Potassium - 143 mg Phosphorus - 150 mg Calcium - 10 mg Magnesium - 49 mg Iron - 1.67 mg Sodium - 5 mg Manganese - 1.091 mg Zinc - 1.25 mg Copper - 0.215 mg Selenium - 4 mcg Also contains trace amounts of other minerals.	Vitamin B1 (thiamine) - 0.103 mg Vitamin B2 (riboflavin) - 0.03 mg Niacin - 2.57 mg Vitamin B6 - 0.08 mg Folate - 13 mcg Vitamin A - 4 IU Vitamin E - 0.26 mg Contains some other vitamins in small amounts.
Sunflower Seeds	One ounce of sunflower seed kernels, dry-roasted without salt contains 5.48 grams of protein, 165 calories and 3.1 grams of dietary fiber.	Potassium - 241 mg Phosphorus - 327 mg Calcium - 20 mg Magnesium - 37 mg Iron - 1.08 mg Sodium - 1 mg Manganese - 0.598 mg Zinc - 1.5 mg Copper - 0.519 mg Selenium - 22.5 mcg Also contains trace amounts of other minerals.	Vitamin C - 0.4 mg Vitamin B1 (thiamine) - 0.03 mg Vitamin B2 (riboflavin) - 0.07 mg Niacin - 1.996 mg Pantothenic Acid - 1.996 mg Vitamin B6 - 0.228 mg Folate - 67 mcg Vitamin A - 3 IU Vitamin E - 7.4 mg Vitamin K - 0.8 mcg Contains some other vitamins in small amounts.
Walnuts	1 ounce (14 halves) English walnuts contain 4.32 mg protein, 185 calories and 1.9 mg fiber.	Potassium - 125 mg Phosphorus - 98 mg Calcium - 28 mg Magnesium - 45 mg Iron - 0.82 mg Sodium - 1 mg Manganese - 0.968 mg Zinc - 0.88 mg Copper - 0.45 mg Selenium - 1.4 mcg Also contains trace amounts of other minerals.	Vitamin C - 0.4 mg Vitamin B1 (thiamine) - 0.097 mg Vitamin B2 (riboflavin) - 0.043 mg Niacin - 0.319 mg Pantothenic Acid - 0.162 mg Vitamin B6 - 0.152 mg Folate - 28 mcg Vitamin A - 6 IU Vitamin E - 0.2 mg Vitamin K - 0.8 mcg Contains some other vitamins in small amounts.

Wheat - Durum	100 grams of durum wheat contain 13.68 grams protein and 339 calories.	Potassium - 431 mg Phosphorus - 508 mg Calcium - 34 mg Magnesium - 144 mg Iron - 3.52 mg Sodium - 2 mg Manganese - 3.012 mg Zinc - 4.16 mg Copper - 0.553 mg Selenium - 89.4 mcg Also contains trace amounts of other minerals.	Vitamin B1 (thiamine) - 0.419 mg Vitamin B2 (riboflavin) - 0.121 mg Niacin - 6.738 mg Pantothenic Acid - 0.935 mg Vitamin B6 - 0.419 mg Folate - 43 mcg Contains some other vitamins in small amounts.
Wheat - Hard Red	100 grams of hard red wheat contain 15.40 grams protein, 329 calories and 12.2 grams of dietary fiber.	Potassium - 340 mg Phosphorus - 332 mg Calcium - 25 mg Magnesium - 124 mg Iron - 3.6 mg Sodium - 2 mg Manganese - 4.055 mg Zinc - 2.78 mg Copper - 0.41 mg Selenium - 70.7 mcg Also contains trace amounts of other minerals.	Vitamin B1 (thiamine) - 0.504 mg Vitamin B2 (riboflavin) - 0.11 mg Niacin - 5.71 mg Pantothenic Acid - 0.935 mg Vitamin B6 - 0.336 mg Folate - 43 mcg Vitamin A - 9 IU Vitamin E - 1.01 mg Vitamin K - 1.9 mcg Contains some other vitamins in small amounts.
Whole Wheat	100 grams of hard white wheat contain 11.31 grams protein, 342 calories and 12.2 grams dietary fiber.	Potassium - 432 mg Phosphorus - 355 mg Calcium - 32 mg Magnesium - 93 mg Iron - 4.56 mg Sodium - 2 mg Manganese - 3.821 mg Zinc - 3.33 mg Copper - 0.363 mg Also contains trace amounts of other minerals.	Vitamin B1 (thiamine) - 0.387 mg Vitamin B2 (riboflavin) - 0.108 mg Niacin - 4.381 mg Pantothenic Acid - 0.954 mg Vitamin B6 - 0.368 mg Folate - 38 mcg Vitamin A - 9 IU Vitamin E - 1.01 mg Vitamin K - 1.9 mcg Contains some other vitamins in small amounts.

Table 3

Best Alkalizing Vegetables with Mineral and Vitamin content details

Vegetable	Amount	Minerals Contained	Vitamins Contained
Alfalfa, sprouted	One cup of raw, sprouted alfalfa seeds contains 1.32 grams of protein, 8 calories and 0.6 grams of dietary fiber.	Potassium - 26 mg Phosphorus - 23 mg Magnesium - 9 mg Calcium - 11 mg Iron - 0.32 mg Sodium - 2 mg Zinc - 0.3 mg Copper - 0.052 mg Manganese - 0.062 mg Selenium - 0.2 mcg Also contains small amounts of other minerals.	Vitamin C - 2.7 mg Vitamin B1 (thiamine) - 0.025 mg Vitamin B2 (riboflavin) - 0.042 mg Niacin - 0.159 mg Pantothenic Acid - 0.186 mg Vitamin B6 - 0.011 mg Folate - 12 mcg Vitamin A - 51 IU Vitamin K - 10.1 mcg Vitamin E - 0.01 mg Contains some other vitamins in small amounts.
Amaranth leaves	One cup of amarant h leaves, cooked, boiled, drained with no added salt has 2.79 grams protein and 28 calories.	Potassium - 846 mg Phosphorus - 95 mg Magnesium - 73 mg Calcium - 276 mg Iron - 2.98 mg Zinc - 1.16 mg Manganese - 1.137 mg Sodium - 28 mg Copper - 0.209 mg Selenium - 1.2 mcg Also contains small amounts of other minerals.	Vitamin C - 54.3 mg Vitamin B1 (thiamine) - 0.026 mg Vitamin B2 (riboflavin) - 0.177 mg Niacin - 0.738 mg Pantothenic Acid - 0.082 mg Vitamin B6 - 0.234 mg Folate - 75 mcg Vitamin A - 3656 IU Contains some other vitamins in small amounts.
Artichoke	One	Potassium - 343	Vitamin C - 8.9

	medium artichoke cooked with no added salt has 3.47 grams protein, 64 calories and 10.3 grams of fiber.	mg Phosphorus - 88 mg Magnesium - 50 mg Calcium - 25 mg Iron - 0.73 mg Zinc - 0.48 mg Copper - 0.152 mg Manganese - 0.27 mg Selenium - 0.2 mcg Sodium - 72 mg Also contains small amounts of other minerals.	mg Niacin - 1.332 mg Vitamin B1 (thiamine) - 0.06 mg Vitamin B2 (riboflavin) - 0.107 mg Vitamin B6 - 0.097 mg Pantothenic Acid - 0.288 mg Folate - 107 mcg Vitamin A - 16 IU Vitamin K - 17.8 mcg Vitamin E - 0.23 mg Contains some other vitamins in small amounts.
Asparagus	Half cup (about 6 spears) cooked with no added salt contains 2.16 grams of protein, 20 calories and 1.8 grams of fiber.	Potassium - 202 mg Phosphorus - 49 mg Calcium - 21 mg Iron - 0.82 mg Sodium - 13 mg Magnesium - 13 mg Zinc - 0.54 mg Copper - 0.149 mg Manganese - 0.139 mg Selenium - 5.5 mcg Also contains small amounts of other minerals.	Vitamin A - 905 IU Vitamin C - 6.9 mg Niacin - 0.976 mg Vitamin B1 (thiamine) - 0.146 mg Vitamin B2 (riboflavin) - 0.125 mg Pantothenic Acid - 0.203 mg Vitamin B6 - 0.071 mg Folate - 134 mcg Vitamin K - 45.5 mcg Vitamin E - 1.35 mg Contains some other vitamins in small amounts.
Bamboo shoots	One cup of bamboo shoots, cooked, boiled, drained with no	Potassium - 640 mg Phosphorus - 24 mg Magnesium - 4 mg Calcium - 14 mg Iron - 0.29 mg	Niacin - 0.36 mg Vitamin B1 (thiamine) - 0.024 mg Vitamin B2 (riboflavin) - 0.06 mg Pantothenic

	added salt has 1.84 grams protein, 14 calories and 1.2 grams dietary fiber.	Sodium - 5 mg Zinc - 0.56 mg Copper - 0.098 mg Manganese - 0.136 mg Selenium - 0.5 mcg Also contains small amounts of other minerals.	Acid - 0.079 mg Vitamin B6 - 0.118 mg Folate - 2 mcg Contains some other vitamins in small amounts.
Bok Choy	One cup of Bok Choy (Pak Choi), cooked, boiled, drained with no added salt has 2.65 grams protein, 20 calories and 1.7 grams dietary fiber.	Potassium - 631 mg Phosphorus - 49 mg Magnesium - 19 mg Calcium - 158 mg Iron - 1.77 mg Zinc - 0.29 mg Copper - 0.032 mg Manganese - 0.245 mg Selenium - 0.7 mcg Sodium - 58 mg Also contains small amounts of other minerals.	Vitamin C - 44.2 mg Niacin - 0.728 mg Vitamin B1 (thiamine) - 0.054 mg Vitamin B2 (riboflavin) - 0.107 mg Pantothenic Acid - 0.134 mg Vitamin B6 - 0.282 mg Folate - 70 mcg Vitamin A - 7223 IU Vitamin E - 0.15 mg Vitamin K - 57.8 mcg Contains some other vitamins in small amounts.
Broccoli	Half cup of broccoli, cooked with no added salt contains 1.86 grams protein, 27 calories and 2.6 grams dietary fiber.	Potassium - 229 mg Phosphorus - 52 mg Calcium - 31 mg Sodium - 32 mg Magnesium - 16 mg Iron - 0.52 mg Zinc - 0.35 mg Copper - 0.048 mg Manganese - 0.151 mg Selenium - 1.2 mcg Also contains small amounts of other minerals.	Vitamin A - 1207 IU Vitamin C - 50.6 mg Niacin - 0.431 mg Vitamin B1 (thiamine) - 0.049 mg Vitamin B2 (riboflavin) - 0.096 mg Vitamin B6 - 0.156 mg Pantothenic Acid - 0.48 mg Folate - 84 mcg Vitamin K - 110 mcg Vitamin E - 1.13 mg Contains some

© Natalie Mitchell

			other vitamins in small amounts.
Brussels Sprouts	One cup of Brussels Sprouts, cooked, boiled, drained with no added salt has 3.98 grams protein, 56 calories and 4.1 grams dietary fiber.	Potassium - 495 mg Phosphorus - 87 mg Magnesium - 31 mg Calcium - 56 mg Iron - 1.87 mg Zinc - 0.51 mg Copper - 0.129 mg Manganese - 0.354 mg Selenium - 2.3 mcg Sodium - 33 mg Also contains small amounts of other minerals.	Vitamin C - 96.7 mg Niacin - 0.947 mg Vitamin B1 (thiamine) - 0.167 mg Vitamin B2 (riboflavin) - 0.125 mg Pantothenic Acid - 0.393 mg Vitamin B6 - 0.278 mg Folate - 94 mcg Vitamin A - 1209 IU Vitamin E - 0.67 mg Vitamin K - 218.9 mcg Contains some other vitamins in small amounts.
Butternut squash	One cup of Butternut squash, cooked, baked, drained with no added salt has 1.84 grams protein and 82 calories.	Potassium - 582 mg Phosphorus - 55 mg Magnesium - 59 mg Calcium - 84 mg Iron - 1.23 mg Zinc - 0.27 mg Copper - 0.133 mg Manganese - 0.353 mg Selenium - 1 mcg Sodium - 8 mg Also contains small amounts of other minerals.	Vitamin C - 31 mg Niacin - 1.986 mg Vitamin B1 (thiamine) - 0.148 mg Vitamin B2 (riboflavin) - 0.035 mg Pantothenic Acid - 0.736 mg Vitamin B6 - 0.254 mg Folate - 39 mcg Vitamin A - 22868 IU Vitamin K - 2 mcg Vitamin E - 2.64 mg Contains some other vitamins in small amounts.
Cabbage	One half cup of cabbage, cooked, boiled, drained	Potassium - 147 mg Phosphorus - 25 mg Magnesium - 11 mg	Vitamin C - 28.1 mg Niacin - 0.186 mg Vitamin B1 (thiamine) -

	with no added salt has 0.95 grams protein, 17 calories and 1.4 grams of dietary fiber.	Calcium - 36 mg Iron - 0.13 mg Sodium - 6 mg Zinc - 0.15 mg Copper - 0.013 mg Manganese - 0.154 mg Selenium - 0.5 mcg Also contains small amounts of other minerals.	0.046 mg Vitamin B2 (riboflavin) - 0.029 mg Vitamin B6 - 0.084 mg Folate - 22 mcg Pantothenic Acid - 0.13 mg Vitamin A - 60 IU Vitamin K - 81.5 mcg Vitamin E - 0.11 mg Contains some other vitamins in small amounts.
Carrots	Half cup cooked with no added salt contains 0.59 grams protein, 27 calories and 2.3 grams fiber.	Potassium - 183 mg Calcium - 23 mg Phosphorus - 23 mg Magnesium - 8 mg Iron - 0.27 mg Sodium - 5 mg Zinc - 0.3 mg Copper - 0.052 mg Manganese - 0.062 mg Selenium - 0.2 mcg Also contains small amounts of other minerals.	Vitamin A - 13286 IU Vitamin C - 2.8 mg Vitamin B1 (thiamine) - 0.051 mg Vitamin B2 (riboflavin) - 0.034 mg Niacin - 0.503 mg Folate - 11 mcg Pantothenic Acid - 0.181 mg Vitamin B6 - 0.119 mg Vitamin K - 10.7 mcg Vitamin E - 0.8 mg Contains some other vitamins in small amounts.
Cauliflower	Half cup cooked with no added salt contains 1.14 grams protein, 14 calories and 1.4 grams fiber.	Potassium - 88 mg Phosphorus - 20 mg Calcium - 10 mg Iron - 0.2 mg Magnesium - 6 mg Sodium - 9 mg Zinc - 0.11 mg Copper - 0.011 mg Manganese - 0.082 mg Selenium - 0.4	Vitamin C - 27.5 mg Niacin - 0.254 mg Vitamin B1 (thiamine) - 0.026 mg Vitamin B2 (riboflavin) - 0.032 mg Folate - 27 mcg Vitamin B6 - 0.107 mg Pantothenic Acid - 0.315 mg

© Natalie Mitchell

		mcg Also contains small amounts of other minerals.	Vitamin A - 7 IU Vitamin K - 8.6 mcg Vitamin E - 0.04 mg Contains some other vitamins in small amounts.
Celeriac	One cup of Celeriac, cooked, boiled, drained with no added salt has 1.49 grams protein, 42 calories and 1.9 grams of dietary fiber.	Potassium - 268 mg Phosphorus - 102 mg Magnesium - 19 mg Calcium - 40 mg Iron - 0.67 mg Sodium - 95 mg Zinc - 0.31 mg Copper - 0.067 mg Manganese - 0.149 mg Selenium - 0.6 mcg Also contains small amounts of other minerals.	Vitamin C - 5.6 mg Niacin - 0.662 mg Vitamin B1 (thiamine) - 0.042 mg Vitamin B2 (riboflavin) - 0.057 mg Vitamin B6 - 0.157 mg Folate - 5 mcg Pantothenic Acid - 0.315 mg Contains some other vitamins in small amounts.
Celery	One cup of celery, cooked, boiled, drained with no added salt has 1.25 grams protein, 27 calories and 2.4 grams of dietary fiber.	Potassium - 426 mg Phosphorus - 38 mg Magnesium - 18 mg Calcium - 63 mg Iron - 0.63 mg Sodium - 136 mg Zinc - 0.21 mg Copper - 0.054 mg Manganese - 0.159 mg Selenium - 1.5 mcg Also contains small amounts of other minerals.	Vitamin C - 9.2 mg Niacin - 0.479 mg Vitamin B1 (thiamine) - 0.064 mg Vitamin B2 (riboflavin) - 0.07 mg Vitamin B6 - 0.129 mg Folate - 33 mcg Pantothenic Acid - 0.292 mg Vitamin A - 782 IU Vitamin K - 56.7 mcg Vitamin E - 0.53 IU Contains some other vitamins in small amounts.
Chinese broccoli	One cup of Chinese broccoli, cooked,	Potassium - 230 mg Phosphorus - 36 mg Magnesium - 16	Vitamin C - 24.8 mg Niacin - 0.385 mg Vitamin

	boiled, drained with no added salt has 1 gram protein, 19 calories and 2.2 grams of dietary fiber.	mg Calcium - 88 mg Iron - 0.49 mg Sodium - 6 mg Zinc - 0.34 mg Copper - 0.054 mg Manganese - 0.232 mg Selenium - 1.1 mcg Also contains small amounts of other minerals.	B1 (thiamine) - 0.084 mg Vitamin B2 (riboflavin) - 0.128 mg Vitamin B6 - 0.062 mg Folate - 87 mcg Pantothenic Acid - 0.14 mg Vitamin A - 1441 IU Vitamin K - 74.6 mcg Vitamin E - 0.42 mg Contains some other vitamins in small amounts.
Chinese cabbage	One cup of Chinese cabbage (pe-tsai), cooked, boiled, drained with no added salt has 1.78 grams protein, 17 calories and 2 grams of dietary fiber.	Potassium - 268 mg Phosphorus - 46 mg Magnesium - 12 mg Calcium - 38 mg Iron - 0.36 mg Sodium - 11 mg Zinc - 0.21 mg Copper - 0.035 mg Manganese - 0.182 mg Selenium - 0.5 mcg Also contains small amounts of other minerals.	Vitamin C - 18.8 mg Niacin - 0.595 mg Vitamin B1 (thiamine) - 0.052 mg Vitamin B2 (riboflavin) - 0.052 mg Vitamin B6 - 0.0211 mg Folate - 63 mcg Pantothenic Acid - 0.095 mg Vitamin A - 1151 IU Contains some other vitamins in small amounts.
Corn	One large ear of yellow corn, cooked with no salt contains 4.02 grams protein, 113 calories and 2.8 grams fiber.	Potassium - 257 mg Phosphorus - 91 mg Magnesium - 31 mg Calcium - 4 mg Selenium - 0.2 mg Iron - 0.53 mg Zinc - 0.73 mg Copper - 0.058 mg Manganese - 0.197 mg Also contains small amounts of other minerals.	Vitamin C - 6.5 mg Niacin - 1.986 mg Vitamin B1 (thiamine) - 0.11 mg Vitamin B2 (riboflavin) - 0.067 mg Vitamin B6 - 0.164 mg Folate - 27 mcg Pantothenic Acid - 0.935 mg Vitamin A - 310 IU Vitamin K - 0.5

			mcg Vitamin E - 0.11 mg Contains some other vitamins in small amounts.
Cucumber	Half a cup of sliced cucumber with skins contains .34 grams protein, 8 calories and .3 grams fiber.	Potassium - 76 mg Phosphorus - 12 mg Magnesium - 7 mg Sodium - 1 mg Calcium - 8 mg Iron - 0.15 mg Zinc - 0.1 mg Copper - 0.021 mg Manganese - 0.041 mg Selenium - 0.2 mcg Also contains small amounts of other minerals.	Vitamin C - 1.5 mg Niacin - 0.051 mg Vitamin B1 (thiamine) - 0.014 mg Vitamin B2 (riboflavin) - 0.017 mg Vitamin B6 - 0.021 mg Folate - 4 mcg Pantothenic Acid - 0.135 mg Vitamin A - 55 IU Vitamin K - 8.5 mcg Vitamin E - 0.02 mg Contains some other vitamins in small amounts.
Daikon Radish	One cup of Daikon Radish(oriental), cooked, boiled, drained with no added salt has 0.98 grams protein, 25 calories and 2.4 grams of dietary fiber.	Potassium - 419 mg Phosphorus - 35 mg Magnesium - 13 mg Calcium - 25 mg Iron - 0.22 mg < Sodium - 19 mg Zinc - 0.19 mg Copper - 0.148 mg Manganese - 0.049 mg Selenium - 1 mcg Also contains small amounts of other minerals.	Vitamin C - 22.2 mg Niacin - 0.221 mg Vitamin B2 (riboflavin) - 0.034 mg Vitamin B6 - 0.056 mg Folate - 25 mcg Pantothenic Acid - 0.168 mg Vitamin K - 0.4 mcg Contains some other vitamins in small amounts.
Eggplant	One cup of eggplant, cooked, boiled, drained	Potassium - 122 mg Phosphorus - 15 mg Magnesium - 11 mg	Vitamin C - 1.3 mg Niacin - 0.594 mg Vitamin B1 (thiamine) -

© Natalie Mitchell

	with no added salt has 0.82 grams protein, 35 calories and 2.5 grams of dietary fiber.	Calcium - 6 mg Iron - 0.25 mg Sodium - 1 mg Zinc - 0.12 mg Copper - 0.058 mg Manganese - 0.112 mg Selenium - 0.1 mcg Also contains small amounts of other minerals.	0.075 mg Vitamin B2 (riboflavin) - 0.02 mg Vitamin B6 - 0.085 mg Folate - 14 mcg Pantothenic Acid - 0.074 mg Vitamin A - 37 IU Vitamin K - 2.9 mcg Vitamin E - 0.41 mg Contains some other vitamins in small amounts.
Fennel	One cup of raw fennel bulb has 1.08 grams protein, 27 calories and 2.7 grams of dietary fiber.	Potassium - 360 mg Phosphorus - 44 mg Magnesium - 15 mg Calcium - 43 mg Iron - 0.64 mg Sodium - 45 mg Zinc - 0.17 mg Copper - 0.057 mg Manganese - 0.166 mg Selenium - 0.6 mcg Also contains small amounts of other minerals.	Vitamin C - 10.4 mg Niacin - 0.557 mg Vitamin B1 (thiamine) - 0.009 mg Vitamin B2 (riboflavin) - 0.028 mg Vitamin B6 - 0.041 mg Folate - 23 mcg Pantothenic Acid - 0.202 mg Vitamin A - 117 IU Contains some other vitamins in small amounts.
French beans	One cup of French beans, mature seeds, cooked, boiled with no added salt has 12.48 grams protein, 228 calories and 16.6 grams of dietary	Potassium - 655 mg Phosphorus - 181 mg Magnesium - 99 mg Calcium - 112 mg Iron - 1.91 mg Sodium - 11 mg Zinc - 1.13 mg Copper - 0.204 mg Manganese - 0.676 mg Selenium - 2.1 mcg Also contains small amounts of	Vitamin C - 2.1 mg Niacin - 0.966 mg Vitamin B1 (thiamine) - 0.23 mg Vitamin B2 (riboflavin) - 0.11 mg Vitamin B6 - 0.186 mg Folate - 133 mcg Pantothenic Acid - 0.393 mg Vitamin A - 5 IU Contains some other vitamins in

	fiber.	other minerals.	small amounts.
Jicama	One hundred grams of jicama, cooked or boiled with no added salt has 0.72 grams protein and 38 calories.	Potassium - 135 mg Phosphorus - 16 mg Magnesium - 11 mg Calcium - 11 mg Iron - 0.57 mg Sodium - 4 mg Zinc - 0.15 mg Copper - 0.046 mg Manganese - 0.057 mg Selenium - 0.7 mcg Also contains small amounts of other minerals.	Vitamin C - 14.1 mg Niacin - 0.19 mg Vitamin B1 (thiamine) - 0.017 mg Vitamin B2 (riboflavin) - 0.028 mg Vitamin B6 - 0.04 mg Folate - 8 mcg Pantothenic Acid - 0.121 mg Vitamin A - 19 IU Contains some other vitamins in small amounts.
Kale	One cup of cooked kale with no added salt contains 2.47 grams protein, 36 calories and 2.6 grams fiber.	Potassium - 296 mg Phosphorus - 36 mg Magnesium - 23 mg Calcium - 94 mg Iron - 1.17 mg Sodium - 30 mg Zinc - 0.31 mg Copper - 0.203 mg Manganese - 0.541 mg Selenium - 1.2 mcg Also contains small amounts of other minerals.	Vitamin A - 17,707 IU Vitamin C - 53.3 mg Niacin - 0.65 mg Vitamin B1 (thiamine) - 0.069 mg Vitamin B2 (riboflavin) - 0.091 mg Vitamin B6 - 0.179 mg Folate - 17 mcg Pantothenic Acid - 0.064 mg Vitamin K - 1062 mcg Vitamin E - 1.1 mg Contains some other vitamins in small amounts.
Leek	One leek, cooked, boiled with no added salt has 1 gram protein, 38 calories and 1.2 grams of	Potassium - 108 mg Phosphorus - 21 mg Magnesium - 17 mg Calcium - 37 mg Iron - 1.36 mg Sodium - 12 mg Zinc - 0.07 mg Copper - 0.077 mg Manganese -	Vitamin C - 5.2 mg Niacin - 0.248 mg Vitamin B1 (thiamine) - 0.032 mg Vitamin B2 (riboflavin) - 0.025 mg Vitamin B6 - 0.14 mg Folate - 30 mcg

© Natalie Mitchell

	dietary fiber.	0.306 mg Selenium - 0.6 mcg Also contains small amounts of other minerals.	Pantothenic Acid - 0.089 mg Vitamin A - 1007 IU Vitamin K - 31.5 mcg Vitamin E - 0.62 mg Contains some other vitamins in small amounts.
Lima Beans	One cup of cooked large lima beans with no added salt contains 14.66 grams protein, 216 calories and 13.2 grams fiber.	Potassium - 955 mg Phosphorus - 209 mg Magnesium - 81 mg Calcium - 32 mg Selenium - 8.5 mg Iron - 4.49 mg Sodium - 4 mg Zinc - 1.79 mg Manganese - 0.97 mg Copper - 0.442 mg Also contains small amounts of other minerals.	Pantothenic Acid - 0.793 mg Niacin - 0.791 mg Vitamin B1 (thiamine) - 0.303 mg Vitamin B2 (riboflavin) - 0.103 mg Vitamin B6 - 0.303 mg Folate - 156 mcg Vitamin K - 3.8 mcg Vitamin E - 0.34 mg Contains some other vitamins in small amounts.
Mushroom	Half a cup of raw mushrooms contains 1.08 grams of protein, 8 calories and 0.3 grams of fiber.	Potassium - 111 mg Phosphorus - 30 mg Magnesium - 3 mg Calcium - 1 mg Iron - 0.17 mg Sodium - 2 mg Zinc - 0.18 mg Copper - 0.111 mg Manganese - 0.016 mg Selenium - 3.3 mcg Also contains small amounts of other minerals.	Vitamin D - 2 IU Niacin - 1.262 mg Vitamin B1 (thiamine) - 0.028 mg Vitamin B2 (riboflavin) - 0.141 mg Vitamin B6 - 0.036 mg Vitamin C - 0.7 mg Pantothenic Acid - 0.524 mg Folate - 6 mcg Contains some other vitamins in small amounts.
Okra	One cup of okra, cooked, boiled, drained,	Potassium - 216 mg Phosphorus - 51 mg Magnesium - 58	Vitamin C - 26.1 mg Niacin - 1.394 mg Vitamin

© Natalie Mitchell

	with no added salt has 3 grams protein, 35 calories and 4 grams of dietary fiber.	mg Calcium - 123 mg Iron - 0.45 mg Sodium - 10 mg Zinc - 0.69 mg Copper - 0.136 mg Manganese - 0.47 mg Selenium - 0.6 mcg Also contains small amounts of other minerals.	B1 (thiamine) - 0.211 mg Vitamin B2 (riboflavin) - 0.088 mg Vitamin B6 - 0.299 mg Folate - 74 mcg Pantothenic Acid - 0.341 mg Vitamin A - 453 IU Vitamin K - 64 mcg Vitamin E - 0.43 mg Contains some other vitamins in small amounts.
Onions	One small onion cooked without salt contains 0.82 grams protein, 26 calories and 0.8 grams of fiber.	Potassium - 100 mg Phosphorus - 21 mg Calcium - 13 mg Iron - 0.14 mg Magnesium - 7 mg Sodium - 2 mg Zinc - 0.13 mg Copper - 0.04 mg Manganese - 0.092 mg Selenium - 0.4 mcg Also contains small amounts other minerals.	Vitamin C - 3.1 mg Niacin - 0.099 mg Vitamin B1 (thiamine) - 0.025 mg Vitamin B2 (riboflavin) - 0.014 mg Vitamin B6 - 0.077 mg Pantothenic Acid - 0.068 mg Folate - 9 mcg Vitamin A - 1 IU Vitamin K - 0.3 mcg Vitamin E - 0.01 mg Contains some other vitamins in small amounts.
Parsnip	One cup of parsnip, cooked, boiled, drained, with no added salt has 2.06 grams protein, 111 calories and 5.6	Potassium - 573 mg Phosphorus - 108 mg Magnesium - 45 mg Calcium - 58 mg Iron - 0.9 mg Sodium - 16 mg Zinc - 0.41 mg Copper - 0.215 mg Manganese - 0.459 mg Selenium - 2.7	Vitamin C - 20.3 mg Niacin - 1.129 mg Vitamin B1 (thiamine) - 0.129 mg Vitamin B2 (riboflavin) - 0.08 mg Vitamin B6 - 0.145 mg Folate - 90 mcg Pantothenic Acid - 0.917 mg

	grams of dietary fiber.	mcg Also contains small amounts of other minerals.	Vitamin K - 1.6 mcg Vitamin E - 1.56 mg Contains some other vitamins in small amounts.
Peas	One cup of boiled peas with no salt added contains 8.58 grams of protein, 134 calories and 8.8 grams of fiber.	Potassium - 434 mg Phosphorus - 187 mg Magnesium - 62 mg Calcium - 43 mg Sodium - 5 mg Selenium - 3.0 mg Iron - 2.46 mg Zinc - 1.9 mg Manganese - 0.84 mg Copper - 0.277 mg Also contains small amounts of other minerals.	Vitamin A - 1282 IU Vitamin C - 22.7 mg Niacin - 3.234 mg Folate - 101 mcg Vitamin B1 (thiamine) - 0.414 mg Vitamin B2 (riboflavin) - 0.238 mg Vitamin B6 - 0.346 mg Pantothenic Acid - 0.245 mg Vitamin K - 41.4 mcg Vitamin E - 0.22 mg Contains some other vitamins in small amounts.
Potatoes	One medium baked potato without salt contains 4.33 grams of protein, 161 calories and 3.8 grams of fiber.	Potassium - 926 mg Phosphorus - 121 mg Magnesium - 48 mg Calcium - 26 mg Iron - 1.87 mg Sodium - 17 mg Zinc - 0.62 mg Copper - 0.204 mg Manganese - 0.379 mg Selenium - 0.7 mcg Also contains small amounts of other minerals.	Vitamin C - 16.6 mg Niacin - 2.439 mg Vitamin B1 (thiamine) - 0.111 mg Vitamin B2 (riboflavin) - 0.083 mg Pantothenic Acid - 0.65 mg Vitamin B6 - 0.538 mg Folate - 48 mcg Vitamin A - 17 IU Vitamin K - 3.5 mcg Vitamin E - 0.07 mg Contains some other vitamins in small amounts.

Pumpkin	One cup of pumpkin, cooked, boiled, drained, with no added salt has 1.76 grams protein, 49 calories and 2.7 grams of dietary fiber.	Potassium - 564 mg Phosphorus - 74 mg Magnesium - 22 mg Calcium - 37 mg Iron - 1.4 mg Sodium - 2 mg Zinc - 0.56 mg Copper - 0.223 mg Manganese - 0.218 mg Selenium - 0.5 mcg Also contains small amounts of other minerals.	Vitamin C - 11.5 mg Niacin - 1.012 mg Vitamin B1 (thiamine) - 0.076 mg Vitamin B2 (riboflavin) - 0.191 mg Vitamin B6 - 0.108 mg Folate - 22 mcg Pantothenic Acid - 0.492 mg Vitamin A - 12230 IU Vitamin K - 2 mcg Vitamin E - 1.96 mg Contains some other vitamins in small amounts.
Radish	One half cup of radishes, raw, has 0.39 grams protein, 9 calories and 0.9 grams of dietary fiber.	Potassium - 135 mg Phosphorus - 12 mg Magnesium - 6 mg Calcium - 14 mg Iron - 0.2 mg Sodium - 23 mg Zinc - 0.16 mg Copper - 0.029 mg Manganese - 0.04 mg Selenium - 0.3 mcg Also contains small amounts of other minerals.	Vitamin C - 8.6 mg Niacin - 0.147 mg Vitamin B1 (thiamine) - 0.007 mg Vitamin B2 (riboflavin) - 0.023 mg Vitamin B6 - 0.041 mg Folate - 14 mcg Pantothenic Acid - 0.096 mg Vitamin A - 4 IU Vitamin K - 0.8 mcg Contains some other vitamins in small amounts.
Rapini	One cup of rapini, raw, has 1.27 grams protein, 9 calories and 1.1 grams of dietary fiber.	Potassium - 78 mg Phosphorus - 29 mg Magnesium - 9 mg Calcium - 43 mg Iron - 0.86 mg Sodium - 13 mg Zinc - 0.31 mg Copper - 0.017 mg	Vitamin C - 8.1 mg Niacin - 0.488 mg Vitamin B1 (thiamine) - 0.065 mg Vitamin B2 (riboflavin) - 0.052 mg Vitamin B6 - 0.068 mg

© Natalie Mitchell

		Manganese - 0.158 mg Selenium - 0.4 mcg Also contains small amounts of other minerals.	Folate - 33 mcg Pantothenic Acid - 0.129 mg Vitamin A - 1049 IU Vitamin K - 89.6 mcg Vitamin E - 0.65 mg Contains some other vitamins in small amounts.
Spinach	One cup of raw spinach contains 0.86 grams of protein, 7 calories and 0.7 grams of fiber.	Potassium - 167 mg Phosphorus - 15 mg Magnesium - 24 mg Calcium - 30 mg Iron - 0.81 mg Sodium - 24 mg Zinc - 0.16 mg Copper - 0.039 mg Manganese - 0.269 mg Selenium - 0.3 mcg Also contains small amounts of other minerals.	Vitamin C - 8.4 mg Niacin - 0.217 mg Vitamin B1 (thiamine) - 0.023 mg Vitamin B2 (riboflavin) - 0.057 mg Vitamin B6 - 0.059 mg Pantothenic Acid - 0.02 mg Folate - 58 mcg Vitamin A - 2813 mg Vitamin K - 144.9 mcg Vitamin E - 0.61 mg Contains some other vitamins in small amounts.
Spirulina (seaweed)	One cup of dried spirulina has 64.37 grams protein, 325 calories and 4 grams of dietary fiber.	Potassium - 1527 mg Phosphorus - 132 mg Magnesium - 218 mg Calcium - 134 mg Iron - 31.92 mg Zinc - 2.24 mg Manganese - 2.128 mg Sodium - 1174 mg Selenium - 8.1 mg Copper - 6.832 mg Also contains small amounts of other minerals.	Vitamin C - 11.3 mg Niacin - 14.358 mg Vitamin B1 (thiamine) - 2.666 mg Vitamin B2 (riboflavin) - 4.11 mg Vitamin B6 - 0.408 mg Pantothenic Acid - 3.898 mg Folate - 105 mcg Vitamin A - 638 mg Vitamin K - 28.6 mcg Vitamin E - 5.6

			mg Contains some other vitamins in small amounts.
Spaghetti squash	One cup of spaghetti squash, cooked, boiled, drained, and with no added salt contains 1.02 grams protein, 42 calories and 2.2 grams of dietary fiber.	Potassium - 181 mg Phosphorus - 22 mg Magnesium - 17 mg Calcium - 33 mg Iron - 0.53 mg Sodium - 28 mg Zinc - 0.31 mg Copper - 0.054 mg Manganese - 0.169 mg Selenium - 0.5 mcg Also contains small amounts of other minerals.	Vitamin C - 5.4 mg Niacin - 1.256 mg Vitamin B1 (thiamine) - 0.059 mg Vitamin B2 (riboflavin) - 0.034 mg Vitamin B6 - 0.153 mg Pantothenic Acid - 0.55 mg Folate - 12 mcg Vitamin A - 170 mg Vitamin K - 1.2 mcg Vitamin E - 0.19 mg Contains some other vitamins in small amounts.
Squash, Summer	One cup of sliced summer squash, boiled with no added salt contains 1.87 grams of protein, 41 calories and 2 grams of fiber.	Potassium - 319 mg Phosphorus - 52 mg Magnesium - 29 mg Calcium - 40 mg Sodium - 2 mg Iron - 0.67 mg Manganese - 0.283 mg Selenium - 0.4 mg Zinc - 0.4 mg Copper - 0.117 mg Also contains small amounts of other minerals.	Vitamin C - 20.9 mg Niacin - .913 mg Vitamin B1 (thiamine) - 0.077 mg Vitamin B2 (riboflavin) - 0.045 mg Vitamin B6 - 0.14 mg Pantothenic Acid - 0.581 mg Folate - 41 mcg Vitamin A - 2011 mg Vitamin K - 7.9 mcg Vitamin E - 0.22 mg Contains some other vitamins in small amounts.
Squash, Winter	One cup of cubed winter squash, baked	Potassium - 494 mg Phosphorus - 39 mg Magnesium - 27	Vitamin C - 19.7 mg Niacin - 1.015 mg Vitamin

	with no added salt contains 1.82 grams of protein, 76 calories and 5.7 grams of fiber.	mg Calcium - 45 mg Sodium - 2 mg Iron - 0.9 mg Zinc - 0.45 mg Copper - 0.168 mg Manganese - 0.383 mg Selenium - 0.8 mcg Also contains small amounts of other minerals.	B1 (thiamine) - 0.033 mg Vitamin B2 (riboflavin) - 0.137 mg Vitamin B6 - 0.33 mg Folate - 41 mcg Pantothenic Acid - 0.48 mg Vitamin A - 10707 mg Vitamin K - 9 mcg Vitamin E - 0.25 mg Contains some other vitamins in small amounts.
Sweet Potatoes	One medium sweet potato baked in its skin contains 2.29 grams of protein, 103 calories and 3.8 grams of fiber.	Potassium - 542 mg Phosphorus - 62 mg Magnesium - 31 mg Calcium - 43 mg Sodium - 41 mg Iron - 0.79 mg Selenium - 0.2 mg Manganese - 0.567 mg Zinc - 0.36 mg Copper - 0.184 mg Also contains small amounts of other minerals.	Vitamin C - 22.3 mg Niacin - 1.695 mg Vitamin B1 (thiamine) - 0.122 mg Vitamin B2 (riboflavin) - 0.121 mg Vitamin B6 - 0.326 mg Pantothenic Acid - 1.008 mg Folate - 7 mcg Vitamin A - 21,909 mg Vitamin K - 2.6 mcg Vitamin E - 0.81 mg Contains some other vitamins in small amounts.
Swiss chard	One cup of Swiss chard, cooked, boiled, drained, has 3.29 grams protein, 35 calories and 3.7 grams of dietary	Potassium - 961 mg Phosphorus - 58 mg Magnesium - 150 mg Calcium - 102 mg Iron - 3.95 mg Sodium - 313 mg Zinc - 0.58 mg Copper - 0.285 mg	Vitamin C - 31.5 mg Niacin - 0.63 mg Vitamin B1 (thiamine) - 0.06 mg Vitamin B2 (riboflavin) - 0.15 mg Vitamin B6 - 0.149 mg Pantothenic Acid - 0.285 mg Folate - 16 mcg

	fiber.	Manganese - 0.585 mg Selenium - 1.6 mcg Also contains small amounts of other minerals.	Vitamin A - 10717 IU Vitamin K - 572.8 mcg Vitamin E - 3.31 mg Contains some other vitamins in small amounts.
Taro	One cup of taro, raw, has 1.56 grams protein, 116 calories and 4.3 grams of dietary fiber.	Potassium - 615 mg Phosphorus - 87 mg Magnesium - 34 mg Calcium - 45 mg Iron - 0.57 mg Sodium - 11 mg Zinc - 0.24 mg Copper - 0.179 mg Manganese - 0.398 mg Selenium - 0.7 mcg Also contains small amounts of other minerals.	Vitamin C - 4.7 mg Niacin - 0.624 mg Vitamin B1 (thiamine) - 0.099 mg Vitamin B2 (riboflavin) - 0.026 mg Vitamin B6 - 0.294 mg Folate - 23 mcg Pantothenic Acid - 0.315 mg Vitamin A - 79 IU Vitamin K - 1 mcg Vitamin E - 2.48 mg Contains some other vitamins in small amounts.
Turnip	One cup of turnips, boiled with no added salt, has 1.11 grams protein, 34 calories and 3.1 grams of dietary fiber.	Potassium - 276 mg Phosphorus - 41 mg Magnesium - 14 mg Calcium - 51 mg Iron - 0.28 mg Zinc - 0.19 mg Copper - 0.003 mg Manganese - 0.111 mg Selenium - 0.3 mcg Also contains small amounts other minerals.	Vitamin C - 18.1 mg Niacin - 0.466 mg Vitamin B1 (thiamine) - 0.042 mg Vitamin B2 (riboflavin) - 0.036 mg Vitamin B6 - 0.105 mg Pantothenic Acid - 0.222 mg Folate - 14 mcg Vitamin K - 0.2 mcg Vitamin E - 0.03 mg Contains some other vitamins in small amounts.
Yellow	One cup	Potassium - 282	Vitamin C - 24.5

squash	of yellow (crookneck) squash, raw, has 1.28 grams protein, 24 calories and 1.3 grams of dietary fiber.	mg Phosphorus - 41 mg Magnesium - 25 mg Calcium - 27 mg Iron - 0.56 mg Sodium - 3 mg Zinc - 0.37 mg Copper - 0.117 mg Manganese - 0.218 mg Selenium - 0.3 mcg Also contains small amounts of other minerals.	mg Niacin - 0.569 mg Vitamin B1 (thiamine) - 0.065 mg Vitamin B2 (riboflavin) - 0.052 mg Vitamin B6 - 0.132 mg Folate - 24 mcg Pantothenic Acid - 0.203 mg Vitamin A - 190 IU Vitamin K - 4.1 mcg Vitamin E - 0.17 mg Contains some other vitamins in small amounts.

You can see from the table above that there really is a large variety of delicious and healthy vegetables available for you to eat and enjoy throughout the year! All these vegetables will provide your body with a continuous alkalizing and healing effect in different degrees and they can be cooked with a myriad of tasty recipes that suit your preferences.

Table 4

Best Alkalizing Beans and Peas with Mineral and Vitamin content

Beans/Peas	Protein/ Fiber	Minerals	Vitamins
Adzuki Beans	100 grams of Adzuki Beans, boiled without salt contain 7.52 grams protein, 128 calories and 7.3 grams dietary fiber.	Potassium - 532 mg Phosphorus - 168 mg Calcium - 28 mg Magnesium - 52 mg Iron - 2 mg Sodium - 8 mg Selenium - 1.2 mcg Zinc - 1.77 mg Manganese - 0.573 mg Copper - 0.298 mg Also contains a small amount of other minerals.	Vitamin B1 (thiamine) - 0.115 mg Vitamin B2 (riboflavin) - 0.064 mg Niacin - 0.717 mg Folate - 121 mcg Pantothenic Acid - 0.430 mg Vitamin B6 - 0.096 mg Vitamin A - 6 IU Contains some other vitamins in small amounts.
Black Beans	100 grams of Black Beans, boiled without salt, contain 8.86 grams protein, 132 calories and 8.7 grams of dietary fiber.	Potassium - 355 mg Phosphorus - 140 mg Calcium - 27 mg Magnesium - 70 mg Iron - 2.1 mg Sodium - 1 mg Manganese - 0.444 mg Zinc - 1.12 mg Copper - 0.209 mg Selenium - 1.2 mcg Also contains trace amounts of other minerals.	Vitamin B1 (thiamine) - 0.244 mg Vitamin B2 (riboflavin) - 0.059 mg Niacin - 0.505 mg Pantothenic Acid - 0.242 mg Vitamin B6 - 0.069 mg Folate - 149 mcg Vitamin A - 6 IU Contains some other vitamins in small amounts.
Black Eye or Cow Peas	100 grams of cooked, Black Eye Peas contain	Potassium - 278 mg Phosphorus - 156 mg Calcium - 24 mg Magnesium - 53 mg	Vitamin B1 (thiamine) - 0.202 mg Vitamin B2 (riboflavin) - 0.055 mg Niacin - 0.495 mg

	7.73 grams protein, 116 calories and 6.5 grams dietary fiber.	Iron - 2.51 mg Sodium - 4 mg Manganese - 0.475 mg Zinc - 1.29 mg Copper - 0.268 mg Selenium - 2.5 mcg Also contains trace amounts of other minerals.	Pantothenic Acid - 0.411 mg Vitamin B6 - 0.1 mg Folate - 208 mcg Vitamin A - 15 IU Vitamin E - 0.28 mg Vitamin K - 1.7 mcg Contains some other vitamins in small amounts.
Broad or Fava Beans	100 grams of Broad Beans contain 7.6 grams of protein, 110 calories and 5.4 grams of dietary fiber.	Potassium - 268 mg Phosphorus - 125 mg Calcium - 36 mg Magnesium - 43 mg Iron - 1.5 mg Sodium - 5 mg Manganese - 0.421 mg Zinc - 1.01 mg Copper - 0.259 mg Selenium - 2.6 mcg Also contains trace amounts of other minerals.	Vitamin C - 0.3 mg Vitamin B1 (thiamine) - 0.097 mg Vitamin B2 (riboflavin) - 0.089 mg Niacin - 0.711 mg Pantothenic Acid - 0.157 mg Vitamin B6 - 0.072 mg Folate - 104 mcg Vitamin A - 15 IU Vitamin E - 0.02 mg Vitamin K - 2.9 mcg Contains some other vitamins in small amounts.
Edamame	100 grams of frozen, unprepared Edamame contain 10.25 grams protein, 110 calories and 4.8 grams dietary fiber.	Potassium - 482 mg Phosphorus - 161 mg Calcium - 60 mg Magnesium - 61 mg Iron - 2.11 mg Sodium - 6 mg Manganese - 1.01 mg Zinc - 1.32 mg Copper - 0.324 mg Also contains trace amounts of other minerals.	Vitamin C - 9.7 mg Vitamin B1 (thiamine) - 0.15 mg Vitamin B2 (riboflavin) - 0.265 mg Niacin - 0.925 mg Pantothenic Acid - 0.535 mg Vitamin B6 - 0.135 mg Folate - 303 mcg Vitamin E - 0.72 mg Vitamin K - 31.4 mcg Contains some other vitamins in small amounts.

Chick Peas/Garbanzo Beans	100 grams of Garbanz o Beans, boiled without salt contain 8.86 grams protein, 164 calories and 7.6 grams of fiber.	Potassium - 291 mg Phosphorus - 168 mg Calcium - 49 mg Magnesium - 48 mg Iron - 2.89 mg Sodium - 7 mg Manganese - 1.03 mg Zinc - 1.53 mg Copper - 0.352 mg Selenium - 3.7 mcg Also contains trace amounts of other minerals.	Vitamin C - 1.3 mg Vitamin B1 (thiamine) - 0.116 mg Vitamin B2 (riboflavin) - 0.063 mg Niacin - 0.526 mg Pantothenic Acid - 0.286 mg Vitamin B6 - 0.139 mg Folate - 172 mcg Vitamin A - 27 IU Vitamin E - 0.35 mg Vitamin K - 4 mcg Contains some other vitamins in small amounts.
Kidney or Red Beans	100 grams of Kidney Beans, boiled without salt, contain 8.67 grams of protein, 127 calories and 7.3 grams dietary fiber.	Potassium - 403 mg Phosphorus - 142 mg Calcium - 28 mg Magnesium - 45 mg Iron - 2.94 mg Sodium - 2 mg Manganese - 0.477 mg Zinc - 1.07 mg Copper - 0.242 mg Selenium - 1.2 mcg Also contains trace amounts of other minerals.	Vitamin C - 1.2 mg Vitamin B1 (thiamine) - 0.216 mg Vitamin B2 (riboflavin) - 0.058 mg Niacin - 0.578 mg Pantothenic Acid - 0.22 mg Vitamin B6 - 0.12 mg Folate - 130 mcg Vitamin E - 0.03 mg Vitamin K - 8.4 mcg Contains some other vitamins in small amounts.
Lima Beans	100 grams of Lima Beans, boiled without salt contain 7.80 grams of protein, 115 calories and 7.0 grams of	Potassium - 508 mg Phosphorus - 111 mg Calcium - 17 mg Magnesium - 43 mg Iron - 2.39 mg Sodium - 2 mg Manganese - 0.516 mg Zinc - 0.95 mg Copper - 0.235 mg Selenium - 4.5	Vitamin B1 (thiamine) - 0.161 mg Vitamin B2 (riboflavin) - 0.055 mg Niacin - 0.421 mg Pantothenic Acid - 0.422 mg Vitamin B6 - 0.161 mg Folate - 83 mcg Vitamin E - 0.18 mg Vitamin K - 2 mcg

	dietary fiber.	mcg Also contains trace amounts of other minerals.	Contains some other vitamins in small amounts.
Mung Beans	100 grams of Mung Beans, boiled without salt, have 7.02 grams of protein, 105 calories and 7.6 grams of dietary fiber.	Potassium - 266 mg Phosphorus - 99 mg Calcium - 27 mg Magnesium - 48 mg Iron - 1.4 mg Sodium - 2 mg Manganese - 0.298 mg Zinc - 0.84 mg Copper - 0.156 mg Selenium - 2.5 mcg Also contains trace amounts of other minerals.	Vitamin B1 (thiamine) - 0.164 mg Vitamin B2 (riboflavin) - 0.061 mg Niacin - 0.577 mg Pantothenic Acid - 0.41 mg Vitamin B6 - 0.067 mg Folate - 159 mcg Vitamin A - 24 IU Vitamin E - 0.15 mg Vitamin K - 2.7 mcg Contains some other vitamins in small amounts.
Navy Beans	100 grams Navy Beans, boiled without salt contain 8.23 grams proteins, 140 calories and 10.5 grams of dietary fiber.	Potassium - 389 mg Phosphorus - 144 mg Calcium - 69 mg Magnesium - 53 mg Iron - 2.36 mg Manganese - 0.527 mg Zinc - 1.03 mg Copper - 0.21 mg Selenium - 2.9 mcg Also contains trace amounts of other minerals.	Vitamin C - 0.9 mg Vitamin B1 (thiamine) - 0.237 mg Vitamin B2 (riboflavin) - 0.066 mg Niacin - 0.649 mg Pantothenic Acid - 0.266 mg Vitamin B6 - 0.138 mg Folate - 140 mcg Vitamin E - 0.01 mg Vitamin K - 0.6 mcg Contains some other vitamins in small amounts.
Pigeon Peas	100 grams of Pigeon Peas boiled without salt contain 6.76 grams proteins,	Potassium -384 mg Phosphorus - 119 mg Calcium - 43 mg Magnesium - 46 mg Iron - 1.11 mg Sodium - 5 mg Manganese - 0.501 mg	Vitamin B1 (thiamine) - 0.146 mg Vitamin B2 (riboflavin) - 0.059 mg Niacin - 0.781 mg Pantothenic Acid - 0.319 mg Vitamin B6 - 0.05 mg

	121 calories and 6.7 grams of dietary fiber.	Zinc - 0.9 mg Copper - 0.269 mg Selenium - 2.9 mcg Also contains trace amounts of other minerals.	Folate - 111 mcg Vitamin A - 3 IU Contains some other vitamins in small amounts.
Pinto Beans	100 grams of Pinto Beans, boiled without salt, contain 9.01 grams of protein, 143 calories and 9 grams fiber.	Potassium - 436 mg Phosphorus - 147 mg Calcium - 46 mg Magnesium - 50 mg Iron - 2.09 mg Sodium - 1 mg Manganese - 0.453 mg Zinc - 0.98 mg Copper - 0.219 mg Selenium - 6.2 mcg Also contains trace amounts of other minerals.	Vitamin C - 0.8 mg Vitamin B1 (thiamine) - 0.193 mg Vitamin B2 (riboflavin) - 0.062 mg Niacin - 0.318 mg Pantothenic Acid - 0.21 mg Vitamin B6 - 0.229 mg Folate - 172 mcg Vitamin E - 0.94 mg Vitamin K - 3.5 mcg Contains some other vitamins in small amounts.
Split Peas	100 grams of Split Peas, boiled, without salt contain 8.34 grams protein, 118 calories and 8.3 grams dietary fiber.	Potassium - 362 mg Phosphorus - 99 mg Calcium - 14 mg Magnesium - 36 mg Iron - 1.29 mg Sodium - 2 mg Manganese - 0.396 mg Zinc - 1 mg Copper - 0.181 mg Selenium - 0.6 mcg Also contains trace amounts of other minerals.	Vitamin C - 0.4 mg Vitamin B1 (thiamine) - 0.19 mg Vitamin B2 (riboflavin) - 0.056 mg Niacin - 0.89 mg Pantothenic Acid - 0.595 mg Vitamin B6 - 0.048 mg Folate - 65 mcg Vitamin A - 7 IU Vitamin E - 0.03 mg Vitamin K - 5 mcg Contains some other vitamins in small amounts.
White Beans	100 grams White Beans, boiled without	Potassium - 463 mg Phosphorus - 169 mg Calcium - 73 mg Magnesium - 68	Vitamin B1 (thiamine) - 0.236 mg Vitamin B2 (riboflavin) - 0.059 mg

	salt, contain 8.97 grams protein, 142 calories and 10.4 grams dietary fiber.	mg Iron - 2.84 mg Manganese - 0.51 mg Zinc - 1.09 mg Copper - 0.149 mg Selenium - 1.3 mcg Also contains trace amounts of other minerals.	Niacin - 0.272 mg Pantothenic Acid - 0.251 mg Vitamin B6 - 0.127 mg Folate - 137 mcg Contains some other vitamins in small amounts.
Winged Beans	100 grams Winged Beans, boiled without salt, contain 10.62 grams of protein and 147 calories.	Potassium - 280 mg Phosphorus - 153 mg Calcium - 142 mg Magnesium - 54 mg Iron - 4.33 mg Sodium - 13 mg Manganese - 1.199 mg Zinc - 1.44 mg Copper - 0.773 mg Selenium - 2.9 mcg Also contains trace amounts of other minerals.	Vitamin B1 (thiamine) - 0.295 mg Vitamin B2 (riboflavin) - 0.129 mg Niacin - 0.83 mg Pantothenic Acid - 0.156 mg Vitamin B6 - 0.047 mg Folate - 10 mcg Contains some other vitamins in small amounts.

References:

Barak V, Halperin T, Kalickman I. "The effect of Sambucol, a black elderberry-based, natural product, on the production of human cytokines: I. Inflammatory cytokines." European Cytokine Network 2001 12(2):290-6.
PLoS ONE, 2014; 9: e88983
Zakay-Rones Z, Thom E, Wollan T, Wadstein J. "Randomized study of the efficacy and safety of oral elderberry extract in the treatment of influenza A and B virus infections." Journal of International Medical Research 2004 32(2):132-40.
Airola, Ph.D., Paavo, How to Get Well, Health Plus, Sherwood, Oregon, 1993.
Altschul, Aaron M. Proteins, Their Chemistry and Politics, Basic Books, New York, 1965.
Barefoot, Robert R. And Carl J. Reich, M.D., The Calcium Factor: The Scientific Secret of Health and Youth, Gilliland Printing Inc., Arkansas City, Kansas, 1996.
Binzel, M.D., Philip E., Alive and Well - One Doctor's Experience with Nutrition in the Treatment of Cancer Patients, American Media. Westlake Village, CA, 1994.
"In my attempts to use nutritional therapy, which includes the use of Laetrile, in the treatment of cancer, I have often been confronted by the Food and Drug Administration and by the State Medical Board. I have fought and, through the grace of God, I have won."
Ehrlich, S. D. (2011, April 3). Saw Palmetto. Retrieved June 6, 2012, from University of Maryland Medical Center-Complimentary Medicine: http://www.umm.edu/altmed/articles/saw-palmetto-000272.htm
National Institute on Aging: Frequently Asked Questions About Testosterone
Mayo Clinic: Saw Palmetto
Lister RE. An open, pilot study to evaluate the potential benefits of coenzyme Q10 combined with Ginkgo biloba extract in fibromyalgia syndrome. J Int Med Res 2002;30:195-9.
Clinical Nutrition. 2003; 78:965–71. Ludwig DS. Clinical update: the low-glycaemic-index diet. *Lancet.* 2007; 369:890–2.
Foster-Powell K, Holt SH, Brand-Miller JC. International table of glycemic index and glycemic load values: 2002. *American Journal of Clinical Nutrition.* 2002; 76:5–56.
Beulens JW, de Bruijne LM, Stolk RP, et al. High dietary glycemic load and glycemic index increase risk of cardiovascular disease among middle-aged women: a population-based follow-up study. *Journal of the American College of Cardiology.* 2007; 50:14–21.
Halton TL, Willett WC, Liu S, et al. Low-carbohydrate-diet score and the risk of coronary heart disease in women. *New England Journal of Medicine.* 2006; 355:1991–2002.
Anderson JW, Randles KM, Kendall CW, Jenkins DJ. Carbohydrate and fiber recommendations for individuals with diabetes: a quantitative assessment and meta-analysis of the evidence. *Journal of the American College of Nutrition.* 2004; 23:5–17.
Hiroshi, Mabushl, et al, "Reduction of Serum Ubiquinone-10 and Ubiquinol-10 Levels By Atorvastatin in Hypercholesterolemic Patients," J. Atheroscler. Thromb. 2005; 12(2):111-119

"Nucleogenesis: Dihydroorotate dehydrogenase," Metabolic Database, www.metabolic-database.com
Ebbeling CB, Leidig MM, Feldman HA, Lovesky MM, Ludwig DS. Effects of a low-glycemic load vs low-fat diet in obese young adults: a randomized trial. *JAMA.* 2007; 297:2092–102.
Maki KC, Rains TM, Kaden VN, Raneri KR, Davidson MH. Effects of a reduced-glycemic-load diet on body weight, body composition, and cardiovascular disease risk markers in overweight and obese adults. *American Journal of Clinical Nutrition.* 2007; 85:724–34.
Chiu CJ, Hubbard LD, Armstrong J, et al. Dietary glycemic index and carbohydrate in relation to early age-related macular degeneration. *American Journal of Clinical Nutrition.* 2006; 83:880–6.
Chavarro JE, Rich-Edwards JW, Rosner BA, Willett WC. A prospective study of dietary carbohydrate quantity and quality in relation to risk of ovulatory infertility. *European Journal of Clinical Nutrition.* 2007.
Higginbotham S, Zhang ZF, Lee IM et al. Dietary glycemic load and risk of colorectal cancer in the Women's Health Study. *J Natl Cancer Inst.* 2004; 96:229-33.
Liu S, Willett WC. Dietary glycemic load and atherothrombotic risk. *Curr Atheroscler Rep.* 2002; 4:454–61.
Willett W, Manson J, Liu S. Glycemic index, glycemic load, and risk of type 2 diabetes. *American Journal of Clinical Nutrition.* 2002; 76:274S–80S.
Foster GD, Wyatt HR, Hill JO, et al. A randomized trial of a low-carbohydrate diet for obesity. *New England Journal of Medicine.* 2003; 348:2082–90.
Samaha FF, Iqbal N, Seshadri P, et al. A low-carbohydrate as compared with a low-fat diet in severe obesity. *New England Journal of Medicine.* 2003; 348:2074–81.
Gardner CD, Kiazand A, Alhassan S, et al. Comparison of the Atkins, Zone, Ornish, and LEARN diets for change in weight and related risk factors among overweight premenopausal women: the A TO Z Weight Loss Study: a randomized trial. *JAMA.* 2007; 297:969–77.Halton TL, Liu S, Manson JE, Hu FB. Low-carbohydrate-diet score and risk of type 2 diabetes in women. *Am J Clin Nutr.* 2008;87:339-46.
Sacks FM, Bray GA, Carey VJ, et al. Comparison of Weight-Loss Diets with Different Compositions of Fat, Protein, and Carbohydrates. *N Engl J Med.* 2009; 360:859-873.
Hoelzl C, Glatt H, Simic T, et al. DNA protective effects of Brussels sprouts: Results of a human intervention study. AACR Meeting Abstracts, Dec 2007; 2007: B67. 2007.
Cordero MD, Moreno-Fernandez AM, deMiguel M, et al. Coenzyme Q10 distribution in blood is altered in patients with fibromyalgia. Clin Biochem 2009;42:732-5.
Lee YJ, Cho WJ, Kim JK, Lee DC. Effects of coenzyme Q10 on arterial stiffness, metabolic parameters, and fatigue in obese subjects: a double-blind randomized controlled study. J Med Food 2011;14:386-90.
Boles RG, Lovett-Barr MR, Preston A, et al. Treatment of cyclic vomiting syndrome with co-enzyme Q10 and amitriptyline, a retrospective study. BMC Neurol 2010;10:10.

Ho MJ, Bellusci A, Wright JM. Blood pressure lowering efficacy of coenzyme Q10 for primary hypertension (review). Cochrane Database Syst Rev 2009;:CD007435.
Budwig, Dr. Johanna, Flax Oil As a True Aid Against Arthritis, Heart Infarction, Cancer and Other Diseases, Apple Publishing Company Ltd., Vancouver, 1996.
Day, Phillip, Cancer - Why We're Still Dying To Know The Truth, Credence Publications, PO Box 3, Tonbridge, Kent TN12 9ZY, United Kingdom.
Diamond, M.D., W. John, W. Lee Cowden, M.D. with Burton Goldberg, An Alternative Medicine Definitive Guide to Cancer, Future Medicine Publishing, Inc., Tiburon, California, 1997.
Erasmus, Ph.D., Udo, Fats that Heal, Fats that Kill, Alive Books, 1993.
Fife, N.D., Bruce, The Coconut Oil Miracle, Avery, New York, 2004.
Fuhrman, M.D., Joel, Eat To Live: The Revolutionary Formula for Fast and Sustained Weight Loss, Little Brown, 2003.
Gerson, M.D., Max, A Cancer Therapy - Results of Fifty Cases and The Cure of Advanced Cancer by Diet Therapy - A Summary of 30 Years of Clinical Experimentation, Gerson Institute, Binita, California, 1990.
Griffin, G. Edward, World Without Cancer, American Media, Westlake Village, California, 1997. Both the book and video can be purchased directly from the author.

Jochems, Ruth, Dr. Moerman's Anti-Cancer Diet, Avery Publishing Group Inc., Garden City Park, New York, 1990. In Holland the vegetarian diet promoted by Dr. Moerman has been recognized by the government as a legitimate treatment for cancer. Results indicate that Dr. Moerman's diet is more effective than standard cancer treatments.
Kendall, Roger V., Building Wellness with DMG - How a breakthrough nutrient gives cancer, autism & cardiovascular patients a second chance at health, Freedom Press, 2003.
Lappe, Frances Moore, Diet for a Small Planet, Ballantine Books, New York, 1992. This book explains the principle of protein complementarity that is the basis of the vegetarian diet. By combining a grain and a legume you produce a protein that is as good as animal protein. Examples include: rice and lentils (rice and dahl - India), corn and beans (Mexico), chick peas and wheat (falafel sandwich - Middle East). This famous bread recipe takes full advantage of protein complementarity: "Take wheat and barley, beans and lentils, millet and spelt; put them in a storage jar and use them to make bread for yourself." - Ezekiel 4:9. A high protein plant diet provides twice the vitamins and minerals of a meat diet, and vastly more fiber, phyto-nutrients, and other required nutrients.
McDaniel, T.C., Disease Reprieve, Xlibris Corporation, 1999. Understanding zeta potential and human health.
McTaggart, Lynne, What Doctors Don't Tell You, First Avon Books, New York, 1998.
Montignac, Michel, Eat Yourself Slim, Alex & Lucas Publishing, 2004.
Pierce, N.D., Carson E., What I Would Do If I Had Cancer Again, 1996.
Robbins, John, Reclaiming Our Health, H J Kramer Inc., Tiburon, California, 1998.

Sharma, M.D., Hari, Freedom from Disease, Veda Publishing, Toronto, Ontario, 1993.

Sharma, M.D., Hari, et al, The Answer To Cancer Is Never Giving It A Chance to Start, Select Books, New York, 2002.
Taylor, Ross, with forward by Olivia Newton-John, Living Simply With Cancer, Cancer Support Association, Perth, Western Australia, 1998.
Whang, Sang, Reverse Aging, Siloam Enterprise, Inc., Englewood Cliffs, NJ, 1994.
Young, M.D., Robert O., The pH Miracle: Balance Your Diet; Reclaim Your Health, Wellness Central, 2003. See also Dr. Young's website.
Clinical Oncology for Medical Students and Physicians, op. cit, pp.32, 34
Spontaneous Regression of Cancer: "The Metabolic Triumph of the Host!", op. cit.,pp. 136, 137.
Manner, HW, Michaelson, TL, and DiSanti, SJ. "Enzymatic Analysis of Normal and Malignant Tissues." Presented at the Illinois State Academy of Science, April 1978. Also, Manner, HW, Michaelson, TL, and DiSanti, SJ, "Amygdalin, Vitamin A and Enzymes Induced Regression of Murine Mammary Adenocarcinomas", Journal of Manipulative and Physiological Therapeutics, Vol 1, No. 4, December 1978. 200 East Roosevelt Road, Lombard, IL 60148 USA
Alvarez-Jubete L, Wijngaard H, Arendt EK et al. Polyphenol composition and in vitro antioxidant activity of amaranth, quinoa buckwheat and wheat as affected by sprouting and baking. Food Chemistry, Volume 119, Issue 2, 15 March 2010, Pages 770-778. 2010.
Bhargava A, Shukla S and Ohri D. Chenopodium quinoa - An Indian perspective. Industrial Crops and Products, Volume 23, Issue 1, January 2006, Pages 73-87. 2006.
Bilalis D, Kakabouki I, Karkanis A et al. Seed and Saponin Production of Organic Quinoa (Chenopodium quinoa Willd.) for different Tillage and Fertilization. otulae Botanicae Horti Agrobotanici Cluj-Napoca Year: 2012 Vol: 40 Issue: 1 Pages/record No.: 42-46. 2012.
Brady K, Ho CT, Rosen RT et al. Effects of processing on the nutraceutical profile of quinoa. Chemistry, Volume 100, Issue 3, 2007, Pages 1209-1216. 2007.
Cordeiro LMC, Reinhardt V, Baggio C et al. Arabinan and arabinan - rich pectic polysaccharides from quinoa (Chenopodium quinoa) seeds: structure and gastroprotective activity. ood Chemistry130. 4 (2012): 937-944. 2012.
Del Castillo V, Lescano G, and Armada M. [Foods formulation for people with celiac disease based on quinoa (Chenopoduim quinoa), cereal flours and starches mixtures]. Arch Latinoam Nutr. 2009 Sep;59(3):332-6. Spanish. 2009.
Vitamin B15 (Pangamic Acid); Properties, Functions, and Use. (Moscow: Science Publishing House, 1965), translated and reprinted by McNaughton Foundation, Sausalito, Calif.
Catalona, et al. Medical World News, 6/23/72, pg 82M California cancer Advisory council, 1963, pg 10 Weilerstein, R. W., ACS Volunteer, 19, #1, 1973
Burger, Hospital Practice, July, 1973, 55-62
Currie & Bagshawe, Lancet, 1, (7492), 708, 1967
Abercrombie, Ca. Res. 22, 525, 1962
Cormack, Ca. Res. 30, (5), 1459, 1970
Catalona, et al. Medical World News, 6/23/72, pg 82M
Jose, Nut. Today, March, 1973, pgs 4-9
Burk & Winzler, VITAMINS AND HORMONES, vol. II, 1944
Adcock et al, Science, 181, 8/31/73, 845-47
Dr. Dean Burk formerly chief of cytochemistry, The National cancer institute, and

Dr. John Yiamouyiannis, Science Director of The National Health Federation, Formerly an editor of chemical Abstracts.
Fairley, Brit. Med. J. 2,1969, 467-473
Burk, McNaughton, Von Ardenne, PanMinerva Med. 13, #12, Dec. 1971
Lea, et al, ca. Res. 35, 2321 -2326, Sept. 1975
The McNaughton Foundation, I.N.D. 6734, April 6, 1970
Nieper, Krebsgeschehen, 4,1972
J.A.M.A. 225, 4, July, 1973, pg 424
Shamberger et al, Proc. Nat, Acad. Sci. May, 1973
Shute & Shute, ALPHA TOCOPHEROL IN CARDIOVASCULAR DISEASE, Ryerson Press, Toronto, Canada, 1954
Ransberger, 10th Int. Cancer Congress, 1970
Wolf & Ransberger, ENZYME THERAPY, Vantage Pr. 1972
Summa; Dipl. Ing. (Chem) Landstuhl, 1972
Reitnauer, Arzneim. Forsch. 22, 1347-61, 1972
Folkman, Ann. Surg. 175, (3). 409-1 6, 1972
Penn, 7th Annual Cancer Conf. 1973
The MEDICAL LETTER, vol. 15, #3 (issue #367) 2/2/73
Kreuger, ADVANCES IN PHARM. & CHEMOTHERAPY, vol x, 1973
Annals New York Academy of Science: 164, 2, 1969
Sorbo, Acta Chem. Scand. 5, 1951, (724-34); 1953 (1129-1136); 1953 (1137-1145)

Clemedson et al, Acta Physiol. Scand. 32, 1954, 245
Engel, Med. Klink. 20, 1790, 1930
DeFermo, Arch. Ital. de Chir. 33: 801, 1933
Saphir,~Endocrinol. 18, 191, 1934
Velasquez & Engel, Endocrinol. 27, 523, 1940
Li, Med. Clin N. Am. 45, 661 -666, May, 1961
Roffo, Bol. Inst. de Med. 21, 41 9-586, 1944
Friedman, Ann. N.Y. Acad. Sci. 80-1 61, 1959 (and refs)
Krebs & Gurchot, Science, 104, 302, 1946
Braunstein, et al, Annals Int. Med. 78:39-45, 1973
Naughton et al, Ca. Res. 35, 1887-1 890, July, 1975
Wide & Gemzell, Acta Endocrinol. 35-261, 1960
Navarro, 9th International Cancer Congress, Toyko, Oct. 1966 reported in HEALTH AND LIGHT, by John Ott, D.Sc., Devin Adair, 1973
Nieper, Agressologie 12, 6,1971, 401-8
Livingston, CANCER: A NEW BREAKTHROUGH, Nash Publishing, Los Angeles, 1972
Benno C. Schmidt, chairman of the Memorial Sloan-Kettering Cancer Center, New York City, chairman of The President's Cancer Panel; address to the A.C.S., California Division, Oct. 12, 1973 (Los Angeles Times)
Yudkin, SWEET AND DANGEROUS, Bantam Books, 1972
Seminars on Healing, The Academy of Parapsychology and Medicine, June 1973
Torrance & Schnabel, Ann. Intern. Med. 6, 732, 1932
Leivy & Schnabel, Am. I. Med. Sd. 183, 381, 1932
Gillette, et al, I. Clin. Invest. 51, 36a, 1972
Gillette, et al, New Eng. J. Med. 290, 654, 1974
Cerami & Manning, Prac. Natl. Acad. Sci. 68, 1180, 1971

© Natalie Mitchell

Gillette et al, ibid, 68, 2791, 1971
Cerami, et al, Fed. Proc. 32, 1668, 1973
Manning, et al, Adv. Exp. Med. Biol. 28, 253, 1972
Houston, Am. Laboratory, 7, #10, October, 1975 (and editorial)
DeLange & Ermans, Am. I. Clin. Nut. 24, 1354, 1971
Barnes, Broda, M.D., HEART ATTACK RARENESS IN THYROID-TREATED PA TIENTS, C.C. Thomas, 1972
Barnes and Galton, HYPOTHYROIDISM, THE UNSUSPECTED ILLNESS, Thomas Y. Crowell, N.Y., Feb. 1976
Smith, J. C. Medical Counterpoint, Nov. 1973
Oberleas, Intntl. Trace Elements Symp. Modern Med., Sept. 16, 1974
New Scientist, 5/2/74
Korant, B.D., Nature, 4/12/74
Klenner, FR., I. So. Med. & Surg. 111, 209, 1949
Stacpoole, P.W., Med. Hyp., March-April, 1975
C.A. Dombradi and S. Foldeak, "Screening Report on the Antitumor Activity of Purified Arctium Lappa Extracts," Tumori, vol. 52, 1966, p. 173, cited in Patricia Spain Ward, "History of Hoxsey Treatment," contract report for the U.S. Congress, Office of Technology Assessment, May 1988.
Kazuyoshi Morita, Tsuneo Kada, and Mitsuo Namiki, "A Desmutagenic Factor Isolated From Burdock (Arctium Lappa Linne)," Mutation Research, vol. 129, 1984, pp. 25-31, cited in Patricia Spain Ward, "History of Hoxsey Treatment," contract report for the U.S. Congress, Office of Technology Assessment, May 1988.
February 1991. 7. "Cancer Commission Was Nothing But a Farce," Bracebridge Examiner, 9 January 1991. 8. Glum, op. cit., p. 136.9. Ibid.

Richard Walters. *Options: The Alternative Cancer Therapy Book.* New York: Avery Penguin Putnam, 1993.

James P. Carter, M.D. *Racketeering in Medicine: The Suppression of Alternatives.* Hampton Roads, 1993.
Ross Pelton and Lee Overholser. *Alternatives in Cancer Therapy.* New York: Simon and Schuster, 1994.
Nicholas A Graham, Martik Tahmasian, Bitika Kohli, Evangelia Komisopoulou, Maggie Zhu, Igor Vivanco, Michael A Teitell, Hong Wu, Antoni Ribas, Roger S Lo, Ingo K Mellinghoff, Paul S Mischel, Thomas G Graeber. **Glucose deprivation activates a metabolic and signaling amplification loop leading to cell death**. *Molecular Systems Biology*, 2012
Is there a role for carbohydrate restriction in the treatment and prevention of cancer? Rainer J Klement and Ulrike Kämmerer; Nutr Metab (Lond). 2011; 8: 75; Published online 2011 October 26
Brewer, A. Keith Ph.D The High ph Therapy for Cancer, Tests on Mice and Humans Pharmacology Biochemistry & Behavior v. 21, supp 1 pg. 15, 1984
Ambrosone CB, Tang L. Cruciferous vegetable intake and cancer prevention: role of nutrigenetics. Cancer Prev Res (Phila Pa). 2009 Apr;2(4):298-300. 2009.
Angeloni C, Leoncini E, Malaguti M, et al. Modulation of phase II enzymes by sulforaphane: implications for its cardioprotective potential. J Agric Food Chem. 2009 Jun 24;57(12):5615-22. 2009.
Antosiewicz J, Ziolkowski W, Kar S et al. Role of reactive oxygen intermediates in

cellular responses to dietary cancer chemopreventive agents. Planta Med. 2008 Oct;74(13):1570-9. 2008.
Agency for Healthcare Research and Quality. Milk thistle: effects on liver disease and cirrhosis and clinical adverse effects. Summary, evidence report/technology assessment: number 21, September 2000.
Asghar Z, Masood Z. Evaluation of antioxidant properties of silymarin and its potential to inhibit peroxyl radicals in vitro. *Pak J Pharm Sci.* 2008 Jul;21(3):249-54.
Banerjee S, Wang Z, Kong D, et al. 3,3'-Diindolylmethane enhances chemosensitivity of multiple chemotherapeutic agents in pancreatic cancer. 3,3'-Diindolylmethane enhances chemosensitivity of multiple chemotherapeutic agents in pancreatic cancer. 2009.
Brat P, George S, Bellamy A, et al. Daily Polyphenol Intake in France from Fruit and Vegetables. J. Nutr. 136:2368-2373, September 2006. 2006.
Bryant CS, Kumar S, Chamala S, et al. Sulforaphane induces cell cycle arrest by protecting RB-E2F-1 complex in epithelial ovarian cancer cells. Molecular Cancer 2010, 9:47. 2010.
Carpenter CL, Yu MC, and London SJ. Dietary isothiocyanates, glutathione S-transferase M1 (GSTM1), and lung cancer risk in African Americans and Caucasians from Los Angeles County, California. Nutr Cancer. 2009;61(4):492-9. 2009.
Christopher B, Sanjeez K, Sreedhar C, et al. Sulforaphane induces cell cycle arrest by protecting RB-E2F-1 complex in epithelial ovarian cancer cells. Molecular Cancer Year: 2010 Vol: 9 Issue: 1 Pages/record No.: 47. 2010.
Clarke JD, Dashwood RH, Ho E. Multi-targeted prevention of cancer by sulforaphane. Cancer Lett. 2008 Oct 8;269 (2):291-304. 2008.
Cornelis MC, El-Sohemy A, Campos H. GSTT1 genotype modifies the association between cruciferous vegetable intake and the risk of myocardial infarction. Am J Clin Nutr. 2007 Sep;86(3):752-8. 2007.
Fowke JH, Morrow JD, Motley S, et al. Brassica vegetable consumption reduces urinary F2-isoprostane levels independent of micronutrient intake. Carcinogenesis, October 1, 2006; 27(10): 2096 - 2102. 2006.
Higdon JV, Delage B, Williams DE, et al. Cruciferous Vegetables and Human Cancer Risk: Epidemiologic Evidence and Mechanistic Basis. Pharmacol Res. 2007 March; 55(3): 224-236. 2007.
Hu J, Straub J, Xiao D, et al. Phenethyl isothiocyanate, a cancer chemopreventive constituent of cruciferous vegetables, inhibits cap-dependent translation by regulating the level and phosphorylation of 4E-BP1. Cancer Res. 2007 Apr 15;67(8):3569-73. 2007.
Hutzen B, Willis W, Jones S, et al. Dietary agent, benzyl isothiocyanate inhibits signal transducer and activator of transcription 3 phosphorylation and collaborates with sulforaphane in the growth suppression of PANC-1 cancer cells. Cancer Cell International 2009, 9:24. 2009.
Jiang H, Shang X, Wu H, et al. Combination treatment with resveratrol and sulforaphane induces apoptosis in human U251 glioma cells. Neurochem Res. 2010 Jan;35(1):152-61. 2010.
Kahlon TS, Chiu MC, and Chapman MH. Steam cooking significantly improves in vitro bile acid binding of collard greens, kale, mustard greens, broccoli, green bell pepper, and cabbage. Nutr Res. 2008 Jun,28 (6):351-7. 2008.
Kelemen LE, Cerhan JR, Lim U, et al. Vegetables, fruit, and antioxidant-related

nutrients and risk of non-Hodgkin lymphoma: a National Cancer Institute-Surveillance, Epidemiology, and End Results population-based case-control study. Am J Clin Nutr. 2006 Jun;83 (6):1401-10. 2006.
Konsue N, Ioannides C. Modulation of carcinogen-metabolising cytochromes P450 in human liver by the chemopreventive phytochemical phenethyl isothiocyanate, a constituent of cruciferous vegetables. Toxicology. 2010 Feb 9;268(3):184-90. 2010.
Kunimasa K, Kobayashi T, Kaji K et al. Antiangiogenic effects of indole-3-carbinol and 3,3'-diindolylmethane are associated with their differential regulation of ERK1/2 and Akt in tube-forming HUVEC. J Nutr. 2010 Jan;140 (1):1-6. 2010.
Lakhan SE, Kirchgessner A, Hofer M. Inflammatory mechanisms in ischemic stroke: therapeutic approaches. Journal of Translational Medicine 2009, 7:97. 2009.
Larsson SC, Andersson SO, Johansson JE, et al. Fruit and vegetable consumption and risk of bladder cancer: a prospective cohort study. Cancer Epidemiol Biomarkers Prev. 2008 Sep;17(9):2519-22. 2008.
Li F, Hullar MAJ, Schwarz Y, et al. Human Gut Bacterial Communities Are Altered by Addition of Cruciferous Vegetables to a Controlled Fruit- and Vegetable-Free Diet. Journal of Nutrition, Vol. 139, No. 9, 1685-1691, September 2009. 2009.
Lin J, Kamat A, Gu J, et al. Dietary intake of vegetables and fruits and the modification effects of GSTM1 and NAT2 genotypes on bladder cancer risk. Cancer Epidemiol Biomarkers Prev. 2009 Jul;18(7):2090-7. 2009.
Machijima Y, Ishikawa C, Sawada S, et al. Anti-adult T-cell leukemia/lymphoma effects of indole-3-carbinol. Retrovirology 2009, 6:7. 2009.
McMillan M, Spinks EA, and Fenwick GR. Preliminary observations on the effect of dietary brussels sprouts on thyroid function. Hum Toxicol. 1986;5(1):15-19. 1986.
Johnson LW, Weinstock RS. The metabolic syndrome: concepts and controversy. *Mayo Clinic Proceedings.* 2006; 81:1615–20.Liese AD, Roach AK, Sparks KC, Marquart L, D'Agostino RB, Jr., Mayer-Davis EJ. Whole-grain intake and insulin sensitivity: the Insulin Resistance Atherosclerosis Study. *American Journal of*
Moore LE, Brennan P, Karami S, et al. Glutathione S-transferase polymorphisms, cruciferous vegetable intake and cancer risk in the Central and Eastern European Kidney Cancer Study. Carcinogenesis. 2007 Sep;28(9):1960-4. Epub 2007 Jul 7. 2007.
Nutrition research reviews/Volume 23/issue 02/ December 2010, p 184-190
Nettleton JA, Steffen LM, Mayer-Davis EJ, et al. Dietary patterns are associated with biochemical markers of inflammation and endothelial activation in the Multi-Ethnic Study of Atherosclerosis (MESA). Am J Clin Nutr. 2006 Jun;83(6):1369-79. 2006.
Rungapamestry V, Duncan AJ, Fuller Z et al. Effect of cooking brassica vegetables on the subsequent hydrolysis and metabolic fate of glucosinolates. Proc Nutr Soc. 2007 Feb;66(1):69-81. 2007.
Silberstein JL, Parsons JK. Evidence-based principles of bladder cancer and diet. Urology. 2010 Feb;75(2):340-6. 2010.
Steinbrecher A, Linseisen J. Dietary Intake of Individual Glucosinolates in Participants of the EPIC-Heidelberg Cohort Study. Ann Nutr Metab 2009;54:87-96. 2009.
Way TD, Kao MC, Lin JK. Apigenin induces apoptosis through proteasomal degradation of HER2/neu in HER2/neu-overexpressing breast cancer cells via the

phosphatidylinositol-3'-kinase/Akt-dependent pathway. J Biol Chem. 2004;279:4479–4489. PubMed
Birt DF, Mitchell D, Gold B, Pour P, Pinch HC. Inhibition of ultraviolet light induced skin carcinogenesis in SKH-1 mice by apigenin, a plant flavonoid. Anticancer Res. 1997;17:85–91. PubMed
The World's Healthiest Foods " Hot Chili Peppers Make Cancer Cells Commit Suicide"
Patel D, Shukla S, Gupta S. Apigenin and cancer chemoprevention: progress, potential and promise. Int J Oncol. 2007;30:233–245. PubMed
Gates MA, Tworoger SS, Hecht JL, De Vivo I, Rosner B, Hankinson SE. A prospective study of dietary flavonoid intake and incidence of epithelial ovarian cancer. Int. J Cancer. 2007;121:2225–223. PubMed
Shukla S, Mishra A, Fu P, MacLennan GT, Resnick MI, Gupta S. Up-regulation of insulin-like growth factor binding protein-3 by apigenin leads to growth inhibition and apoptosis of 22Rv1 xenograft in athymic nude mice. FASEB J. 2005;19:2042–2044. PubMed
Tang L, Zirpoli GR, Guru K, et al. Consumption of Raw Cruciferous Vegetables is Inversely Associated with Bladder Cancer Risk. 2007 Apr 15;67(8):3569-73. 2007.
Tang L, Zirpoli GR, Jayaprakash V, et al. Cruciferous vegetable intake is inversely associated with lung cancer risk among smokers: a case-control study. BMC Cancer 2010, 10:162. 2010.
Tarozzi A, Morroni F, Merlicco A, et al. Sulforaphane as an inducer of glutathione prevents oxidative stress-induced cell death in a dopaminergic-like neuroblastoma cell line. J Neurochem. 2009 Dec;111(5):1161-71. 2009.
Thompson CA, Habermann TM, Wang AH, et al. Antioxidant intake from fruits, vegetables and other sources and risk of non-Hodgkin's lymphoma: the Iowa Women's Health Study. Int J Cancer. 2010 Feb 15;126(4):992-1003. 2010.
Zhang Y. Allyl isothiocyanate as a cancer chemopreventive phytochemical. Mol Nutr Food Res. 2010 Jan;54(1):127-35. 2010.

Printed in Great Britain
by Amazon